The
Walnut Creek
WISH

CREEKTOWN DISCOVERIES

The Walnut Creek WISH

WANDA E. BRUNSTETTER

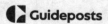

Published by Guideposts
100 Reserve Road, Suite E200
Danbury, CT 06810
Guideposts.org

This Guideposts edition is published by special arrangement with Barbour Books is a registered trademark of Barbour Publishing.

All scripture quotations, unless otherwise noted, are taken from the King James Version of the Bible.

Scripture quotations marked NIV are taken from the HOLY BIBLE, NEW INTERNATIONAL VERSION®. NIV®. Copyright © 1973, 1978, 1984, 2011 by Biblica, Inc.™ Used by permission. All rights reserved worldwide.

All German-Dutch words are taken from the *Revised Pennsylvania German Dictionary* found in Lancaster County, Pennsylvania.

This book is a work of fiction. Names, characters, places, and incidents are either products of the author's imagination or used fictitiously. Any similarity to actual people, organizations, and/or events is purely coincidental.

Image Credit: Richard Brunstetter III
Cover Design: Buffy Cooper

ISBN 978-1-961126-29-9 (softcover)
ISBN 978-1-961126-27-5 (epub)

Printed in the United States of America.
10 9 8 7 6 5 4 3 2 1

Dedication

To my cousin Lois, whose joyous
attitude has always been contagious.
And to our Amish friend Orley, whose wisdom
and advice have helped so many people.
With special thanks to my granddaughter Daun,
who shared with me her personal insights
regarding hotel management.

~

Be still, and know that I am God.
PSALM 46:10

Prologue

"What do ya think about this old *schlidde*?" Orley Troyer held the item up for his wife's inspection. "Should we make an offer on it, Lois?"

Her brows furrowed. "It would have to be a low offer, because if you're thinking of putting the sled in our antique store for resale, I doubt you'd make much of a profit."

Orley nodded and put the item down. The old relic was not in the best shape. Not only was the paint faded, but the rope to pull the sled was missing, as well as one side of the steering controls. Lois was right—it was unlikely that anyone would want to buy the antiquated item.

"Let's see what's over there. Maybe we'll find some old dishes." Looking bright-eyed, Lois pointed to a table where none of the other people who'd come to this yard sale were looking right now.

"You go ahead," Orley responded. "I'm gonna walk around for a bit and see what else I can find."

"Okay." With her head held high and the narrow ties on her white head covering swishing from side to side, Lois headed off toward the table full of dishes and glass items.

Orley smiled. Although his sweet wife had recently turned forty-eight, in his eyes she still looked just as young and pretty as the day they'd gotten married, twenty-eight years ago. Lois was also the kindest woman he'd ever known, always thinking of others and willing to help anyone she met. He felt blessed to have married such a caring woman.

Orley glanced at some of the other tables, but almost involuntarily, his feet took him back to the sled. There was no logical reason for it, but Orley felt drawn to the item.

As he stared at the dilapidated sled, an odd feeling came over him—the one he experienced whenever he felt attracted to an item with seemingly no worth.

Orley ran his fingers over the wooden slats. *I won't be the least bit surprised if someone doesn't come into our store and buy this sled. I'm almost certain that it will have a deep meaning for that person too.*

Chapter 1

Canton, Ohio

Rhonda Davis stood in front of her bedroom window looking out at the dismal weather. Spring brought flowers but also rain. She hated wet weather and had since she was a girl, forced to walk to and from school in the rain, wind, and sometimes snow. Rhonda's father had always left for work too early to drop her off at school, and Rhonda's mother hadn't gotten her driver's license until Rhonda was in her first year of college.

"Talk about a late bloomer," she mumbled, turning away from the window. "Why'd my mom have to be afraid of everything when I was a girl?" Even now, at the age of fifty-eight, Rhonda's mother rarely did anything exciting. She preferred to stay at home and knit things that no one really wanted, rather than taking trips, getting involved in charity events, or trying a new hobby. Mom's greatest attribute was her cooking skills and the ability to play the piano.

Rhonda had always seen her mother as mousy and rather boring.

Rhonda's thirty-seven-year-old sister, Gwen, lived a boring, rather quiet life with her husband, Chad, and three children.

By the time Rhonda started high school, she had determined to make something of herself. That decision included getting a college degree and majoring in business. In her second year of college, she'd met Jeff, and two years later they were married. For the first two years, Rhonda had been satisfied with her job as assistant manager of a large hotel in Canton. But by the time she and Jeff had been married five years, Rhonda's desire to have children outweighed any accomplishments she'd made with her job. The doctor had said there was nothing physically wrong with her or Jeff that would prevent Rhonda from getting pregnant, but even after another three years, all efforts of her conceiving a child had been unsuccessful. Rhonda had finally quit hoping for a baby and thrown herself into her work at the hotel, which she now managed full time. She and Jeff had been married twelve years, and all they had to show for it was a modern townhouse, an expensive sports car, a luxury SUV, and a chasm of disinterest between them.

Rhonda figured that unless something happened to turn the tide, she and Jeff would soon be heading down the road to divorce.

"And why not?" she mumbled, picking up her hairbrush and pulling it through her shoulder-length hair. "The only thing my husband and I have in common now is that we're both married to our jobs. We can barely say a civil word to each other anymore."

She set her brush back on the dresser and laid a hand against her breastbone, releasing a heavy sigh. *If I'd known how things would turn out, I would never have married Jeff.*

Still wearing her robe, Rhonda left her room and walked to the closet in the hallway. *I wonder if that old box of junk is still in there. The one that holds some of my past. I really should dump that stuff since it doesn't serve any real purpose.*

She opened the door and looked around for a few seconds. "Yes, it's still here." Her instinct was to go through the items one more time, so she hauled the box back to the bedroom and placed it on the end of the bed. *I don't know why I've bothered to keep this stuff or go back to look at it from time to time.*

Rhonda lifted the lid and moved her hand around inside. She pulled out a silly old card from her sister that she'd made in the second grade. Rhonda couldn't help but smile. *I remember this one well. Gwen and I sure had some fun when we were kids.*

Rhonda set the card back in the box and pulled out a couple of dainty plastic red roses. *Ah, yes. . .this was on the small birthday* cake Jeff got me when we were dating in college. Those were great days we had together back then. Of course, we were younger and had no real problems to deal with.

Rhonda felt something soft and withdrew an embroidered handkerchief. It had been embellished with two little bells, and small bluish flowers adorned it. She held it against her chest and sighed. *This is from my wedding day, and there's the blue I needed to complete that old traditional rhyme: Something old, something new, something borrowed, something blue.*

Rhonda breathed out a puff of air. *Of course, that old saying is about bringing good luck, which I don't really believe in. A person makes their own luck, based on how hard they work to get what they want.*

She picked through a few more items and paused, holding a little book in her hand. Rhonda stared at the pocket-sized New Testament. It had been a gift from her paternal grandmother, who had since passed away. Rhonda's fingers opened it to the first page. *To my granddaughter Rhonda: May you find comfort in the words of this book. Love, Grandma Haskell.*

Rhonda's smile soon faded, because the truth was, she had no use for a Bible. Even so, she would hold on to it for sentimental reasons. Although this was her Bible, she'd never read any of it. She had, however, hoped to pass the Testament to her own daughter some-day, but it looked as though all hope was lost in that department.

She placed it back in the box and felt an overwhelming urge to cry. Rhonda's frame stiffened as she got control of her emotions while carrying the box back to the closet. Then she closed the door and returned to her room.

Rhonda stepped over to her closet and picked out something presentable to wear to work. She chose a pair of gray slacks along with a colorful blouse and placed them on the bed. On her days off, Rhonda often went shopping for new clothes to add to her wardrobe, but nothing ever seemed good enough or brought any measure of satisfaction. Managing the busy hotel had become bor-ing, and she felt like her life was going nowhere.

Downstairs in the kitchen, Rhonda found her husband sitting at the table with a cup of coffee in one hand and the newspaper spread out in front of him.

"Morning, sleepyhead. I thought maybe you were planning to spend the day in bed." He glanced up at the clock on the wall across from him, then dropped his gaze to the newspaper again.

"I don't have the luxury of sleeping all day, and you should know it. In case you forgot to look at the schedule I have posted, I need to be at work soon." Rhonda gestured to the bulletin board hanging on the wall near her desk. "And I don't usually get dressed like this to stay home for the day." Her tone was filled with sarcasm as she reached into a cabinet and withdrew a breakfast bar.

Jeff's upper lip curled slightly before he took a drink of coffee. "You and your schedules and reminder notes. Why does everything you do have to be put on paper?"

Rhonda poured herself a cup of coffee and took the seat across from him. "Without my lists, I might neglect to do something important each day." She pointed a perfectly manicured finger at him, although she wasn't sure why since his concentration seemed to be fully on whatever he was reading. "Those lists are also for your benefit, so you'll know when I'll be here and what my work schedule is. You'd do well to write some lists of your own instead of relying on your memory, which sometimes fails you."

Jeff's facial features tightened as he looked up from the newspaper and glared at her. His pale blue eyes held no sparkle, as they had when they were dating and even in the early years of their marriage. There was a time when Rhonda would have looked at her husband's face and thought he was the most handsome man on earth. But those days had faded like an old pair of jeans. These days, Rhonda barely noticed the distinguishing mark of the dimple in Jeff's chin, which she used to think was cute. Like this morning, she was more likely to observe the growth on his face, indicating that he hadn't shaved in several days.

"I don't need any stupid lists, Rhonda. I know my own daily schedule." Jeff's voice had an edge to it.

Rhonda blew on her coffee and took a sip. "Whatever you say, dear. I'm sure you never forget anything either." She unwrapped her bar and took a bite.

"I didn't say that. Just said I don't need any lists."

Rhonda continued to nibble on her meager breakfast. This was a pointless conversation and a waste of her time. She never got anywhere making suggestions to Jeff.

He finished his coffee and set the mug down with a thud. "Know what I think we should do?"

She swallowed. "About what?"

"About us and the way our life as a married couple has become."

"You mean boring and flat, devoid of the love we once felt for each other?" Rhonda couldn't keep the bitterness from her tone. She took the last bite of the bar and tossed the wrapper into the garbage.

He blinked rapidly, while the rest of his face went slack. "Surely you don't mean that."

Rhonda finished the rest of her coffee and got up from the table. "Admit it. You and I both know that there's not much left between us. You have your restaurant to run, and I have my job at the hotel. We only see each other for a short time every morning and evening, and when we're together, we hardly have a civil word to say to one another."

"It doesn't have to be that way. We could start over."

"Yeah, right." She kept her focus on the empty cup as she rinsed it out thoroughly and placed it on the top rack in the dishwasher.

"I'm serious, Rhonda, and I believe I know what we should do."

She folded her arms. "And what would that be—renew our vows so we can make more promises to love and cherish that we're not going to keep?"

He shook his head. "We oughta sell our townhouse here in Canton and move to one of the smaller, more rural communities."

Sucking air in noisily through her top teeth, she lifted her gaze to the ceiling. "You've got to be kidding. Like that would change anything."

"No, I'm not kidding." Jeff tapped the table, bringing her focus back to his unshaven face. "I've been looking at the ads for homes being sold in some of the smaller communities that are predominately made up of Amish families. You can't get any more laid back than that."

Rhonda moved back to the table and stood next to Jeff's chair. "Have you forgotten that both of our jobs are here in Canton, or do you need a reminder note for that too?"

"Very funny." He pointed to the newspaper. "Here's a nice-looking home in Walnut Creek. It has a bit of land with it, and there's going to be an open house there this Sunday. I think we should go take a look."

Rhonda carved her long fingers through the ends of her hair, holding it back away from her face and then releasing it again. "Have you not heard anything I've said? We can't move to Walnut Creek or any other rural community. Our jobs are here, and. . ."

"Yeah, but if we moved there, we could slow our pace when we're not at work. We've been arguing a lot lately, and it might be good for our marriage if we start over someplace new."

She shook her head vigorously. "I am not going to quit my job at the hotel. That would put more stress on us, because it's not likely that we could find good-paying jobs in Walnut Creek or any of the other smaller towns."

Jeff flapped his hand at her. "We can commute. Canton isn't that far from some of the smaller communities. Why don't we drive over to Walnut Creek Sunday afternoon and take the tour? There may be a few other homes for sale in the area too. Please say you'll at least think about it."

Rhonda lifted her hands so the palms pointed upward. "Okay, I'll give it some thought." She started to move away from the table but turned back to face him. "Who knows—moving might actually end up being a good thing."

Jeff offered her a half-smile. "You think so?"

"In one way at least. It would give you a reason to throw out some of that old stuff you've piled up in our garage and basement."

He shrugged. "We'll have to wait and see about that."

Chapter 2

Walnut Creek

"I can't believe I let you talk me into this," Rhonda complained as the town of Walnut Creek came into view. "It's ridiculous to think that moving here, or anywhere else for that matter, is going to improve our lives in any way."

Before Jeff could respond, Rhonda continued with her tirade. "It took us about forty minutes to get here, and there wasn't much Sunday traffic. But on weekdays the commute probably takes longer, so we'd have to get up earlier in order to be on time for work." She paused to take a breath. "So, the whole idea of moving here seems rather foolish to me."

Jeff's jaw clenched as he gripped the wheel of his SUV. "You could have said no when I suggested coming to look at the house I found in the newspaper."

"Oh sure, and listen to you gripe about it until I finally gave in and agreed to waste a perfectly good afternoon." She gave a huff. "Whenever you want something, you try to wear me down until I finally agree to it."

"Do not. You're exaggerating."

"Are you kidding me? What do you want, Jeff—some examples?"

He glanced over at Rhonda, then back at the road, waiting for his GPS to tell him when to make the next turn. "Let's change the subject, shall we?"

"Better yet, let's not say anything at all. That's safer, don't you think?" Rhonda stared out the window.

Jeff bit back a caustic retort. Hopefully, his wife's negative attitude and condemnation would improve once they toured the house. Then again, if Rhonda didn't like the place, she might be in a worse mood on the way home and would have no trouble reminding Jeff what a waste of time it had been to tour the house or make the drive to Walnut Creek.

⁓

When Jeff pulled his rig up in front of a white ranch-style house with FOR SALE and OPEN HOUSE signs, Rhonda was surprised to see how welcoming it looked. She thought the spacious front porch, low-pitched roof, and large windows made the home quite appealing. Although, since they hadn't seen the inside of the house yet, Rhonda would keep her opinion to herself. No doubt there would be things she wouldn't like about the interior, in which case she would veto the idea of making an offer on the place.

"Looks like a nice house, don't you think?" Jeff bumped Rhonda's arm, bringing her thoughts to a halt.

"Um. . .well, the exterior has a pleasing appearance."

"Right, and it has the benefit of being on one level." He scrunched up his face. "I don't know about you, but I'm kind of sick of trudging up and down all the steps in our townhouse."

Rhonda shrugged. "Stairs aren't so bad. It's a good cardio workout and helps keep us fit."

Jeff opened his door and got out of the SUV. "You coming?"

"Of course. That is why we drove all this way." Rhonda exited the vehicle and followed him up the walk leading to the house. It was an easy climb to the porch, with just two steps. A two-seated swing sat on one end of the porch with two comfy-looking throw pillows. A small bistro table with two chairs was positioned on the other end of the porch.

It was a lovely spring day, and several birds twittered from the maple tree in the front yard. Rhonda fought the temptation to take a seat on the swing and absorb the peacefulness for a while, but she reminded herself that this wasn't her home, so she had no right to take such liberties.

The front door opened, and a well-dressed, middle-aged woman greeted them with a smile. "I'm Shelly Lockhart." She handed Jeff a business card along with a flyer that listed some information about the home and property it sat upon. "Please come in and feel free to look around. I'll be in the kitchen, so if you have any questions, let me know."

"Thank you." They stepped into the foyer, and when the Realtor turned to the left, Jeff headed down the hall to the right. The first room they came to had been set up as an office, but there was a closet, so it could easily be a bedroom if whoever bought the home wanted it to be.

Of course, if we lived here, I'd keep this as my office, Rhonda thought. *It would be nice to sit in front of the window with my laptop and look out at the green grass, trees, and the field across the road, instead of staring at the row of townhouses behind ours.*

Jeff didn't say much as he perused the office space, and he didn't stay in the room long either. Rhonda figured this particular room hadn't impressed him too much.

They moved on to the next room, farther down on the left side of the hall. It was quite large, with plenty of room for the four-poster king-sized bed, two end tables, and two matching dressers. On the opposite side of the room was a small sofa and a rocking chair. A large-screen TV hung on the wall, with a gas fireplace underneath.

"Wow!" Jeff whistled. "Now this is what I call a master bedroom. I wouldn't mind coming home to this every night."

"Let's check out the master bath." Rhonda gestured to the french doors separating the bedroom from the bathroom.

Upon entering the room, she looked at each area in awe. The bathroom included a large vanity with double sinks, a deep soaking tub, a walk-in shower with two shower heads, and a smaller area for the toilet with a door for privacy.

Walking back toward the french doors, Rhonda saw another door. She opened it to reveal a spacious master closet. She couldn't think of a single negative thing about this master suite.

Jeff moved closer and gave her arm a tap. "Pretty nice, huh?"

"I'll say. I wonder what else this house has to offer."

"Well, let's go find out." Jeff stepped out of the room and led the way back down the hall. At the end, they found two more bedrooms with a nice-sized bathroom between them. While not as large as the master bath, it had a double-sink vanity, toilet, and a shower/tub combination. There was also a closet with plenty of room for linens.

One of the bedrooms had a wallpapered border, sporting colorful balloons, up where the wall met the ceiling. A crib sat against one wall, and a white dresser with some balloons painted on the drawers had been positioned on the other side of the room, which was obviously a nursery.

Rhonda swallowed against the constriction that had formed in her throat. She then looked over at Jeff and grimaced. "I wasn't expecting this."

"Neither was I." He seemed to be looking at the room with disdain. "I'm ready to move on. How about you?"

Rhonda nodded in agreement. She didn't need the reminder that they had no children. *If we did decide to buy this home, the first thing I'd do is take off the balloon border in this room and paint the walls a neutral color.*

She turned toward the door. "Let's see what other rooms are in this house."

Across from the nursery was a decent-sized laundry room with a washer and dryer, as well as a utility sink and plenty of cabinets for storage.

The final room at the end of the hall was the largest of all and had been set up with a pool table, snack bar, several comfortable-looking chairs, and another large-screen TV.

With eyes wide, Jeff lifted both hands over his head and

waved them back and forth as though directing a choir. "This is it, Rhonda—my man cave!"

She rolled her eyes. "In your dreams. This place is so nice I bet we can't afford it."

He handed her the flyer the Realtor had given him. "Take a look. It's not as bad as you might think."

Rhonda studied the piece of paper. She had to admit if they sold their townhouse, buying this home might actually be doable. She turned to face Jeff. "We haven't seen the kitchen, dining room, or living room yet, so let's not get too excited about this end of the house. The rest of the home might not be to our liking at all."

"You're right, we do need to check out those rooms. I also want to see what the garage has to offer, as well as the backyard."

"Okay, then let's start with the garage since it's on this end of the house."

"Unless you'd rather check out the kitchen while I look at the garage."

Rhonda shook her head. "Since my sweet little sports car would be parked in there, along with your big vehicle, I want to see how much room we'd have."

"Okay." Jeff opened the door and went down the one step into the garage.

Rhonda followed. Because the homeowners were away during the open house, the garage was empty, but its size surprised her. A third bay meant more than enough room for two vehicles, along with plenty of shelves and cupboards for storage, as well as a large freezer, which sat near the door. Above them was a trap door, which meant there was overhead space for more storage.

"I like what I'm seeing here." Jeff's face broke into a wide grin and he rubbed his hands briskly together. "Plenty of room to display my collectibles, either here or in that TV/game room."

Rhonda bristled. "I was hoping if we moved from the town-house that you'd get rid of all that junk."

His brows furrowed. "It's not junk. Some of my items are valuable."

"Good, then you should sell them so we'll have extra money for our savings or as a down payment for this or some other house."

Jeff pursed his lips. "I'll think about it. Right now, though, why don't we take a look at what's on the other end of this home?"

"Good idea. I'm eager to see how the kitchen is laid out." Rhonda started back down the hall and heard Jeff's footsteps behind her.

After they'd gone past the bedrooms, Rhonda looked to her right and spotted the formal living room. No TV there—that was a good thing. This cozy room was a place for visiting, with no distractions. *Of course, other than our immediate families, it's doubtful we would have many visitors, since we don't know anyone living here in Walnut Creek.*

Moving on, they came to another bathroom—this one was smaller, with just a toilet and sink. It had been cheerfully decorated with a woodsy, outdoor theme.

A few more steps down the hall, and to the left they found the formal dining room with plenty of area for the large table and china hutch that took up most of the space. It was more than adequate for serving holiday meals or giving a dinner party, should a person choose to have one.

At the end of the hall on this side of the house was the kitchen. It was another big room, with a table and chairs at one end, along with a roll-top desk and a serving cart. The stovetop, double ovens, and refrigerator were on the other end of the kitchen. In front of the sunny window was an extra-deep, two-sided sink, with plenty of counter space on both sides. Four tall chairs sat around the island in the middle of the room.

"This would be a fun kitchen to cook in," Rhonda murmured. "If I had time for that sort of thing."

"If we had this kitchen, I think we'd both make the time for cooking," Jeff responded. "Our kitchen in the townhouse pales in comparison to this one."

Rhonda couldn't argue with that. Everything about this lovely home was head and shoulders above the place they currently owned.

The Realtor joined them by the island and gestured to another room to the right of the kitchen. "Please look at the family room, and then go out the back door from there to the covered patio where you can see the one-acre yard. Feel free to wander around and explore it."

When they entered the family room, which had also been decorated with a woodsy theme, Rhonda paused to look at the gas fireplace with a wooden mantle above. *How fun it would be to decorate the area above the brick fireplace with holiday themes throughout the year. But when would I find the time for that?* she asked herself.

Jeff bumped her arm. "Let's go outside. I'm eager to see the big yard."

"It's big all right," Rhonda said after they stepped out the door. "There's a lot of lawn to be mowed." She made a sweeping gesture with her arm.

"That's what riding lawnmowers are for."

She rolled her eyes. "We don't have one of those, or any other kind of mower, since the HOAs we pay monthly cover ground maintenance for the small area of grass in our yard."

Ignoring her comment, Jeff rushed forward, leaving Rhonda on the patio. "Come on," he shouted. "You've gotta see the pond out here. It includes a waterfall, and there are some fancy-looking goldfish as well."

"Oh, boy, now he's sold." Rhonda made her way to where Jeff stood. She had to admit, the addition of the pond made this yard quite inviting. *How nice it would be to sit out here and do nothing but relax. But then when would I find the time for that? Maybe on my days off?*

While Rhonda stood by the pond, watching the fish swim around, Jeff walked the perimeter of the yard.

"There's a good-sized storage shed for tools and a lawn mower on the other side of the house," Jeff told Rhonda when he returned to her side. "The home and yard have just about everything we could want, and there's plenty of room to put in a hot tub or even a swimming pool if we wanted to."

Rhonda shook her head. "You're getting carried away, Jeff. This home and yard are too big for just the two of us."

"I want it, and if you're honest with yourself, I bet you do too. Just think how great it would be to come home from work every day to a place this peaceful."

"It is serene, but—"

"Let's put an offer on it before someone else snaps it up. A place this nice probably won't be on the market very long." Jeff put his arm around her waist. "Think about it, Rhonda—if we move here, it'll be good for our marriage." The enthusiasm in her husband's tone could not go unnoticed. Neither could the way his face seemed to light up.

"We can't make a snap decision about something so big right now. We need time to think it over—weigh the pros and cons of making such a move."

"I get that, but we don't want to lose the place either." Jeff's tone went from enthusiastic to sounding desperate. Was he really that determined to make their marriage better, or was he merely caught up in the idea of living in such a nice home in a quiet rural area?

"I cannot feel good about putting in an offer today. Can we at least sleep on it before making a decision?"

"Yeah, okay." Jeff pulled Rhonda into his arms and gave her a kiss that nearly took her breath away. It had been a long time since he'd kissed her like that, and she almost agreed to buy the house, right there on the spot. Rhonda held herself in check, though. A snap decision based on the hope that their struggling marriage would suddenly be okay was not a good idea. They both needed time to talk about this and think things through.

Chapter 3

Canton

Monday morning when the alarm buzzed by her side of the bed, it was all Rhonda could do to pull herself upright and turn it off. She'd had trouble getting to sleep last night, thinking about the home she and Jeff had looked at in Walnut Creek. So many questions and concerns had encompassed her thoughts, making it hard to come up with a decision about whether they should make an offer on the house.

Rhonda yawned as she sat remembering their drive into Walnut Creek. It was a quaint place with small businesses dotting the area, but there were many homes spaced out on large properties.

If they did get the home they'd seen, some of their extra down time would go into taking care of a yard, which they weren't used to doing. Due to her job, Rhonda's time was limited, and she'd have to adjust her new routine to include the longer commute. Even so, she couldn't help thinking about how nice the rural countryside looked and that maybe yard work could become a way to de-stress.

Rhonda couldn't get over seeing the Plain people riding in those little black buggies drawn by horses. She tapped her chin. *They sure live simply in the way they get around and even how they dress. I wonder what it would be like to get to know some of them.*

Rhonda's mind kept going over the pros and cons of moving. Their home would be great for having overnight company, and they could take guests out for the day to many places in the area. The community of Walnut Creek was set up nicely for tourism, with its meat-and-cheese stores, Amish furniture stores, and many other Amish-owned businesses. Rhonda thought Walnut Creek would be a nice place to live, but she wasn't convinced that living there could really help her and Jeff's marriage.

She glanced over at her husband, lying on his side with his back to her. He hadn't even lifted his head from the pillow, despite the irritating buzz of the alarm clock.

Did he have a restless night too? she asked herself. *Does Jeff have as many misgivings as I do about whether to sell the townhouse and move to Walnut Creek?*

Rhonda got up and padded over to the window in her bare feet. She opened the blinds to let some sunlight in and hopefully wake her husband.

Jeff groaned and put one hand over his eyes. "Please tell me it's not morning already."

"It is, and the alarm went off. Didn't you hear it?"

"I tried not to."

She moved over to the bed and shook his leg through the covers. "Come on, we need to get ready for work or we'll be late."

He pulled the sheet over his head. "I don't care. I didn't get enough sleep last night."

"Neither did I, because my thoughts were consumed with that house we saw yesterday."

"Same here." Jeff pushed the covers aside and sat up. "I weighed the pros and cons, and I think we should get it."

Rhonda reached around and massaged the back of her neck, trying to get the kinks out. "It's not that simple, Jeff."

"It is to me. You liked the place and so did I. We need to go for it before someone else does."

"I don't see how it's possible when we haven't even put this place on the market, let alone sold it." She turned to face the window again. "In order to buy a new home, we'd have to sell the townhouse. I mean, how else would we pay for it, Jeff?"

He got out of bed and joined her at the window. "We can make a down payment with money from our savings and then take out a loan for the balance we'd owe on the house in Walnut Creek. Then as soon as this place sells, we can pay off the new place."

"That sounds simple enough, but there are two things that might get in the way of that."

He tipped his head. "Such as?"

Rhonda held up one finger. "The amount we'd get from this house might be less than what we'd need to pay off the loan."

"And the second thing?"

"There are no guarantees that our townhouse would sell right away. We might end up making payments on a loan that would take a long time to pay off and end up stuck with the townhouse and all of its expenses too."

"I doubt that would happen, but if it should, we could rent or even lease this place and use the money we'd get every month to make our payment to the bank for the loan."

Rhonda bit the inside of her cheek as she continued to rub the back of her neck. "I don't know. . .it's risky, and I'm not sure it would be smart to rent out the townhouse. I've heard horror stories about people who own rentals and how terrible the renters leave the place when it's time to move out."

Jeff took hold of Rhonda's shoulders and gave them a gentle squeeze. "Life is full of risks, but if we don't throw caution to the wind once in a while and take chances, we could miss out on something exceptional."

"Can we talk about this during breakfast? Right now, I need to take a shower and get ready for work."

"Sure, honey." Jeff smiled. "Since I don't have to be at the restaurant until almost noon, I'll fix breakfast for us this morning."

Rhonda blinked rapidly as she stared at him.

"Don't look so surprised. I do know how to cook you know. Don't forget, that's what I used to do professionally before I bought my own restaurant."

"Of course, I know you can cook. I just can't remember the last time you offered to fix breakfast. You usually spend the time before leaving for work reading the newspaper or the antique magazine your dad subscribed to for you last Christmas."

"Well, today is different." Jeff kissed Rhonda's cheek. "I'll see you downstairs soon."

"Okay." Rhonda slipped on her robe and headed to the bathroom. *I wonder if Jeff will fix something I really like with the hope of getting me to agree to buy that house we can't really afford unless our place here sells.* She released a heavy sigh. *Decisions. . .decisions. . . decisions. . . I sure hope we make the right one.*

Jeff finished the final layer of yogurt for the parfaits he'd decided to make for breakfast, and he added a few sliced strawberries on top of each one. He sure hoped he could sway his wife into agreeing to get the house in Walnut Creek. He still couldn't get over the layout of that big home, and the large-screen television seemed to beckon him.

I'd like to come home to that place in the evenings and stretch out in my very own man cave. That room was unbelievable. I'd have a lot of fun watching all my favorite movies that Rhonda doesn't like. Jeff shook his head. *It's no fun here at the townhouse sharing the same TV—especially when we don't always want to watch the same shows.*

He set their parfaits in the refrigerator to chill and put away everything he'd used to prepare them. He then rinsed out the sponge by the sink and wiped down the messy surfaces. Except for the few dirty dishes that Jeff still needed to rinse off and wash, it looked like he hadn't done anything in the kitchen. He was pleased with the effort he had put into making breakfast so far and hoped all this would be worth it in the end.

Jeff's mind wandered as he used a sponge to scrub the small cutting board he'd used for slicing the strawberries. *I really, really hope we can get that house. I know Rhonda would like me to downsize my collection, but for now I'm gonna keep all my stuff, because I've worked hard to get them.*

Assuming Rhonda would be ready to eat soon, Jeff took out their chilled parfait glasses layered with vanilla and yogurt granola and placed them on the table—one near his spot and the other in front of Rhonda's usual place at the table. Just in time too, because a moment later, she entered the room.

He offered her his best smile. "Would you like a piece of toast or a bagel, along with your yogurt parfait?"

Eyeing the table, Rhonda gave a slow shake of her head. "You really know how to impress a woman, don't you?"

"I do my best." Jeff winked at her. "Especially for a woman as beautiful as you."

Her lips pressed together in a slight grimace as she took a seat at the table. "You wouldn't be trying to butter me up so I'll agree to buy that house, would you?"

Jeff's ears warmed. She'd found him out, and he couldn't deny it. "That did have something to do with me fixing breakfast," he admitted, "but I also wanted to do something nice for you."

She gave a quick nod. "Thank you for that."

Jeff pulled out a chair to join her at the table, but before he could sit down, his cell phone rang. He recognized the Realtor's name from yesterday in the caller ID, so he answered right away. "Hello."

"Hello, Mr. Davis. This is Shelly Lockhart. I wanted to let you know that several other people have shown an interest in the house you and your wife toured yesterday. So, if you are seriously interested in the home, I would suggest you consider putting an offer on it today."

Jeff's heartbeat raced a bit as he glanced over at Rhonda. With raised eyebrows, she leaned forward in her chair.

"Umm...well, I'll need to talk this over with my wife. Can I call you back in a few minutes?"

"Of course, but please don't take too long. My assistant just informed me that someone else is on the verge of making an offer on the same house."

"I'll get back to you right away."

When Jeff clicked off the phone, he sank into his chair and quickly related to Rhonda all that the Realtor had said. "So, I think we should agree to pay a bit more than the asking price, to make sure our offer is accepted."

"I'm not sure that's a good idea." Rhonda's voice sounded tense. "Maybe we should talk to your dad, or even my mom, and get their input."

Jeff lifted his gaze to the ceiling. "That's really a great idea, Rhonda. I'm sure your timid mother, who doesn't believe in taking chances, would be most helpful in giving us sound advice."

"Okay, I get what you mean, and maybe you're right. But you could talk to your dad about it. He has a level head for business."

"I've already spoken to him."

She tipped her head. "Oh? When was that?"

"Last night. You'd already gone up to bed, so I decided to give my dad a call."

"I see. What did he have to say about the situation?"

"He said the decision was ours to make, but if it were him and his business wasn't in Cleveland, he'd jump at the chance to move to Walnut Creek, where the pace is much slower."

Jeff glanced at the clock on the far wall. "We're wasting time, Rhonda. We need to give the Realtor an answer before it's too late."

She fiddled with the spoon on her placemat for several seconds. "How much more do you think we should offer?"

"How about another ten thousand dollars?"

She combed her fingers through the ends of her shiny brown hair before nodding. "Okay, let's go for it, but if our offer gets accepted, then we'd better get this place on the market right away."

At six o'clock that evening, Rhonda climbed into her car and rolled down her windows for some fresh air. It had been difficult to get through her day at work without thinking about the offer they'd made on the house of her dreams that morning after breakfast.

Although Rhonda hadn't been thrilled about taking on a mortgage payment while waiting for their townhouse to sell, the idea of living in Walnut Creek seemed like heaven right now.

Eager to get home, Rhonda started her car. She'd had a rough day at the hotel, and a few times she'd felt like quitting.

But I can't quit my job, she told herself. *We need the extra income to make ends meet, and we'll need it even more if our offer is accepted on the house.*

Rhonda would be disappointed if they lost out on the home in Walnut Creek to a higher offer. But maybe it would be for the best. At least they wouldn't be taking on a huge debt, unsure of when or if their townhouse might sell.

By the time Rhonda got home, she'd worked herself into a dither. She was glad to see Jeff's vehicle parked in the driveway and hoped that he might have started supper, because she didn't feel like cooking.

When Rhonda entered the house, Jeff greeted her with a wide grin. "The bank called me today, and we are pre-approved for the loan." He stepped forward and took hold of her hand. "And here's some even better news—Shelly Lockhart, the Realtor from Walnut Creek, called to let us know that our offer was accepted by the seller." He pulled Rhonda into his arms and gave her a strong hug. "We got the house, honey. Can you believe it? We actually got the house!"

Rhonda's thoughts became fuzzy to the point that she could hardly think or speak. "We. . .we did?"

"Yes, it's officially a done deal, and we've been approved for our loan. So now we need to get in touch with a Realtor here in Canton and get our townhouse on the market."

Perspiration broke out on Rhonda's forehead, and her stomach tightened. Although she still felt squeamish about all of this, she had to admit that she had fallen in love with that beautiful house. *And who knows*, she thought, *maybe Jeff was right when he said that moving to the rural area and owning a lovely home might be good for our marriage and improve things for us.* For the moment, at least, things looked more promising than they had in several years.

Chapter 4

"What are you doing over there on your computer? Since we both have the day off, shouldn't you be helping me pack boxes?" Jeff called across the room to Rhonda.

She looked away from her work and turned to him with a frown. "I'm responding to an important email from the hotel's corporate office, so this takes precedence over putting stuff in boxes. Besides, our townhouse hasn't sold yet, so I don't see what the rush is to get our things packed."

Jeff closed the box he'd been working on and marched across the room with both hands on his hips. "Need I remind you that by the end of this month the deal on our new home in Walnut Creek will close?"

"I realize that, but—"

"Once it closes, we will sign the final papers and get the keys. After that, we'll be free to move in."

Rhonda gave a brief nod. "Understood, but that doesn't mean we need to rush. There's some painting that will need to be done there, and I'll want to clean all the carpets." Rhonda was tempted to stop talking and get back to her unfinished email, but she decided to say something else before Jeff put in his two cents. She was too late.

"Listen, Rhonda, I don't see any reason why we can't wait till we're moved in to paint the rooms you're not happy with."

She gave a huff. "I don't want to fill rooms up with furniture and then have to move it all out to accommodate painting. It'll be much easier to paint with no furniture in the way."

"Any furniture you'll want to put in the rooms that need a fresh coat of paint can be stored in that oversized garage until the rooms are ready."

She shook her head. "That doesn't make sense, Jeff. For once, can't we do something my way instead of yours?"

His face flamed as he squinted at her. "My way, huh? As I recall, I'm the one who usually has to back down and do what you want."

"That's not true, and you know it. I agreed to buy the house in Walnut Creek even though I wasn't comfortable with the fact that our place here hasn't sold."

"True, but that's because you want the new place as much as I do."

Jeff was right. Rhonda did want that lovely home, but she wouldn't give in and admit it. Besides, her feelings about the house had nothing to do with whether they should move into the new house when the deal closed or wait until the painting could be done.

"We can talk later about what date we'll move in." Jeff got right in Rhonda's face. "But for now, what's it gonna be? Will you help me box things up in a couple of the rooms today?"

She released a heavy sigh before responding sarcastically: "Okay, okay, since you asked so nicely. Just let me finish this email and then I'll start filling a box."

He smiled. "Thank you."

She turned back to the computer. *As much as I might wish it, I seriously doubt that things will be better between me and Jeff by moving to a rural area.*

⌒

Jeff and Rhonda had been packing boxes for nearly three hours when Rhonda announced that she was hungry and stopped to fix lunch. "Would you like me to make you a sandwich?" she asked, bending down to tap Jeff's shoulder.

"Umm. . .yeah, sure. Just set it on the kitchen counter. I'll be in to get it as soon as I finish with this box."

"Okay, but what kind of sandwich do you want? There's some egg salad left from yesterday, or I can make you a ham and cheese if you prefer."

He shrugged. "I don't care. Whatever you make is fine with me."

Her brows lowered. "Really? You'll eat liverwurst if I fix it?"

Jeff wrinkled his nose. "No, not that, but I'm not worried since I haven't seen any liverwurst in our refrigerator lately."

"So, which one would you like me to make you—ham and cheese or egg salad?"

"I'll go with the ham and cheese."

"What would you like to drink?"

"A glass of water works for me."

"Okay." Rhonda exited the room, leaving Jeff to finish packing the box of old comic books he'd begun collecting since he was a teenager. There was no way he could leave those behind. Rhonda had asked him to throw them out, but he'd adamantly said no, mentioning that they were probably worth some good money.

Jeff put the last of the books into the box, sealed it with tape, and then put a label across the top. With a marking pen, he wrote the words "For Jeff's Man Cave."

Continuing to kneel in front of the box, he thought about how much bigger their new place was compared to this tiny townhouse. Regardless of what his wife thought, there would be plenty of room to display all his antiques and collectibles.

Jeff grinned and picked up a bag full of old marbles to put in the next box. He could hardly wait to visit Memory Keepers, the antique store he'd seen the day he and Rhonda had gone to their new house for the inspection. Jeff was eager to see what kind of collectibles they had that he could either buy or trade. In fact, on his first free day after he and Rhonda moved into their new place, Jeff planned to visit Memory Keepers.

Walnut Creek

"I can see why this store is called Memory Keepers," an older English woman said soon after she'd entered Lois and Orley Troyer's antique shop. "I see so many things here that remind me of my childhood and some of the things I used to see in my grandmother's house." She released a sigh. "I'll always cherish those wonderful memories."

Lois smiled from behind the front counter, where customers paid for their purchases. "Yes, many people who have visited our store have said something similar to that. I suppose all the fancy gadgets we see in our fast-paced modern world will be seen as antiques someday and people will look on them with fond memories."

The woman tipped her head to one side. "I'm surprised to hear you say that, since you Amish live a plain life, without a bunch of modern things."

"That is true," Lois said, "but I was thinking more in line with English ways rather than ours. But some Amish communities have become more progressive and have begun using cell phones, solar power, and battery-operated lights."

The woman's brows lifted. "Really? I didn't know that. But then, since I'm not from around here, I don't know much about the Amish other than what I've read or seen on TV."

"You can't believe even half of what you see or hear on TV or in the newspapers," Orley said as he strode from the back of the store up to the counter. "A lot of people have the wrong impression about us Amish. They assume without getting the facts."

The English woman's cheeks colored. "Yes, sir, I am aware of that. I only meant. . ." She stopped talking and turned toward the door. "Perhaps what I'm looking for is not here."

Certain that Orley must have hurt the woman's feelings, Lois quickly stepped out from behind the counter and apologized on her husband's behalf. "We tend to be a little touchy sometimes, whenever people criticize or misjudge our ways."

"I suppose everyone does." The woman gave a brief shrug and walked out the door.

Lois turned to face Orley. "You might want to be more careful what you say to our customers, Husband. Some folks, like that woman, won't be receptive to your blunt comments."

The wrinkles in Orley's forehead deepened. "Guess you're right. I'll work harder on my communication skills." He gave Lois's arm a gentle squeeze and shuffled off toward the back of the building again.

Lois lifted her gaze toward the ceiling. *I don't know what's gotten into that man of mine. He's usually quite friendly and all smiles with our customers, but today Orley was just the opposite. I hope he gets over whatever is bothering him before the next customer comes through our door.*

Since there were no customers at the moment, Lois went to the small room at the back of the store and grabbed her lunch. Orley had already opened his and taken a seat at the small table. He looked over at Lois with a sheepish expression. "Maybe I got a little grumpy with that English woman because I needed to eat."

She looked at him and scrunched up her nose. "Seriously?"

"Guess I need to work a little harder on my manners." He took a bite of his meat loaf sandwich and smacked his lips. "Mmm, this is good, *Fraa*. You sure make a tasty sandwich."

"*Danki*. I also brought some rich chocolate brownies with that mint frosting you like so much."

"You spoil me with your good cooking." Orley lifted the sandwich. "I'm going to enjoy this first, but I can't wait for the dessert." He tapped his insulated container. "A cup of hot *kaffi* from this thermos will go well with the brownie."

Lois couldn't help but smile, seeing the satisfied expression on her husband's face as he ate his sandwich. Sometimes, if there weren't any customers, they'd eat together in this back room. With the door to the room kept open, one of them would see if a shopper came in. They'd also be alerted by the jingle of the bell attached to the front door.

Lois reached into her lunch bag for her sandwich and took a bite. *I'm happy to say that this is good and my absolute favorite way to have leftover meat loaf.*

"If things stay slow today, would you like to head home early?" Orley asked after he'd taken another bite.

"I don't know. Why don't we wait and see how it goes?"

"That suits me just fine."

As she sat with her husband, enjoying their noon meal, Lois thought about the years they'd worked together in their antique shop. There'd been so many different items they had brought in and refurbished so that the old things could find new homes. It seemed odd to her that some people couldn't see that about their own families. Just because someone grew old didn't mean their worth was gone. Aging loved ones deserved the comfort of knowing they were loved.

Lois heard the front door open. She wiped her mouth with a napkin. "I'll take care of the customer so can you stay and finish your lunch."

"Danki." Orley grinned and reached for his bag of chips.

Lois hurried to the main floor and spotted an older man looking at a crystal vase.

"Good afternoon." Lois opened a piece of wrapped mint candy from the counter and popped it into her mouth.

"Yes, it is." He motioned to the container. "That's sure a pretty glass vase."

She nodded.

He moved ahead, looking around intently at some of the other antique merchandise.

Lois was curious, as the man seemed to be searching for something. "Are you looking for anything particular today?"

"I'm not sure. I mean, well, actually yes. I am looking for a gift for my wife." He paused for a moment. "She likes old things, so I figured I'd stop in here and see what you might have to offer."

"Does your wife collect anything in particular?" Lois questioned.

The man scratched his head. "She does have a few glass pieces around our home—like animal figurines, teacups with saucers, and plates that hang on the wall with different themes."

"We have some teacups and saucers along that wall." Lois pointed in that direction.

The man went over and picked out one of them. "Ah yes, I think my wife would like this."

Lois took the cup for him and stepped around to the back of the counter while the customer continued browsing. She thought it was nice that the gentleman was aware of what his wife liked. Apparently, he wasn't concerned about adding to one of her collections. *Some people don't appreciate their spouse's collections,* she mused. *I think we need to step back and allow our loved ones a little enjoyment in this life.*

It wasn't long before the man found two more old teacups he liked. He brought them up to the register, along with a decorative plate. "I'm going to get these for her too."

Lois rang up the amount and wrapped each of the items in heavy paper. The man got out his wallet and removed the amount of cash needed. He watched her carefully put each piece into the bag and then handed Lois the money.

Lois counted the change back to him. "I hope your wife enjoys her gifts."

He put his money away and picked up the bag. "I'm sure she will. I'm glad I came in here to have a look around. I may be back some other time. You have a nice variety of things here."

"Thank you." Lois watched the man go out the door. She then returned to the back room to finish her lunch.

Orley had eaten his food and now held open *The Budget* newspaper. "How'd it go out there?"

"Good. We sold three of those pretty teacups and saucers and a plate."

"That's nice." He rustled the paper after he'd turned the page.

Lois picked up the rest of her sandwich and started eating. Her husband was an avid reader and could pick up about anything to feed his need.

"What are you reading?"

"I'm looking at an ad for a new tractor." He winked.

"Seriously?" She popped the last bite into her mouth.

"No, but I am thinking of getting a new buggy."

"We have one already, Husband."

"*Jah,* but it's old. I have enough antiques around here." He chuckled. "I think it's time to invest in a new carriage." His gaze returned to the newspaper.

Lois shook her head and got out her brownie, placing it on a paper plate.

Orley looked up from the paper. "You'll like it, dear, I promise you."

"Are you talking about a new buggy?"

"Nope, I meant the brownie." He gave her a silly grin.

She chuckled. "You can have some of mine if you like."

"Okay, just one bite, and then I'll leave you alone." He picked up his fork, took a piece of the brownie, and popped it into his mouth. "Mmm . . . *gut* stuff."

Lois sampled hers. "You're right. It is good. I'm glad my mother gave me her recipe."

"I like her Dutch apple pie recipe too. Always good around the holidays."

She nodded. "Mom was into sweets and liked to try different desserts, so she'd get quite creative in the kitchen. Once she tried to make us a chocolate soufflé." Lois forked another bite into her mouth.

"How did it turn out?"

"It never did."

"Why?"

"Because we were too noisy, and it always fell." She laughed and finished the remainder of her brownie.

"Good one." He went back to reading again.

"Say, I was wondering if you could move that dresser for me out there in our show room."

"Which one?"

"The cherry-wood one. I'd like to add some things to it—maybe dress it up with some décor we have and see if someone takes an interest in it."

"I suppose. When do you want me to move it?"

"How about now?" Lois stood and put away her things from lunch.

Orley set aside his paper and also stood. "Sounds good."

They made their way to the dresser with Lois leading the way. It was a nice piece and in good shape for its age. Orley carefully moved it out to the place where Lois pointed. But then Lois didn't like the empty spot where it had been and wanted to move another piece of furniture to fill the space.

"Wait." Orley lifted his hand.

"What's the matter?"

"Are we going to move every piece of furniture around in this room?"

"Of course not. We're about done here. I just need you to slide that desk over a couple of feet." She pointed.

"Okay." Orley came around and pulled it into place.

"There, that's better." Lois looked at the dresser. "I'll start playing with some things to make it stand out a bit more."

"Sounds good." He turned and headed for the back room.

Lois watched him exit the main area and chuckled. *I'm sure he is going back to that paper to read it cover to cover. I'm glad we don't own a used bookstore. I'd never get any help out of him.*

Chapter 5

"There it is, hon. Aren't you excited?" Jeff pointed straight ahead as they approached their beautiful new home. "Can you believe this place is actually ours? What an awesome way to finish off the second week of May."

Rhonda couldn't mistake the excitement in her husband's voice as he drove his SUV up the driveway. She didn't want to throw cold water on their new venture, but she still had some misgivings about their hasty decision to buy this home, especially since their townhouse hadn't sold yet. Instead of voicing her thoughts, however, Rhonda smiled and said, "I wonder how long it'll be before the movers get here."

"Shouldn't be too long. I gave them good directions, and I'm sure they'll GPS it." Jeff set the brake and turned off the engine. "Let's go inside. We'll wait for them there."

"We could just wait on the front porch, since there's no furniture in the house yet." Rhonda gestured to the porch swing that the previous owners had graciously left behind for them.

Jeff shook his head. "There'll be plenty of time for sitting outside now that the warm spring weather has arrived. Right now, I'd like to go inside and walk through the whole house so we can be sure of where we want everything to go once the movers arrive."

"Good idea. I brought some signs along that I made up the other day. The numbers on them coordinate with what's written on each of the boxes we packed. I'll put the signs in the appropriate rooms so the men will know what goes where." Rhonda reached for her briefcase and stepped out of the vehicle. She'd planned to drive her car here today, but it was in the shop having some work done and wouldn't be ready until sometime next week. But that didn't matter, since she had put in for a few days' vacation in order to unpack boxes and get settled into their new home. Jeff would also be taking some time away from his restaurant, leaving it in the capable hands of his manager, Russ. Rhonda looked forward to some time away from the hotel, where she wouldn't have to deal with all the problems that went with managing the business. Times like last week, when three employees didn't show up for work without warning or explanation, left her with a pounding headache.

Rhonda hurried across the yard to catch up with Jeff. By the time she stepped onto the porch, he'd already put his newly acquired key in the lock and opened the front door. Prepared to follow him inside, Jeff caught Rhonda by surprise when he turned and swept her into his arms.

"Why—what are you doing?" she asked breathlessly.

"I'm carrying my bride across the threshold of our new forever home."

Nothing's forever, she almost said but decided not to ruin Jeff's exuberance as they entered the house.

"I can't believe it's ours." Rhonda smiled. "The empty living room seems to echo the sound made by my voice."

"For now it does, but once our furniture and the boxes start filling the empty rooms, the echoes will fade."

She couldn't wait to see this room and all the other parts of the house once they were filled with their belongings. Rhonda wondered how long it would take to unload the moving van when it arrived. The first order of business after their bedroom furniture had been put in place was to make up the bed so they could sleep in it this evening. There'd be no sleeping on a blow-up mattress, like they'd done on the night they'd moved into the townhouse at a later hour than planned.

"Now don't drop me," Rhonda murmured against Jeff's chest. "I weigh a few more pounds than I did on our wedding night."

"You're still a slender woman and just as beautiful as the day I married you."

"Thank you for saying that."

"It's the truth."

Her skin tingled beneath the warmth of his embrace. Once fully inside, and after Rhonda's feet had touched the floor, Jeff drew her into his arms and gave her such a meaningful kiss that it made Rhonda forget about the quarrel they'd had last night over another box of old things she'd asked him to get rid of. He'd ignored her, of course, and they'd ended up going to bed angry, without even saying a muffled *good night*.

Rhonda hoped there would be better days ahead, and if Jeff's heart-melting kiss was any indication of what was to come, she felt a ray of hope for them. Now if their townhouse would only sell, she could relax and enjoy the thrill of living in their beautiful new home.

Seated on the front porch with his teeth gritting so hard his jaw ached, Jeff checked the time on his cell phone. "They should've been here by now." He looked over at Rhonda, sitting beside him doing something on her iPad. "I wonder what's keeping those movers."

"If you're that worried about it, why don't you call the moving company? I'm sure they can contact the man who's driving the van," she said.

Staring out toward the road, Jeff tapped the phone against his knee. If he could will that moving van to show up right now, he sure would. "If they're not here in the next ten minutes, I will give that company a call. They need to know that the men they've hired are unreliable and more than a little tardy." He got up from the porch swing and began to pace as his agitation grew.

"For heaven's sake, Jeff, you need to calm down and try to relax."

Jeff's facial muscles tightened as he turned to face his wife. "I can't calm down. With every minute that passes without those movers showing up, I'm getting more irritated."

"That's obvious, and it's not good for your health." Rhonda pointed to the nicely greened lawn in their front yard. "Why don't you put some of your aggression to good use and jog around the house a few times?"

He frowned at the smirk on her face. "This is not funny, and I don't understand why you're so calm about the movers being late. You are the punctual one who never wants to be late for work or any appointment."

"But it's not me we're talking about—it's the movers."

"Exactly." Jeff looked at his cell phone again. "Pretty soon another hour will have passed with no moving truck in sight." He took in a few quick breaths. Normally, Jeff was the more laid back one in the family, but today was an exception. This was the kind of house he'd always wanted to own, and Jeff was eager to get their furniture and other belongings brought in so he and Rhonda could begin their new life.

He looked away from his phone and grimaced. "I don't want us to be unloading things at midnight, like we did when we moved into the townhouse. I want to have this all done today."

"We will, and you need to stop worrying. You becoming upset is not getting us anywhere."

"I can't help it. The movers should've been here by now. It's not that many miles from our townhouse in Canton to Walnut Creek, and that truck should be moving along a lot faster than one of those horse and buggies we saw on the way here."

Continuing to pace the length of the porch, Jeff paused to glance out at the road occasionally. Finally, he called the moving company, but no one answered, so he left a disgruntled message. Jeff hoped someone would return his call soon.

"Sometimes I think we oughta go back to the days when making a phone call meant you'd be likely to speak to a real person," Jeff muttered. "I'm sick and tired of always having to leave a message for someone who may or may not call back. I wish life could be less complicated, but I guess living in this century, that's not gonna happen."

Rhonda made no comment. She seemed engrossed in whatever she was doing on her iPad.

Jeff was on the verge of calling the moving company a second time when he heard the rumble of a vehicle coming down the road. A few seconds later, an oversized moving van turned up their driveway.

"Well, it's about time." Jeff turned to face Rhonda. "Would you please go inside and hit the buttons to open the garage doors? I'll direct the van to park outside, between the first and second bay. That way they can unload all the boxes into the garage."

"Sure." Rhonda left the swing and went in through the front door.

After directing the van to the spot where he wanted it parked, Jeff was tempted to storm over to the driver, who had just gotten out of the vehicle, but he held himself in check. No point in getting the man riled up when furniture and boxes needed to be unloaded in a timely and careful manner.

The middle-aged driver stepped up to Jeff, and a few seconds later, a younger man got out of the truck and joined the two. "Sorry we're late," the older one said. "We had a flat tire on the way here, and then our GPS messed us up and we took a wrong turn off the Interstate." His sweaty forehead creased, and he pulled a hanky from his back pocket to wipe off the moisture.

"It's okay. You're here now, and that's all that matters." Jeff heaved a sigh and led the way to the open garage doors. Hopefully, things would go better from this point on.

⁓

"I still think we should have painted this room before we moved all our stuff in." Rhonda felt hot tears behind her eyes as she surveyed what had once been a young child's room. *If only. . .*

Jeff slipped his arm around her waist. "Since we didn't ask the movers to put any of the boxes in this room, it shouldn't be a problem for us to get it painted soon."

"How about tomorrow? If we go after some paint in the morning, we should be able to have it done in a few hours."

"That won't fly. Tomorrow's Sunday, and you won't find much open here in Walnut Creek on what many people consider should be a day of rest." He shook his head. "I sure don't want to drive all the way to one of the bigger towns to look for paint."

"Maybe we could go to the hardware store in Millersburg tonight," Rhonda suggested. "It's not that far from here, and I'll bet it's still open."

Jeff yawned and stretched his arms over his head. "I am too tired to go anywhere, and I'm sure you must be too. We both worked hard today after the movers left, getting our bedroom furniture set up so we can sleep tonight—not to mention the things we did in the living room, dining room, and kitchen. We really got a lot done, which is why we're both beat."

Rhonda couldn't deny her fatigue. She'd forgotten how tiring moving into a new place could be. *Tiring and stressful*, she thought, looking around the nursery before turning out the light. "Guess I'll take a warm shower and get ready for bed. Maybe I'll feel more energetic in the morning."

Rhonda started down the hall toward the master bedroom. "Are you coming, Jeff?" she called over her shoulder.

"I'll be there soon. I wanna take a quick look at the news."

Rhonda halted her footsteps and turned to face him. "I assume you mean you'll be checking the news via your cell phone?"

He swiped a hand across his forehead before shaking his head. "Thought I might go out to my man cave and turn on the TV."

Her brows squished together. "Are you kidding me? When did you have time to set up your television?"

"While you were in the kitchen getting things semi-organized."

She anchored both hands firmly against her hips and frowned.

"As I recall, you said you were going to see if there was room to park your vehicle in the garage. You also stated that you planned to set the grill outside on the patio so we could barbecue some steaks tomorrow afternoon."

"I did say that, and since the bay where I should be parking my vehicle is full of boxes, I parked it outside, near the third bay, which also has boxes, and came back inside." Jeff dropped his gaze to the floor. "Figured it wouldn't take long to set up the grill tomorrow afternoon, so I opted to get the TV up and running instead."

"I see." Rhonda looked upward, disparagingly shaking her head. "Don't wake me when you come to bed, because I'm sure it'll be late." She hurried into their room and closed the door before he could offer a response.

"Not that anything Jeff could say would matter anyway," Rhonda muttered as she laid a fresh towel out for the bath she'd decided to take instead of a shower. Some things would probably never change—like Jeff's addiction to his precious large-screen TV and all his nonsensical collections.

A minute later, he bounded into their bedroom with a sappy grin. "Rhonda, come see how nice the TV looks in the man cave."

"Right now?"

"Yeah, and I've got it on that home remodeling show you like so much. You know—the one with your favorite twin hosts."

"Okay, I'm coming, but I won't be watching it very long, because I want to take a bath." Rhonda followed him down the hall and into what she felt sure would be Jeff's favorite room.

Sure enough, her favorite fixer-upper program was on. It did look great on the large screen Jeff had displayed on the wall. Rhonda found herself taking a seat in one of the recliners.

"So, what do you think? Pretty cool, huh?" He grinned like a child with a new toy.

"Maybe this man cave thing isn't such a bad idea after all, as long as I—"

"I know, right?" He sat next to her for a moment, but soon his trigger finger hit the remote button, which changed what they'd watched briefly to another program.

"Hey, I thought you brought me out here to watch my remodeling program." Rhonda's brows furrowed.

"Well, I did, but there are so many other channels to watch." Jeff hit the remote button a few more times.

She stood up. "Okay, on that note, I'm going back to getting ready for my bath."

"All right, enjoy yourself. I'll be right here or, more to the point, probably in my recliner, checking out what else there is to watch."

"Have fun." Disgusted, Rhonda headed back to their room. She figured Jeff would probably end up falling asleep in that chair of his, and come morning, he wouldn't even remember the last thing he'd been watching.

Well, there was nothing she could do about it, and what she needed most right now was the opportunity to soak away the pain from working so hard all day. Hopefully, the warm water would also release some of the tension she felt in every part of her body.

Tears sprang to her eyes. *As long as Jeff puts his own needs ahead of mine, things will never get better between us. Even though we are now living in the house of my dreams, I doubt it will ever fill the void in my heart and soul.*

She moved across the bathroom as though in a daze and knelt beside the oversized tub to turn on the water. *Maybe I'm just overly tired tonight. After a good night's sleep, perhaps things will look brighter in the morning.*

Chapter 6

Canton

Sitting behind the desk in her office at the hotel, Rhonda was going over a list of things that needed to be done in several rooms on the second floor. Truth was, most of the hotel needed some upgrades, but the email Rhonda had received from the corporate office this morning informed her that only the necessary upgrades and repairs could be done at this time. So, now it was a matter of picking and choosing which rooms had priority over others.

I know the rooms with the balconies out front on the second level are normally the prime requests. And we have two larger suites with full-sized refrigerators that are popular with families. Rhonda shifted on her chair. *Too bad there isn't enough money to pay for all those rooms needing to be renovated right now.*

"I hate making decisions like these," Rhonda mumbled.

"Were you talking to yourself or me?"

Rhonda turned at the sound of the morning desk clerk's voice. She hadn't heard Lori come into her office. "I was grumbling to myself," she replied, hoping the smile she'd managed to put on her face looked sincere.

"Hotel problems, I assume?" Lori moved closer to Rhonda's desk.

"Yes, but then that's nothing new." Rhonda gave a small laugh. "It goes with the title of hotel manager, don't you know?"

The blond, curly-haired young woman gave a nod. "With me

being pregnant and my crazy hormones acting up at times, I'm glad I am not in your position. My job can get pretty stressful on occasion, but I don't have nearly as many responsibilities as you're faced with each day. You must really like your job to put up with all the crazy stuff you're expected to resolve."

Rhonda shrugged. "I just do the best that I can." She watched Lori gently rubbing her stomach, wondering how it must feel to be pregnant. It was hard not to be envious of Lori's excitement over her upcoming birth. Her mild-mannered employee seemed content and cheerful as she sometimes hummed while doing the most mundane things at the hotel.

Rhonda's responsibilities here had become a part of her life. She'd enjoyed all the challenges that went with it at first. But lately, Rhonda had found herself daydreaming about how nice it would be if she could stay home all the time and enjoy the beautiful house she and Jeff had been living in for almost two weeks. With every passing day, it became more difficult to pull herself out of bed and get ready for work. What Rhonda wished she could do was putter around the yard, planting new flowers and shrubs, or recline on a lounger near the pond, absorbing the sun and listening to the gentle twitter of the birds making a home in their yard.

Pushing her wishful thoughts to the back of her mind, Rhonda turned her attention back to Lori again. "Did you come to see me for something specific, and is anyone minding the check-in desk while you're gone?"

A red hue erupted on Lori's normally pale cheeks as she shifted from one leg to the other. "I. . .uh. . .left the desk unattended, thinking I'd only be gone a few minutes and would hear the bell if anyone came to check in."

Rhonda tipped her head. "Where's Zach? He's also working today, right?"

Lori gave a quick shake of her head. "He never showed up."

"Really? Well, he didn't call in sick or let me know he wouldn't be coming in."

"I never heard anything either. Zach should have been here two hours ago, and now that leaves me at the desk by myself, with no one to fill in for me while I eat lunch or take a break."

"Well, he'd better have a mighty good excuse for his unexplained absence." Rhonda rose from her chair and gave Lori's arm a pat. "I'll help out today whenever you need to be away from the desk."

With lips parted, Lori released a noisy breath. "Thank you, Mrs. Davis. I bet you're the best manager this hotel's ever had."

"I don't know about that, but I always try to do a good job and cover all the bases."

Lori hummed a gentle melody as she went out the door and headed for the hotel lobby.

Rhonda followed. She hoped the rest of the day went quickly—she couldn't wait to go home.

Walnut Creek

Although this was not Jeff's normal day off, he'd turned the restaurant over to Russ's capable hands and taken off two hours early. There was a lot that still needed to be done in the way of unpacking boxes, but Jeff had other ideas this afternoon.

After driving a short way from his house, Jeff turned onto the street where several shops were located. He'd had his eye on one in particular and hadn't taken the time to visit there yet. With any luck, he might find something to his liking and go home with a prize to put on display somewhere in their new home.

If Rhonda knew what I was up to, she'd say a trip to the antique shop was a waste of my time and that I shouldn't spend money on something I don't need.

A short time later, Jeff pulled his rig in front of Memory Keepers Antique Store. It was an old building but appeared to be well cared for. The flower boxes outside bloomed with vibrant colors, and looking through the clear windows, he could see some of the treasures within.

Jeff's heart raced at the thought of spending the next hour or so browsing through a shop full of nostalgic things. His fascination with antiques and collectibles had begun when he was a boy, and it had never left him. In fact, the older he'd got, the more fascinated he'd become with things to collect. Some of the items he owned included vintage bottles and glass canning jars. Jeff also had a good many insulators, a few old-fashioned milk cans, and several ornate oil lamps. Then there were jars full of outdated buttons, buckles, and marbles in many sizes and colors.

Jeff got out of his SUV, and when he entered the old-style building, a slightly musty odor awakened his senses. He was greeted near the door by a middle-aged Amish man dressed in plain clothes and sporting a full beard but no mustache.

"Good afternoon. Welcome to Memory Keepers." The older man extended his arm and gave Jeff a hearty handshake. "I'm Orley Troyer, the co-owner of this establishment. Feel free to look around and let me or my wife know if you have any questions or are looking for anything in particular."

"I will, thanks." *Between the way this man is dressed and being in here with all these antiques, I feel like I've stepped back in time.* Jeff had sometimes wondered if he would have been happier if he'd been born in a different era.

Without offering his name, Jeff turned away. He was about to wander off, when the Amish man said, "Is this your first time visiting our store? Don't think I've seen you in here before."

"My wife and I are new to the area," Jeff explained. "I'm a collector of old things and have wanted to check out your shop since we moved here almost two weeks ago."

Orley smiled as he fingered his beard. "I'm glad you stopped by . . .uh, what's your name?"

"Jeff Davis."

"Where'd ya move here from?"

"Canton. I own a restaurant there, and my wife manages a hotel in that town."

"So, you both have to commute to your jobs?"

"Yep." Jeff figured if he didn't walk away soon, the Amish guy would engage him in more unnecessary conversation. "Guess I'll take a look around now and see if anything in your store catches my eye."

"Certainly. As I said before, if you have any questions, just let me or my wife know. Lois is in the back room, but I'm sure she'll be out soon."

"Thanks." Jeff hurried off before the Amish fellow could say anything more. He wondered if all Amish men were as friendly and talkative as this one seemed to be.

Everywhere Jeff looked, he saw interesting items. A lot of old-looking trinkets hung on the high walls of the three sides of the interior. Some things had even been hung from the ceiling, like a couple of old bicycles and a few pedal cars. The owners used the shop's space effectively to house and display all its treasures.

Toward the back of the store, an old sled was propped against the wall. It was the kind Jeff and his cousin Larry used when they were boys and visited their grandparents on a snowy winter day. Being a few years older than Jeff, his brothers, Eric and Stan, hadn't shown much interest in the sled. But Jeff and his cousin used to argue over who would get the first ride down the hill behind their grandpa and grandma's house. When Grandpa died, Larry had been the recipient of the sled, as stipulated in Grandpa's will. Jeff was none too happy about it, but there wasn't much he could do. He'd had a sick feeling in the pit of his stomach the day Grandma had given the sled to Larry, while all Jeff got was a jar of old marbles to add to his collection. While he appreciated the marbles, they didn't have the same meaning for Jeff as the sled. Since Jeff's brothers didn't care about the old relic, they hadn't understood why he'd been upset when their cousin took the sled home that afternoon. While not as devastating as losing his mother to cancer the year before his grandfather's death, Jeff had mourned the loss of the old sled he'd wanted so badly.

He studied the sled here in the antique store a little closer and determined that it was very similar to the one he'd missed out on. Definitely from the same era as his grandfather's.

With a satisfied smile, Jeff picked up the sled and carried it to the front counter where the Amish man stood.

"That's an old one, and I've done a few repairs, so it's in fairly good shape," Orley commented.

"I agree. Can you hold it for me? I'd like to look around a bit more."

"Sure, no problem. I'll put it back behind the counter till you're ready to pay."

"Thanks." Jeff handed the sled to Orley and headed off to see what other goodies he could find.

Approaching a table where several items were for sale, he noticed an old yellowed plaque that quoted a Bible verse:

Be still, and know that I am God.
—Psalm 46:10

A sense of bitterness welled in Jeff's soul. He remembered the day the family's minister had read that verse before praying for Jeff's mother during the worst part of her illness.

I believed God would take away Mom's cancer, but she died anyway. A lump formed in Jeff's throat. *When the doctor told us that there was no physical reason Rhonda could not conceive, I prayed again, but no children came.* Rhonda had wanted to adopt, but Jeff said no. He had determined that if God wanted them to have children, He would have answered Jeff's prayer.

With a shake of his head, Jeff moved away from the table. *So much for praying and believing. I don't see how my dad could keep going to church and reading his Bible all these years.*

Out of the mood to look any further, Jeff made his way back to the register. "I'll pay for the sled now," he told Orley.

"Didn't see anything else that caught your fancy, huh?"

Jeff shrugged his shoulders. "I didn't look at everything, but I need to get home now anyway. Maybe I'll stop in some other time and see what else you have."

"I'll look forward to seeing you again." Orley's wide smile appeared genuine—not forced like some people's.

Jeff looked at the sled. *I can't wait to take this home and put it on display. I wonder what Rhonda will think of it. When I tell her that I've found a replacement, very much like the one my grandpa had, maybe she'll understand why I bought it.*

Jeff paid for the sled, picked it up, and said goodbye to the Amish man. There was something about the pleasant fellow that made Jeff look forward to coming back to Memory Keepers sometime soon.

~

After the English man left with his sled, since there was no one else in the store, Orley went to the back room to speak with Lois. She'd been in there for close to an hour, and he wondered what was taking her so long.

Upon entering the room, Orley found his wife sitting at her desk, tapping her pen, while wearing a perplexed expression.

"What have ya been up to in here? I expected you'd be out helping me soon."

"Helping do what?" She looked up at him. "Is the store full of customers right now?"

Orley shook his head. "Just one since you came back here, but he left a few minutes ago."

"Oh, then I'm sure you managed fine without me." Lois set her pen aside and scooped up whatever she'd been working on. Then she placed the notebook in a manila folder and put it in her tote bag. "Was it a new customer or someone we've met before?"

"The man's name is Jeff Davis, and it was the first time he's visited our store. Said he and his wife recently moved to Walnut Creek." Orley placed both hands on the desk. "He bought that old sled we acquired some weeks ago and said he might be back to look at other things sometime."

"That's good." Lois started for the door. "Are you coming, Husband, or do you need to stay here for a while and take a break?" She gestured to the chair she'd occupied.

"I'm fine—no need for me to sit here by myself."

"All right then. If you don't have anything else to do, would you mind helping me rearrange some of the things we put on that sale table yesterday?"

"Sure, no problem." Orley followed Lois out to the main part of the store. As they approached the table in question, he remembered how Jeff had looked at some of the items on it and scrunched up his face. Then he'd quickly made a beeline for the register to pay for the sled. *I can't be sure*, Orley thought, *but I have a feeling there's more to that fellow than just an interest in antiques. Sure hope I get the opportunity to talk to him again.*

Chapter 7

When Rhonda arrived home from work shortly before five that evening, Jeff waved at her from where he sat on the front porch swing. Since he'd said he planned to take off early in order to do some more unpacking, she figured he'd be inside doing that or at least finishing dinner preparations.

"You'll never guess what I bought today," he said when she stepped onto the porch.

"Some groceries, I hope."

Jeff shook his head. "Didn't know we needed any."

With her arms crossed, Rhonda squinted at him. "The grocery list was lying on the kitchen table. I mentioned it to you this morning."

"Sorry, I forgot." Jeff's tone of voice sounded apologetic, but his expression didn't convey any remorse.

She leaned against the porch railing, enjoying the warmth of being outside on this lovely evening in May. "If you bought something today but it wasn't groceries, where did you go shopping?"

"I made a stop at Memory Keepers Antique Store here in Walnut Creek." Jeff's eyes appeared bluer than normal as he grinned up at her. "I discovered something I've been hoping to find for a long time."

She tipped her head slightly. "What would that be?"

"A sled."

Her brows lifted. "Would you please repeat that?"

"I bought a sled." Jeff leaned forward with one hand on his knee.

"It looks almost exactly like the one my grandpa used to own. In the wintertime, whenever we visited our grandparents, my cousin Larry and I would take turns sledding down the hill behind Grandpa and Grandma's house. Once in a while, my brothers would get in on the act too." Jeff paused and sat staring into the yard with a faraway look in his eyes. "Those were some good times, and I wanted a sled like that for my own."

Rhonda felt sure her husband had more to say, so she waited for him to continue.

Nearly a minute passed, and then Jeff's eyebrows pulled close and down, creating a forehead crease. "Larry got that old sled when Grandpa died, and I got a jar of marbles."

"It's nice that he left you both something. I assume his other grandchildren were recipients of some treasured item your grandfather owned too?"

Jeff gave a nod. "Eric got a pocketknife and Stan received Grandpa's harmonica."

"Did your brother know how to play it?"

"Not really, but I remember once when we were all sitting around a bonfire in my grandparents' yard, Grandpa got out the harmonica and played several songs for us." Jeff stared off into space again, and then he looked back at Rhonda. "Stan was interested in the harmonica at first, but after trying it once, he gave up and said it was too hard."

Rhonda wasn't sure what all of this had to do with the sled Jeff had just purchased, but she took a seat on the swing beside him and waited to see if he would say anything more.

"I wanted that old sled of Grandpa's really bad, and I've been on the lookout for one, but until today I've had no luck."

"You've never mentioned the sled to me before."

"I had no reason to until now." Jeff took hold of her hand. "Come inside with me and I'll show you."

Rhonda's mouth opened to ask why he'd taken it in the house, but before she could voice the question, Jeff stood and pulled her to her feet.

"It's in my man cave."

That figures. Rhonda didn't voice her thoughts. Instead, she followed Jeff into the house and down the hall. When they stepped into the room, her eyes widened. An old, worn-out-looking sled that in her opinion should have been thrown away hung in a prominent spot on the wall adjacent to where Jeff had put his large-screen TV.

"What do you think, hon? Isn't it a beauty?" The exuberance in Jeff's voice was clearly evident not to mention the satisfied-looking gleam in his eyes.

Rhonda cleared her throat before responding to Jeff's question. "There's no doubt that the sled is quite old." She pointed to the object in question. "I understand if seeing it brought back some childhood memories, but you're not a kid anymore, Jeff. Besides, since we have no children of our own, you'll have no one to pass the sled on to when you're gone."

His joyous expression faded. "I didn't need that reminder." Jeff looked up at the sled. "I can enjoy the sled while I'm here for whatever time I have left on this earth. I may even take a ride on it when the snow falls this winter."

She resisted the temptation to roll her eyes and mention that the piece of property their home sat upon had no hill for sledding. "I would prefer that you not have the old relic hanging here in the house."

"How come?"

Rhonda gestured to the sled. "Our new home is a showpiece, and there's nothing attractive about that sled."

Jeff stared at the sled for several seconds then reached up and took it off the wall. "Fine, I'll hang it in the garage on the side where I'll eventually park my rig, and you won't have to look at it."

Before Rhonda could comment, Jeff marched out of the room. She cringed when she heard the door leading to the garage open and slam shut. She'd gotten her way, but was it worth the price? Now she'd no doubt be fixing dinner by herself.

~

"Rhonda couldn't even say she was happy that I'd found an old sled that looks like my grandpa's or say one thing nice about it," Jeff muttered as he hung the antique on the garage wall. This wasn't the place where he wanted it to be, but Jeff got his hammer and added a nail in a decent spot so that when he pulled into the garage, the sled would be right where it could be admired. He'd brought it out here to keep the peace but saw no logical reason the sled couldn't have remained in his man cave. *I don't tell her how to decorate her home office, so I hope my wife doesn't ask me to move the TV out here too. If she does, that'll be the last straw.*

Jeff stood looking up at the sled. *Sure wish it was winter right now and I could try it out. Of course, I'd have to find the right-size hill for it without a lot of trees.* A wide smile spread across Jeff's face. *Think I'll take a drive this Sunday and check out the land that's farther out. Holmes County has lots of hills. I just need to find a suitable one that's not on someone's property. Maybe Rhonda would like to join me. It'll give us a chance to see more of the countryside. Maybe we could go right after lunch.*

———

A feeling of guilt crept in as Rhonda entered the kitchen to fix their evening meal. Jeff had been excited when he'd told her about the sled he'd bought, and she had thrown cold water all over his enthusiasm. Rhonda wasn't opposed to the idea of her husband having a few collectibles, but Jeff had more than he needed. The money he'd spent on them added up, and now, with a mortgage here, and a townhouse they still hadn't gotten a single offer on, she couldn't help being concerned about their finances.

An idea popped into her head, and setting the meal preparations aside, Rhonda left the kitchen. She entered the garage moments later and found Jeff on his knees in front of an open box full of collectibles. "How much do you think all the stuff you've accumulated over the years is worth?" she asked, squatting down beside him.

He jerked his head. "Umm. . .I don't know. I'd have to look up the value of each item on the internet or maybe in the antique collectors' catalog I get every month. Why do you ask?"

"Since we haven't sold the townhouse yet and there's no guarantee that an offer will come in soon, it might be a good idea if you sold some of your things, and then we could put the money into our savings account."

Jeff flinched as though he'd been injured in some way. "You're kidding, right?"

She shook her head. "We need some extra money as a buffer, Jeff."

"We're not going under financially. You have your job at the hotel, and my restaurant is doing well."

"I can't argue with that, but if the townhouse doesn't sell soon..."

"Let's give it another few weeks, and then I'll consider selling a few items that would bring in enough money to make it worth the sacrifice."

Rhonda looked away and gathered her thoughts. How could it be a sacrifice to part with a few old items that as far as she knew held no sentimental value? Other than the sled, of course. Jeff had made it clear that he'd bought the relic because it reminded him of the one his grandfather had owned.

Rhonda stood. "We can talk about this later. I'm hungry, so I am going back to the kitchen to get dinner finished. Are you coming, Jeff?"

"I'll be there as soon as I find a spot for the stuff in this box."

Rhonda's lips pressed together as she tromped out of the garage. *If I know my husband, he'll probably be out here for hours, and I'll end up eating my meal alone.*

Rhonda was almost to the kitchen when the doorbell rang. *Oh, great. I wonder who that could be. I hope it's not someone selling something.*

She hurried to the front door, and when she opened it, every muscle in her body tightened. "Mom! Wh–what are you doing here?" Rhonda glanced outside and saw her mother's ten-year-old gray minivan parked in the driveway. It wasn't like she needed a vehicle that big, since she lived alone and rarely had passengers.

"Is that any way to greet the woman who gave birth to you thirty-five years ago?" Rhonda's mother pushed a wayward piece of light brown hair behind her ear. "I figured it was about time I came by to see your new place." She gave Rhonda a hug. "You said you would call when you were ready for company, but I couldn't wait any longer for an invitation."

Feeling a sense of powerlessness, Rhonda forced herself to put on a happy face. "I'm glad you're here. Come in, Mom, and I'll show you around the place, but you'll have to excuse the fact that there are still some boxes sitting around we haven't unpacked yet." *Perfect timing, Mother. Now I'll feel obligated to invite you to join us for supper.* Rhonda glanced over her shoulder, hoping her husband had heard the bell. *Come out of the garage, Jeff. I could really use your support right now—especially if my mother starts asking too many questions about our reasons for choosing this home or begins nitpicking things.*

"I hope you haven't been overdoing it with all the work here that needs to be done. No doubt you and Jeff will be busy sorting through boxes for quite a while yet." Her mother paused and grabbed a hankie to wipe her nose. "Sorry about that. Spring allergies, don't you know?"

Rhonda nodded. "I hear the pollen count is higher than normal right now."

"True. It's the time of year when things are budding, but my doctor gave me something new to help with my condition."

"I hope the medicine works and you'll get some relief."

"I hope so too." Her mother glanced around. "This is quite the house. As big as it is, I'm sure it will cost a lot of money to cool in the summer and heat during the winter, not to mention your monthly payments on such a big home probably won't be cheap."

"Once we sell the townhouse, it will free us up financially."

"I'm sure it will, but until then, you two will have to pinch pennies."

"It's not that bad. I'm certain we can work through it all without a problem." No way would Rhonda admit her concerns.

Mom glanced at a nice-sized picture hanging on the wall where they stood in the hall. "Is that new?"

"Yes, Jeff got it for me."

"It looks expensive."

Rhonda reached up to rub a pulsating spot between her brows. At the moment, she wished that her mother had remained the mousy little woman who'd been afraid to take chances and didn't offer unwanted advice. But the divorce from Rhonda's dad and two years of counseling had changed all that. She still could hardly believe it, but within the last few years, Mom had gone from bashful to bold.

Chapter 8

Since it was time to eat, and Rhonda's stomach had begun to growl, she invited her mother to stay for supper with a promise of touring the house after the meal. Of course, Mom had happily agreed, saying she didn't get to see her youngest daughter often enough.

"The reason we see each other so seldom is because we both have jobs," Rhonda replied as she cut up some fresh veggies to go with the chicken and rice she'd put in the slow cooker that morning. "And when you're not working, you keep busy with Gwen and her family. If Jeff and I had children, we'd probably see you a lot more."

Mom took plates from the cupboard and set the table. "Speaking of Jeff...where is that good-looking son-in-law of mine? Since you asked me to set the table for three, I assume he must be joining us for supper."

"Yes, Jeff is here. He's out in the garage going through a box of antiques I am hoping he will get rid of."

"Collecting antiques can be an expensive hobby." Mom looked at Rhonda. "Now where do you keep your silverware?"

Maybe if Mom gets side-tracked, she'll drop the subject of antiques. I don't want to discuss it anymore. "They're right over there, in the drawer below the toaster." Rhonda pointed.

"Your new kitchen is the biggest I've ever been in." Mom slowly shook her head as she retrieved the utensils. "It's so full of storage. Why, I believe you have enough space for two families."

Rhonda hoped her mother wasn't dropping a hint that she'd like to move in with them. That would never work out. Besides, since Mom's house was close to Gwen's, Rhonda figured she ought to be satisfied.

"The kitchen is just right for us." Rhonda responded. "It's nice to have some elbow room."

Her mother stepped over to the table and placed the forks, knives, and spoons at each setting. "I understand. The kitchen in your townhouse was quite small."

Mom looked at the fancy clock on the far wall. "So, Jeff is out in the garage sorting his collectibles. That's got to be an expensive hobby." She returned to the cupboard for glasses. "His restaurant must be doing pretty well for him to be able to collect antiques, not to mention buying this beautiful home, which I'm sure must have been quite pricey." Her forehead creased as she turned to face Rhonda. "I hope you're not living beyond your means."

I had hoped Mom would let that subject go. I don't want to discuss this with her right now or any other time for that matter. Looking her mother straight in the eyes, Rhonda said in a low, firm voice, "Jeff and I are doing fine financially."

"Did I hear my name mentioned?" Jeff entered the room and gave Rhonda's mother a hug. "It's good to see you, June. I saw a minivan parked out front and figured it was yours. How have you been?"

She moved her head quickly up and down. "I'm doing well. How about you?"

Jeff glanced at Rhonda then back at her mother. "Can't complain. Has Rhonda shown you around the house?"

"Not yet." Rhonda spoke before her mother could respond to his question. "Dinner's ready, and I invited Mom to eat with us. I'll give her the grand tour after we finish our meal."

"Okay." Jeff moved closer to Rhonda. "Is there anything I can do to help?"

Yes, don't make my mother feel so welcome that she won't know when to go home. Rhonda shook her head. "Food's ready, so if you've washed your hands, you can go ahead and have a seat."

"I washed up in the utility room after I was done in the garage."

Rhonda wanted to ask what he'd decided to do with all the things in that box but changed her mind. It was a topic that could wait until later—when her curious mother was not around.

Jeff pulled out the chair at the head of the table and sat down. "That chicken sure smells good. I bet it will taste even better."

Rhonda forced a smile and looked at her mother. "Feel free to be seated. I just need to set the food on the table and then we'll eat."

"I can help," Mom offered.

Rhonda handed her the dish of veggies. "I'll get the rice and chicken, so you're free to sit down now."

"Okay."

Mom sat in the chair to the right of Jeff, and after Rhonda placed the rest of the food on the table, she seated herself on her husband's left.

Rhonda was about to pass the platter of chicken to Jeff when she noticed her mother's bowed head and closed eyes. *That's weird. Is she praying?* Although Rhonda and her sister had been sent to Sunday school and Bible school a few times when they'd stayed at their grandmother's house during childhood, her parents hadn't been churchgoers, and religion had never been much of a topic in their home. Rhonda and her sister hadn't even been taught to offer prayers at the table or before going to bed.

Rhonda sat quietly waiting for her mother to open her eyes and was glad that her husband did the same. Jeff did look over at Rhonda with a quizzical expression, however.

Once Rhonda's mother opened her eyes and lifted her head, Rhonda handed the chicken to Jeff. He took two pieces and set the platter next to Mom.

After each of them filled their plates, Rhonda looked at Jeff again, hoping he would get some conversation going, because she was at a loss for words. Apparently, Jeff was too. Of course, it would have been difficult to speak with his mouth full of chicken.

Mom remained quiet for a few minutes as she ate some of the rice, then she set her fork down, cleared her throat a few times, and said, "Gwen and I have been attending a Bible study at the church not far from our homes."

Rhonda nearly choked on the carrot she'd put in her mouth. She quickly washed it down with a drink of water. "Wh—when did you start going to church?"

"A few months ago. Gwen sent the kids to Sunday school at first, and then she and Scott began attending church services." Mom paused for a drink of water. "Shortly thereafter, they invited me to join them, and we've all been going ever since."

"This is the first time you've said anything about it to me. Why the big secret, Mom?" Rhonda's face heated, and her pulse began to race.

"It's no secret, really. It's just not something I wanted to discuss with you over the phone."

Rhonda shrugged. "What is there to discuss?"

"Well, I. . ."

"Let's change the subject, shall we?" Rhonda lifted the plate of veggies and held them out to her mother. "Would you like some more carrot or celery sticks?"

"No, thanks, I'm fine with what I have on my plate."

They finished their meal with minimal conversation, which was centered mostly around the pleasantly warm weather they'd been having this spring.

"From what I saw of your front yard and large front porch, it seems you'll have some nice places to relax during the summer months," Mom commented.

"Yeah, and the backyard's really great too." Jeff pushed away from the table and stood. "Rhonda, you can show your mother around the house while I put the dishes in the dishwasher. When I'm done, I'll meet you two out back by the pond."

Mom's eyes widened. "A pond? Oh, how nice that must be."

"Yep, and it's full of some colorful fish."

"I'll be eager to see it."

Rhonda left her chair and motioned for her mother to do the same. "If you'll follow me, I'll give you the grand tour."

As they went from room to room, Rhonda's mother gave several positive comments and even stated that she hoped Rhonda and Jeff would make many wonderful memories in this beautiful home.

When they entered the guest room that had been used as a nursery by the previous owners and was yet to be repainted, Mom slipped her arm around Rhonda's waist. "This would certainly make a lovely room for a baby. I wish you and Jeff would reconsider adoption."

A stab of regret shot through Rhonda like an arrow piercing its mark, but she pushed it aside. "As you already know, Jeff has never wanted to adopt, and I'd rather not talk about it." Rhonda stepped out of the room and felt relief when she saw that her mother had followed.

"Well, that concludes the tour of the house." Rhonda moved down the hall in the direction of the front door. Hopefully, her mother would take the hint and head for home without going out back to see the pond.

"I haven't seen the backyard yet. I'm sure Jeff must be waiting for us out there by now."

"Um. . .yeah, that's right." Rhonda felt more than a little rattled, especially after the mention of them adopting a baby. *Why did Mom have to bring that topic up? I wish I hadn't shown her the guest room with those balloons on the wall. For that matter, I wish Mom hadn't come here at all.*

~

Jeff took a seat on a wooden bench near the far end of the pond. He held a container of fish food in his hand but wouldn't feed them until Rhonda and June showed up. He thought his mother-in-law might get a kick out of watching the fish swim to the top with their mouths opened wide in eagerness to be fed. Having a pond with fish was great, but it also meant work, as the water would need to be kept clean without harsh chemicals that could harm the fish. The filter for the pump that ran the waterfall would also require regular maintenance. Even so, Jeff figured the tranquility it brought was worth all the work.

"Oh, my. . .what a lovely yard!"

Jeff turned at the sound of his mother-in-law's voice. "Come on over and see our exotic fish." He waited until June and Rhonda joined him, then he sprinkled a bit of food in the water. The fish swam over as quickly as he had expected.

June laughed. "Just look at them go after that food. They carry on like they're starving."

"Yep. It's an everyday occurrence too." Jeff handed the container to her. "Would you like to feed them?"

"Sure."

"Just be careful you don't put in too much," he warned. "Over-feeding can cause serious problems."

"Don't worry. I'll go easy."

While June fed the fish, Jeff looked over at Rhonda, who stood quietly to one side with her arms folded. Her somber expression made him wonder if something had occurred between the two women. Rhonda had mentioned several times in the past that she'd never gotten along well with her mom. Their perception of things clashed, even when Rhonda was a girl. According to Rhonda, her sister had been the favored one—at least where their mother was concerned. Rhonda had gotten along with her dad fairly well, until he'd left his wife for another woman ten years ago. Rhonda hadn't spoken to him since, and from that time on, her relationship with her mother had continued to decline. Although Jeff hadn't asked, he wondered if his wife blamed her mother for the divorce. *Could June have done something to drive her husband into the arms of another woman?*

Jeff's thoughts reverted to the present when Rhonda's mother handed him the fish food. "Thanks for letting me feed them; it was fun. I bet my granddaughters would enjoy seeing your pond and getting the chance to feed the fish."

"Sure. Anytime you're here, you're welcome to feed the fish, and so are the girls."

"If Gwen decides to bring the kids over, please tell her to call first to make sure we're at home," Rhonda stated.

"Don't worry. I'll make certain she calls you first. I probably should have done that too, instead of making an impulsive decision and showing up without an invitation."

"It's okay. We're glad we were here when you came by." Jeff

looked at his wife. "Right, Rhonda?"

"Umm. . .yes, of course."

"I should be on my way home soon. No doubt my cat, Ginger, will be waiting for her evening meal." Her lips curved in a pleasant-looking smile as she looked at Jeff and then Rhonda. "I have a little housewarming gift for you, but I left it in my car. If you'd like to walk out with me, I'll give it to you."

"Okay." Rhonda's expression was one of eagerness, and Jeff figured it had more to do with the fact that June would be leaving soon than it did with whatever the gift was that she'd brought for them.

"We can walk around front rather than going through the house." Jeff led the way, and the women followed.

When they got to June's minivan, she opened the back door and withdrew a maroon-colored gift bag with white tissue paper sticking out of the opening. "I think this will go nicely in the front entrance of your home." She handed the bag to Rhonda.

"Should I open it now?"

"Yes, please do."

Rhonda reached into the sack and pulled out a beige-colored plaque with the words *God Bless Our Home* in bold, black letters.

A lock of hair fell on June's cheek as she tipped her head slightly to one side. "I hope you like it."

Jeff couldn't wait to hear his wife's response. He would let her comment before he said anything.

"It was nice of you to think of us." Rhonda had managed to put what Jeff felt sure was a fake smile on her face.

"Yes, thanks for the gift, June." Jeff hoped he sounded sincere. Seeing this wall hanging with the word *God* on it made him think about the plaque he'd seen at the antique store this afternoon. If there was one thing Jeff and Rhonda agreed upon, it was that they didn't need any part of religion in their home. While others, like Rhonda's mom and sister, might feel the need for that kind of thing, Jeff felt sure that he and Rhonda could make it through life on their own, without any help from God.

Chapter 9

"Let's go for a Sunday afternoon ride," Jeff suggested after he and Rhonda had finished eating their lunch on the back patio. "I hear tell from one of my employees that this area has a lot of nice open land. I'd like to see what some of the countryside looks like here in Holmes County."

"Seriously?" Rhonda's jaw clenched as she tapped her foot under the patio table. "What happened to our plans to open more boxes today? And don't forget that one of our guest rooms still needs to be painted."

"We unloaded several boxes this morning, and I figured we could both use a break this afternoon." Jeff finished the last of his lemonade. "Come on, honey, let's do something fun for a while. You know what they say about 'all work and no play.'"

She rolled her eyes and sighed. "Okay, but I don't want to be gone too long. There's still plenty we should get done around here, and since we both have to work tomorrow, we need to go to bed at a decent hour. No staying up till midnight, watching TV either."

Jeff bobbed his head. "No problem. We won't be gone more than a few hours."

"Promise?"

"Of course. When you're ready to come back home, just say the word."

"It's nice to sit out here on the front porch and relax, jah?" Orley smiled at Lois.

She nodded. "I can't think of anyone I'd rather spend my Sunday afternoon with."

He reached across the short span between them and took hold of her hand. "My feelings exactly. I knew the day we got married that I was one lucky fellow."

Heat rushed to Lois's cheeks, and she fanned her face with her free hand. Orley's compliments always made her blush—especially when he looked at her with such a tender expression, the way he was now.

"Our church service was good today, wasn't it?" she asked.

"Jah," Orley agreed. "The minister's sermon on loving our neighbors was a good reminder of how we should treat others."

Lois gave a decisive nod. "I appreciated his use of 1 John 4:12: 'If we love one another, God dwelleth in us, and his love is perfected in us.'"

"That's a good one, all right. But then there are many other fine verses that speak of love for others."

Lois glanced out toward the road in front of their property. "Did you notice how that vehicle slowed down in front of our place? I thought for a minute that it was going to stop or drive on in here, but then it finally moved on."

"I did make a mental note of it," Orley said. "Figured it was probably someone out taking a leisurely Sunday drive or heading somewhere they weren't familiar with. That can happen when people from out of the area don't know the back roads."

"True." Lois let go of Orley's hand and stood.

"Where ya goin'?"

"In the house to get some refreshments." Lois moved her brows up and down. "When we first got home from church, I saw you eyeballing those brownies I made yesterday."

He snickered and gave his belly a thump. "I wouldn't say no if you brought some of those tasty morsels out for us to enjoy."

"No problem, Husband. I'll pour us some iced tea as well." Lois stepped into the house and closed the screen door behind her. What a nice day this was turning out to be.

"It's sure pretty out here in the country," Jeff commented as he turned onto County Road 172. He glanced over at Rhonda, and she gave a noncommittal shrug.

"There are a lot of Amish farms out this way, and the ones I'm seeing so far are very well kept."

"I've noticed too and am amazed at the large gardens alongside or out in front of all the white homes we've driven by already," Rhonda said. "There were also no electrical wires running to their homes, and I've seen several houses with black carriages parked outside."

"Did you see those horses and buggies pulling out of that driveway a ways back?"

"How could I have missed them? They were all driving so slow." Rhonda spoke in a tone of agitation.

Jeff grimaced. His wife was obviously not having the good time he'd hoped she would on their little jaunt. "Those Amish must have been heading home from church."

"I didn't see any church buildings."

"They take turns holding Sunday services in each member's home, barn, or other large building on their property," Jeff explained.

"Who told you that?"

"No one. I read about it on the internet when I was looking up information on the Amish way of life."

"Why would you want to know about that?" she questioned.

"Just curious is all. Since we live in the heart of Amish country, I thought it would be a good idea to learn something about the culture of the Plain people who reside here."

"I see."

They rode in silence for a while, until Jeff noticed a house on the right side of the road with a nice-sized hill that looked perfect for sledding. He slowed the SUV for a better look and was tempted to stop. On second thought, he decided to keep going.

Jeff glanced over at Rhonda. Her eyes were closed, with her head leaning against the headrest of her seat. He wondered if she was bored or trying to take a nap.

After traveling a bit farther, he turned the vehicle around and headed in the direction from which they'd come. When his rig approached the place where he'd seen the nice hill, Jeff noticed a man and a woman dressed in plain clothes sitting on the front porch.

On an impulse, Jeff pulled his SUV into the yard. At the same time, Rhonda opened her eyes and leaned forward. "Wh–where are we, and why are you stopping here?"

"See that hill over there?" Jeff pointed.

"Yes. What about it?"

"I'm pretty sure it's part of the property that belongs to the people who live here." Jeff's anticipation mounted. "I'm gonna stop and talk to them about it."

Rhonda blinked rapidly as her dark brows squished together. "Why would you want to talk to complete strangers about a hill on their property?"

"Because it would be the perfect place to try out my old sled, and I'll need to get their permission to use it."

"Have you lost your mind, Jeff? Winter is six months away, and there won't be snow on the ground until then, if we get any at all this year."

He frowned at her. "Don't ya think I know that? I just want to pave the way so that when the time comes, I'll have a place to go sledding."

She wrinkled her nose. "Okay, Jeff, whatever you say."

Ignoring his wife's sarcasm, Jeff drove his rig up the driveway.

As he drew closer to the house, Jeff was surprised to discover that the Amish man on the porch was Orley Troyer, the owner of the antique store he had visited. He chuckled. "What are the odds?"

Rhonda looked at Jeff with a curious expression. "What are you talking about?"

"That's the man who sold me the sled, and I bet the woman sitting beside Orley is his wife. What a coincidence. I can't wait to talk to them." Jeff opened the door and got out. "You coming, Rhonda?"

She shook her head. "I'll wait here, but please don't take too long. We need to get home soon so we can—"

Without waiting for his wife to finish her sentence, Jeff sprinted for the house. He was almost there when Orley stepped off the porch and greeted him. "Well, hello there, Jeff." With a wide smile, Orley extended his hand.

Jeff shook it eagerly. "You remember me?"

"Of course. I remember most of my customers—especially the ones who buy old sleds." Orley's smile remained fixed as he gave a quick wink. "Come on up to the porch. I want you to meet my wife."

Jeff glanced back at his vehicle, where Rhonda waited, wondering if he should include her too. After a few second's deliberation, he gave a wave and then motioned for her to join them on the porch. Based on the sour-grapes expression on Rhonda's face when she got out of his rig, Jeff figured if he didn't find a way to redeem himself, he might be sleeping in a recliner in his man cave tonight. In all honesty, though, sleeping out there wouldn't be the worst thing, because he liked his little getaway room. But Jeff thought better of the idea and decided to do something nice for Rhonda to keep the peace.

When Rhonda joined him on the porch, Orley and Jeff introduced their wives.

"Please take a seat and join us for some iced tea and brownies." Lois offered them a pleasant smile as she motioned to the two empty chairs next to the ones she and Orley now occupied.

"I'll get your beverages." Lois rose from her seat.

"Oh, don't bother on our account. We can't stay long anyhow. Right, Jeff?" Rhonda's question was spoken in a near whisper.

Before Jeff could respond, Lois went inside, and Orley spoke up. "Surely you can stay long enough for a glass of cold tea and some of these." He lifted the plate of brownies that had been sitting on the small table between his and Lois's chairs.

"Sounds good to me." Jeff plucked a chocolate goody off the plate and took a bite. "Yum. . .this is sure tasty. You should try one, Rhonda."

"No, thanks. I'm not hungry right now. I'm also trying to avoid eating too many sweets." She sat with her arms crossed and a stoic expression.

Jeff brushed some brownie crumbs off the front of his shirt. *Yep. I'm probably gonna be sleepin' in the man cave tonight. I wish my uptight wife could just relax and enjoy herself with these nice folks.*

Lois returned a few minutes later and handed Rhonda and Jeff each a glass of iced tea. Jeff took a drink and smacked his lips. "Thanks. This sure hits the spot."

Rhonda drank her tea too, and Jeff felt relieved when she looked at Lois and said, "Thank you."

"You're probably wondering why we dropped by, since I had no idea you lived here." Jeff directed his statement to Orley.

The older man smiled as he gave a nod. "I'll admit, I was surprised to see you."

With no hesitation, Jeff made known his desire to go sledding on their hill when winter brought snow. He ended by asking if they would mind.

"I'm guessing you're eager to try out that old sled?" The twinkle in Orley's eyes said he already knew the answer.

Jeff nodded enthusiastically.

"I have no problem with it, and I might be tempted to try a little sledding myself." Orley looked over at Lois. "What do you say, Fraa? Would you have any objections to me and Jeff going sledding on our hill?"

"Of course not," she quickly answered.

"Maybe you womenfolk would like to join us."

Lois gave her husband what Jeff felt sure was a playful pinch. "No, thanks. I'll just watch from the sidelines and warm your insides with some hot chocolate when you're done having fun."

Jeff wasn't about to ask Rhonda if she'd like to go sledding—not with the way her posture had slumped.

In need of a change of subject, Jeff observed, "This is a nice place you have here."

"Thanks. Lois and I have lived in this home since we got married."

"Do you have a big family to help take care of your home and yard?" The question came from Rhonda and seemed to be directed to Lois.

The middle-aged woman shook her head. "It's just Orley and me. We've never been blessed with children."

"Neither have we." Rhonda placed one hand against her chest and released an audible sigh. "But I keep busy managing a hotel in Canton, and Jeff has his own restaurant to occupy his time. We also recently purchased a new home in the area and still have a lot of unpacking to do, so our lives are plenty busy." Rhonda nudged Jeff's arm. "We should go and let these two enjoy the rest of their Sunday in peace and quiet."

Jeff knew he'd better do as she'd suggested or he could end up sleeping outside on a chaise lounge tonight instead of in the comfort of his favorite recliner. It was nice to visit with the Amish couple. They seemed like good folks. But Rhonda had a point—Orley and Lois could probably use some time alone.

He stood and thanked Orley and his wife for taking time out to visit with them and also for the refreshments Lois had provided.

"You're welcome," the Troyers said in unison.

"Come by here or stop in at the store anytime you like," Orley added.

Jeff gave a nod. "Thanks, I will."

Once their goodbyes had been said, Rhonda and Jeff got into his all-wheel-drive vehicle. As they headed in the direction of home, Rhonda decided it would be best if she remained quiet. She was irritated that they'd wasted so much time at the Amish couple's home when they should have been unpacking more boxes. Rhonda also thought it was ridiculous that Jeff had thought he needed to find a hill so he could go sledding. He wasn't a little kid anymore, and he ought to grow up and face his responsibilities as a man. Rhonda hoped that by the time winter arrived, her impetuous husband would forget about the silly notion of going sledding with the Amish man.

She rubbed her throbbing temples. Between her mother dropping by unannounced a few days ago and Jeff's unexpected stop at the Amish couple's home, Rhonda felt more stressed than ever.

Jeff bumped Rhonda's arm. "Aren't the Troyers a nice couple?"

She shrugged. "They seem to be, but then first impressions are not always accurate. The Troyers may not be as nice as you think."

"Don't be so judgmental, Rhonda. I believe they are genuine people. Remember, I spoke to Orley at his antique store, and he acted the same way toward me then as he did today."

She pursed her lips. "Oh yes, I'm sure. He wanted your business, after all."

"No, I'm certain it was more than that. Orley seemed genuinely—"

"I hope you don't keep making trips to that store—unless it's to sell off some of your antiques or collectibles that have some monetary value." She tapped Jeff's arm. "I assume they buy items at their store as well as sell."

"Probably, but I haven't decided if or when I'd be willing to part with any of my collections." Jeff kept his focus straight ahead.

Rhonda's fingers clenched her purse straps. *We'll see about that.*

Chapter 10

Canton

Monday morning Jeff arrived at his restaurant an hour before opening in order to put a few of his collectibles on display. He couldn't help being a little excited about doing this and hoped for some possible feedback from his employees and the patrons who would see his antiques. And by bringing the items to his business, Jeff would still be able to enjoy them.

Rhonda might not be too thrilled when she finds out I haven't sold any of my collectibles, he thought. *I don't intend to at this point either.*

Last night, Jeff had told Rhonda that he would be clearing out some of his memorabilia this morning, and she seemed relieved. Jeff had not specified, however, that he'd be taking them to his restaurant to put on display. He assumed his wife thought he planned to sell the items. His announcement, plus a little bit of time spent unpacking some more boxes after they'd gotten home from the Troyers had apparently been enough to keep him from having to sleep in the man cave. Of course, sleeping there would have meant more time to watch TV.

"Mornin', Boss," his manager said. "Do you have any more boxes to bring in?"

"Nope, this is all for now, Russ. I brought some of my antiques to put out on display." Jeff opened the lid and showed his faithful employee the contents. "Some will go on this shelf, and I'll place the milk bottles on the tables as a decoration."

Russ leaned in closer. "Those look like nice pieces."

"Thanks. It's taken me a while to collect all these bottles." Jeff set the big box down and carefully took out one item at a time, arranging several of them on the shelf. When finished, he stood back and eyed his work. *I like how this looks. It wasn't such a bad idea after all.*

"Hey Boss, can you come over and take a look at the new menus we had printed?"

Jeff turned at the sound of Russ's voice. "Oh, yeah, I've been so busy I kinda forgot about those." He joined the middle-aged man he'd hired three years ago and looked at the counter where one of the menus had been set out.

"They look pretty good." Jeff smiled. "Hopefully, the new breakfast items we've added will be a favorite with our morning customers."

"Don't see why they wouldn't be. All the items we've currently offered have sold well." Russ bobbed his balding head. "The locals and many from outside the area come here to enjoy the downhome cooking we serve."

"I'd like to think so. That is what my restaurant is noted for— nothing fancy, just simple but tasty, nourishing meals like down-to-earth folks would get at home."

"Only better. Right, Boss?"

Before Jeff could respond to his manager's question, he heard the rumble of a truck out back. "I bet that's the delivery we've been waiting for. Would you mind opening the back doors for them to bring in the boxes?"

"Sure, I'll take care of it right now." Russ hurried toward the back of the restaurant.

Jeff picked up an old milk bottle from the box and placed it in the center of one of the tables. With the proper amount of water, and some fresh-cut flowers placed inside, the glass bottle would make a nice centerpiece. Since Jeff had brought several other bottles like this one from home, he could put them on most of the tables.

Those that didn't get a milk bottle would get something else—either a different kind of old bottle or a small glass canning jar.

Or, he thought, *I might drop by the Troyers' antique store on the way home this afternoon and see if they have some other kinds of milk bottles.*

Jeff cringed when his mind shifted gears, taking him back to a day when he was a boy, and he'd searched for and found an old soda-pop bottle in one of his grandpa's sheds, set way back on his grandparents' property. Jeff hadn't realized it until later, but the overgrown path he'd followed to the shed had left him with a nasty case of poison ivy. Due to the severe itching he'd dealt with for several days, Jeff had almost given up on the idea of collecting old bottles. But his fascination with antiques and collectibles had won out, and he'd kept pursuing his hobby, sometimes taking risks to dig up or scrounge around in search of old things.

The business phone rang, putting Jeff's thoughts on hold. He hurried over and answered, "Jeff's Red Barn Restaurant."

"Hey, Son, how's it going?"

Jeff reached up and rubbed the bridge of his nose. "Everything's fine, Dad. How come you're calling me on the business line instead of my cell phone?"

"I tried that number and all I got was your voice mail, so I figured I might catch you at the restaurant."

"And so you did. Anything new with you?" Jeff wasn't about to admit to his father that he'd left his cell phone at home that morning. *He might think I'm irresponsible.*

"Actually, there is something new in my life, but I'd like to wait and tell you in person. Is it okay if I drive down this weekend? I'd like to see your new place and spend a little time visiting with you and your lovely wife."

Jeff shifted the receiver to his other ear. "I'll be busy most of Saturday, painting one of our guest rooms, but Sunday is free. At least I hope it is, unless Rhonda comes up with some other project for me."

"The drive from Cleveland will take me about an hour and a

half, and I wouldn't be able to come until church is over, which wouldn't give us as much time to talk as I'd like. How about if I come Saturday morning? I'll help you do the painting."

Jeff tapped his fingers on the countertop as he thought about the promise he'd made to his wife last night, agreeing to paint the guest room this coming weekend. "Yeah, Dad, Saturday would be fine, and I appreciate your offer to help paint. Between the two of us, we can get the job done twice as fast as I would painting the room by myself."

"Great. I'll see you around 9:00 a.m. on Saturday. Or is that too early?"

"Nine's fine. Talk to you soon, Dad."

After Jeff said goodbye, he bonked his head. *Sure hope I did the right thing. Since Dad and I don't see eye-to-eye on his Christian viewpoints, I'll have to be careful what I say if that topic comes up. I don't want to end the day feeling stressed out, the way Rhonda did after her mother dropped by our house unannounced.*

Jeff picked up another antique milk bottle to set on the next table. *At least my wife and I are like-minded when it comes to our lack of religious beliefs. If I could just make her understand how important old relics like this are to me. Sure wish she shared my interest in antiques.*

A knock sounded on Rhonda's office door, and she looked up from her paperwork. "Come in."

A few seconds later, Lori stepped into the room, wearing a deep frown. "I. . .I have some bad news." With fluttery hand movements, she spoke in an emotion-choked voice.

"What is it? You're obviously upset."

"Thirty mattresses and box springs were just delivered, and they're sitting in the middle of the hotel lobby."

"Did you tell the people who delivered the mattresses what rooms they should be put in?"

"I. . .I couldn't; they unloaded them quickly and then took off."

Lori's hands dropped limply to her sides. "I didn't even know the mattresses were being delivered today. Did you?"

"No, I did not. All the corporate office told me was that the company they had ordered them from would let me know when they had a firm delivery date." Rhonda gathered her wits about her and stood. "Please get a hold of the maintenance man and all the housekeepers. You can watch the desk while the rest of us haul the mattresses and box springs to their appropriate rooms."

"Okay." Lori placed both hands on her belly as she hurried from the office.

Rhonda leaned against her desk and brought a shaky hand to her forehead. Last night she'd been upset with Jeff when he'd quit helping her unpack boxes and gone in to watch TV, and now this? *How much more stress can I handle?* At the moment, she wished she could walk away from this job, go home, and sit by the pond for the rest of the day with a cold drink in her hands.

But I can't quit, Rhonda told herself. *We'd never be able to make the mortgage payment every month if I weren't working. If we'd just get an offer on the townhouse, it would help.*

With a determination she didn't feel, Rhonda forced herself to leave the room and head for the lobby to face the items waiting for her and the rest of the employees.

~

Walnut Creek

Orley had been talking with an Amish man named Jake Miller from their church district, when he caught sight of Lois wearing her dark outer bonnet and carrying one of her larger purses as she headed for the front door.

He excused himself from Jake and hurried over to Lois. "Are you going somewhere?"

She gave a brief nod. "I. . .I have an errand to run."

"How long will you be gone?"

"It shouldn't take long." Lois offered Orley a close-lipped smile and rushed out the door.

His brows furrowed. *I wonder why my fraa always has so many errands to run. She's seemed a bit preoccupied here of late too. I hope Lois isn't keeping anything from me.* He watched out the window as she walked briskly down the sidewalk. *Maybe she hasn't been feeling well and has gone off to see the doctor without telling me. Think I'm gonna come right out and ask her about it when she gets back to the store.*

Orley returned to his customer, who now had an antique clock in his possession. "Would you take fifty dollars less for this than what you have on the sticker?" Jake asked.

Orley reached up and gave his earlobe a tug. "I could knock twenty-five off for you. Would that be agreeable?"

The man tilted his head from side to side a few seconds then grinned and said, "It's a deal."

Orley got out a cardboard box and some packing material and met Jake up front at the register. He wrapped the clock securely and placed it carefully inside the box.

Jake pulled out his wallet and paid Orley in cash. "My fraa's *gebottsdaag* is next week, and this will be a nice gift for her."

Orley smiled. "I hope Edna likes it, and please tell her happy birthday from me and Lois."

"I will." Jake picked up the box, and with a little whistle, he strode out the front door.

Since there were no other customers in the store, Orley decided this would be a good time to go into the back room and get himself a snack. He'd only made it halfway there when the bell above the door jangled. He turned and saw Jeff Davis step in.

"Well, this is a pleasant surprise," Orley said. "I was hoping I would get to see you again. Just didn't expect it would be this soon."

Jeff smiled. "I'm on a mission."

Orley tipped his head. "And what would that be?"

"I'm giving my restaurant a facelift and need some old milk bottles for the rest of my tables that currently have no centerpiece."

"I believe I can help with that." Orley pointed to a shelf on the left side of the room. "There are plenty of milk bottles in different sizes and shapes to pick from."

"Sounds good. I'll take a look." Jeff moved to the other side of the room, and Orley followed.

"Lois and I enjoyed our brief visit with you and your wife yesterday."

"I appreciated it too."

"And your wife? Did Rhonda like visiting with us?" It was probably a bold question, but the words slipped off Orley's tongue before he thought it through.

Jeff's cheeks reddened. "I believe she did, but she was a little put out with me for staying at your place too long and then not getting enough unpacking done at home."

"Sunday is supposed to be a day of rest," Orley stated. "Maybe some time away from unloading boxes was good for both of you."

"Yeah, that's how I felt, but Rhonda tends to be a workaholic. And I had promised her that we'd get a lot of unpacking done over the weekend, which didn't happen, even though I did get a few boxes unloaded." Jeff sighed as he rubbed the back of his neck. "Things have been strained between me and my wife for some time, and I had hoped by moving to a more relaxed atmosphere and settling into a new home that things would get better. I sure wish there was something I could do to make things better between us and cause Rhonda to smile whenever she looks at me."

Orley leaned in closer. "Would you like my advice?"

"Uh. . .sure."

"Maybe you should give your wife a nice gift or a pretty bouquet. Lois has always responded favorably whenever I've given her special gifts or flowers."

Jeff slowly nodded. "That's not bad advice. Thanks for the suggestion."

Orley grinned. "You're most welcome. You'll have to drop by again and let me know if your wife responded well to your gesture."

"I'll do that, and before going home, I think I will go to the local flower shop and get a nice bouquet for Rhonda."

Orley gave Jeff's shoulder a few taps. "Next time you come by the store, you should bring your wife with you. I'm sure Lois would enjoy getting better acquainted with Rhonda."

"Okay, I'll give her that invitation." Jeff pointed to the shelf overhead. "Now about those bottles. . ."

Soon after Jeff left the store, Lois returned.

"Are you feeling okay?" Orley asked, stepping up to her.

Tipping her head to one side, Lois pursed her lips. "I'm fine. Why do you ask?"

"Oh, no particular reason. You just haven't seemed like yourself here of late. If there was something wrong, you'd tell me, wouldn't you?"

Lois gave Orley's arm a gentle squeeze. "There's nothing wrong, Husband. If I didn't feel well, I would speak up."

Although Orley felt relieved, he still wondered why Lois always had so many errands to run and why she never explained where she planned on going. It seemed like a mystery to him—one he had no answers for.

Before Orley got the chance to ask Lois anything more, an English man and a woman came into the store. They didn't appear to be together, so Orley asked the man if he needed assistance while Lois spoke with the woman.

Once Orley directed the man to the section where old tools were displayed, he stood off to one side with his arms folded. *If I don't get busy with something this evening and end up forgetting about it, I plan to ask Lois a few more questions. I don't want to be suspicious, but I do have a feeling she's hiding something from me.*

Chapter 11

When Jeff pulled his rig in front of the garage, he was disappointed to see that Rhonda's car wasn't there. Since he'd taken the time to stop at the antique store and then the flower shop, he figured his wife would be home from work by now.

Maybe something came up at the hotel and she had to work later than usual, he reasoned. *Or she might have made a stop on the way home to pick up some groceries or a take-out meal for our supper.*

Jeff got out of his vehicle and reached into the backseat to get the dozen red roses he'd purchased for Rhonda. The florist had placed the flowers inside cone-shaped plastic wrap, and Jeff wanted to put them in a vase with some water as soon as possible.

He hurried up the walk and stepped onto the porch then put his key in the door and turned the knob. Upon entering, Jeff headed straight for the kitchen to look for a vase. After searching through all the cupboards, Jeff came to the conclusion that there were no vases in the kitchen. Most likely they were still in a box in the garage.

"We've gotta get the rest of those boxes opened and things put away," he muttered. "They're taking up the space where we should be parking our vehicles."

Jeff snapped his fingers when an idea popped into his head. *An old canning jar would make the perfect vase for the flowers.* He left the roses on the table and hurried out to the garage.

When Rhonda drove into the yard, she saw Jeff's SUV parked outside the garage. "Good, he's home. I hope he got supper started."

Every muscle in Rhonda's body ached. She couldn't wait to spend some time in the soaking tub. Hauling mattresses and box springs into guest rooms was not on her list of managerial duties. When Rhonda had been hired for the job, she'd been told that she would be responsible for recruiting, training, and supervising the staff. She would also be expected to manage budgets, maintain financial records, plan maintenance work, set up hotel events, and book rooms. In addition to all that, Rhonda would need to handle customer complaints, promote and market the business, and make sure the hotel complied with health and safety regulations and licensing laws. There was no question about it—Rhonda had a lot on her plate. But the job provided a decent salary, and keeping busy helped take her mind off troubles at home or conflicts with her mother and sometimes her sister.

Rhonda reached for the carnations, protected by plastic wrap, and got out of the car. The flowers at the check-in counter had been replaced today. Since they still had some life left in them, Rhonda had brought them home to enjoy and add a little brightness to the rest of her day rather than throw the flowers out.

When Rhonda entered the kitchen, she was surprised to see red roses on the kitchen table.

Now how did those get there? Could Jeff have bought them? She poked her tongue against the inside of her cheek. *Today's not my birthday, our anniversary, or any other special occasion, so what would have prompted him to buy flowers?*

Opening the door under the kitchen sink, she took out two cut-glass vases. After filling them with water, she put the carnations in one vase and the roses in the other. Then, placing them both on the table, she headed down the hall in search of Jeff.

Rhonda was halfway between the kitchen and living room when she saw Jeff coming toward her with an old canning jar in his hand.

"Oh, good, you're home; I have something for you." Jeff gave Rhonda a kiss on the cheek.

"You mean the roses?"

"Yeah. I picked them up at the flower shop in town. Do you like them?"

"They're beautiful, and as you know, my favorite flower." She tipped her head back to give him better eye contact. "Was there any particular reason you bought me flowers?"

"Just wanted to do something special for you."

"Thank you."

He smiled and held up the jar. "I couldn't find any vases, so I went out to the garage and found this in one of the boxes."

"No need for that now. I had put a couple of vases under the kitchen sink."

"I never thought to look there." Jeff thumped the side of his head. "Dummy me."

Rhonda shook her head. "You're not dumb. Guess I should have mentioned that I had put them there, but since you rarely buy me flowers. . ." Her voice trailed off. "Sorry, I just meant that. . ."

"It's okay. I'll work a little harder at being more attentive." He caressed her cheek with his thumb. "You look tired. Did you have a rough day at the hotel?"

She touched both temples while closing her eyes. "You have no idea."

"What happened?"

Rhonda opened her eyes and clasped his hand. "Let's go to the kitchen. I'll tell you about it while I fix supper."

"I have a better idea." Jeff gave Rhonda what appeared to be a heartfelt smile. "You can sit at the table, and I'll fix us something to eat."

Rhonda pressed a palm against her chest. "Thank you, Jeff. I would appreciate that very much."

When they entered the kitchen, Jeff's gaze went to the table where she'd set the two vases filled with flowers. "You bought yourself some flowers too?" His brows lifted high on his forehead.

"No, they came from the hotel lobby and were replaced by a new bouquet," she explained. "Since the carnations had a few days' life left in them, I didn't want to throw the pretty flowers out. Besides, I'd hoped their lovely aroma and soft, muted pink color might help me relax."

Jeff set the glass jar on the counter, pulled Rhonda into his arms, and gently patted her back. "I'm sorry you had a rough day. I wish we both had jobs that could be done from home so we'd have more time to be here at our beautiful place."

Rhonda took a seat at the table. "This house and property are like a sanctuary for me. At the end of a workday, I find myself more eager than ever to come home." She released a lingering sigh. "Although working from home is a pleasant thought, it's not likely to happen since both of our jobs require us to be in Canton."

"True." Jeff opened the refrigerator and took out two bison-burger patties from the bottom freezer. "I'll thaw these in the micro-wave and then cook 'em on the outdoor grill. How's that sound?"

"Delicious." Rhonda's stomach growled, reminding her that she'd missed lunch today due to all the craziness with the mattresses and a few other disturbances.

"You went in a little earlier than usual this morning. How did your day go at the restaurant?" she asked, keeping her focus on Jeff.

"Not too bad. And I'll get to the reason why I went to work earlier, but first I'll mention something else. We got our new menus, and the fresh items we offered seemed to be well liked by the cus-tomers who ordered them."

"That's good. A little change is always nice. It gives people a reason to keep coming back."

"Yeah." Jeff placed the meat patties on a plate. "And now the reason as to why I went to work earlier. I wanted to spend some time changing things up a bit, to give the restaurant a more country feel. I decided that the decor should go along with what folks might expect when they come into a restaurant that resembles an old barn."

"What did you do to accomplish that?"

"I set some of my old bottles and jars on the tables as center-pieces. I also put some on a few shelves up on the walls." He glanced over at her and grinned. "Now you won't have to worry about lookin' at those old relics sitting around here."

While Rhonda would have preferred that her husband had sold some of his bottles and jars, at least he had taken them out of the garage and most likely emptied another box in the process. Determined not to say anything negative that could spoil this pleasant time of being together, Rhonda kept her thoughts to herself.

He cleared his throat. "Did you hear what I said, Rhonda?"

"Umm. . .you mean about the old relics?"

"No, actually I had moved on to another topic."

"What about?"

"I was telling you that if I hadn't left my cell phone at home this morning, I could have gotten some pictures of the tables and you could have seen how nice they look now."

"You'll be there tomorrow, so you can take some pictures then."

"Good point." Jeff put the plate in the microwave and set the timer to defrost the patties. "I got a phone call from my dad today."

"That's nice."

"Being caught off guard, I asked him why he was calling me on the business line instead of my cell phone."

"Did you explain that you'd left it at home?"

"No. I felt embarrassed and dumb at the same time when dad said all he'd gotten was my voice mail, which was why he called the restaurant's number."

"Don't let it bother you. We all forget things at times." Rhonda shifted in her seat. "How's everything going with him?"

"Okay, I guess. He asked if he could come here on Saturday, and when I mentioned that I'd be painting the guest room, he volunteered to help." Jeff moistened his lips with the tip of his tongue. "Are you okay with that?"

"Certainly. Especially since it means that spare room will get done, and we can finally use it for overnight guests." She sucked in her lower lip. "Although, I can't imagine who would ever spend the night. With my mom and sister living in New Philly, it's not likely that they'd ever need to stay all night with us."

"What about your nieces?" Jeff asked. "It might be fun to have Megan and Kimberly sleep over some weekends."

"I'll give that idea some thought." Rhonda leaned close to the vase filled with roses and inhaled deeply of their fragrant aroma. *Having Gwen's girls stay here for even one night would only remind me that Jeff and I have no children of our own.* She clenched her fingers while holding them in her lap. *Do I really need that reminder?*

Redirecting her thoughts, Rhonda focused on the beautiful bouquet from Jeff. It had been a long time since he'd given her flowers, and she appreciated the sweet gesture.

I need to make an effort to do more thoughtful things for him too. She tapped her fingers. *Let's see now. . .should I make a list. . .*

———

"This is a mighty good chicken-and-rice casserole you fixed for our *nachtesse* this evening." Orley looked across the table at Lois and smiled.

"Danki. I made our supper dish this morning before we left for the store, so when we got home, all I had to do was warm it in the oven."

He wiped his mouth on a napkin and leaned a bit closer to her. "There's something I've wanted to ask you."

She quirked an eyebrow. "What's that?"

"Do you still enjoy working at the store, like you did when we first opened the business? Or have you become bored with it?"

"Of course, I'm not bored. What made you ask such a question?"

"For the past month or so, you've been gone from the store more than usual, running errands and who knows what else? When we first opened Memory Keepers, you seemed to like it, but here lately you appear to be preoccupied with other things."

Lois waved his question aside. "Everything is fine. I've just had more errands to run lately."

Orley decided to be more direct with his next question. "What kind of errands have you had to run that've taken you away from the store several times a week for the past few months?"

Small circles of red erupted on Lois's cheeks. "Why would

you care about that? Are you worried that I may have been buying things I don't need?"

He shook his head vigorously. "Of course not. I'm just curious since you are gone a lot."

"Oh, I go here and there. It seems like there's always so many things to be done."

"Well, um. . ."

Their conversation was interrupted when a knock sounded on the front door. Orley rose from his seat. "I'll go see who that is." He hurried from the room.

⁓

Lois got up and cleared the table. During the couple trips made back and forth from the dining room, she glanced at her mending basket. *My, my, that basket of mine has a pile of work needing to be done. With so many other things I'm expected to do, I don't know when I'll get around to doing any mending.*

After placing all the dishes and silverware on the counter, she ran warm water and liquid detergent into the kitchen sink. She'd only gotten the dishes put into the water when Orley returned to the kitchen and announced that their closest neighbor's cows had gotten out, and some of them were roaming around in their yard.

"So, I'm going out to help Abe round up the cows and get them herded back over to his pasture."

"I hope it goes well, and please be careful."

"I will. Don't worry. See you soon." Orley quickly exited the room.

As Lois washed the dishes, she thought about the brief conversation she and Orley had at the table. It appeared that her husband didn't trust her and felt the need to ask those questions. She wished there were something she could do to put his mind at ease.

As Lois sloshed the sponge across one of the plates and scrubbed it thoroughly, she looked out the window at Orley and their neighbor herding the cows out of their yard. *No matter how busy I am with other things, I'll make a concentrated effort to spend more time with him, either here at home or at the shop. Hopefully, that will put my husband's concerns to rest.*

Chapter 12

At nine o'clock sharp, Jeff glanced out the kitchen window and saw his dad's convertible pull into the yard. The sporty-looking vehicle he drove was an eye catcher for a man in his midfifties.

What's up with my dad? I don't get it. When he and Mom were together, he drove an older sedan, and he seemed okay with it. Why the sudden change? Jeff shook his head and tried to compose himself.

"My dad's here," he called to Rhonda.

She stepped into the kitchen from the dining room, where she'd been unloading a box of her good dishes into the hutch. "Should I let him in, or did you want to greet your dad at the door?"

"Guess we could do it together." Jeff moved closer to Rhonda and put his arm around her waist. They walked down the hall, and he opened the front door.

Jeff watched as his father got out of the car and came up the walkway carrying a canvas satchel. Dad's trim but muscular body and full head of dark hair made him look much younger than his fifty-seven years. Jeff hoped he would look that good when he reached his father's age.

"It's good to see you, Son," Dad said when he'd stepped onto the porch. "And you as well, Rhonda." He greeted Jeff with a hearty handshake and a hug and then hugged Rhonda.

"Hi, Dad. Nice to see you too." Jeff invited his father inside.

"Welcome to our home, Don." Rhonda motioned to the three boxes stacked in the entryway. "As you can see, we haven't fully unpacked yet. It's my goal today to open these and find a suitable place for everything inside."

Jeff's father gave an ample, white-toothed smile. "As big as this place looks from the outside, I'm guessing there'll be more than enough room for all of your things." He set his satchel on the floor. "How about giving me a tour of the house before we begin painting?"

Just look at his teeth. I've never seen them look so white. Jeff tried not to stare and gave a hearty nod. "Of course. That's what I'd planned to do." He couldn't help wondering if his wife had also noticed his dad's bright smile.

"I have some laundry to do, so I'd better get that out of the way before I start unloading more boxes." Rhonda smiled at Jeff and his dad. "By the time you two finish painting the guest room, it'll probably be time for lunch, so I'll have something ready for you to eat around one."

"Sounds good to me," Jeff's dad said. "No doubt we'll be hungry by then."

While Rhonda headed off to the utility room, Jeff's first stop was to show his dad the dining room and kitchen.

"Pretty nice. Looks like this place has a lot to offer," Dad commented after seeing both rooms.

"Yeah, but wait till you see the rest of the house." Jeff couldn't help feeling a bit proud. To his way of thinking, having a home this nice was proof of his success as a businessman. And to be honest, he wanted to impress his father. Although Jeff's younger brothers, Eric and Stan, were both married with three children apiece, neither of them lived in above-average houses. Eric was a journeyman electrician, but he didn't own the business. Stan taught choir and band at a high school in Cleveland. There was nothing extraordinary about his home either.

Jeff continued with the tour of his house. The whole time, Dad commented on how big the place was and mentioned all the work it would take to keep it up, not to mention the expenses involved.

"I hope you and Rhonda didn't bite off more than you can chew by buying this place," he said, looking at Jeff with a serious expression.

"I'm not concerned about the extra work. In fact, it's relaxing to putter around in the yard." Jeff reached around to rub the back of his hot neck. *Can't my dad just be happy for me without having to make unnecessary comments?*

"Too bad your job isn't closer to home," Dad said. "I imagine the commute will get old after a while."

Jeff's features tightened as he shook his head firmly. "I don't mind the drive. Gives me time to think about things while I'm heading to and from work." *If my dad were the Christian he always says he is, then he shouldn't be so critical. I wonder if Dad throws cold water on anything Eric or Stan chooses to do. Guess it's a good thing I don't live close to him anymore, or we might butt heads the way we often did in the past.*

"Let's take a look at the garage now," Jeff said, moving their conversation in another direction. "There's something I'd like to show you."

When they entered the garage, Jeff pointed out the old sled hanging on the farthest wall.

"Say, that looks like your grandpa's old sled." Dad moved closer and seemed to be scrutinizing the item. "But that makes no sense. When my dad died, his will stated that he wanted your cousin Larry to have it." He put his hand on Jeff's shoulder. "I remember how disappointed you were when Larry walked off with the sled and you got a jar of old marbles."

Jeff lowered his head and shuffled his feet against the concrete floor. "It may seem silly to you, but I've always searched for a sled like the one Grandpa used to have and hoped I'd find one."

"It's not silly, Son. You enjoyed using the old relic when you were a kid, and I'm glad you found one so similar."

Jeff looked up. "Really, Dad?"

"Of course. I'm also happy that you and Rhonda have this nice home." Dad looked directly at Jeff. "Sorry if I came off earlier as though I didn't support your decision to move here. I'm just concerned that you may have taken on too much—especially since you now have a mortgage plus a townhouse that hasn't sold yet."

"It's okay. Our old place will sell soon." Jeff placed one hand against his belly. "I feel it in my gut."

"That's good, but a little prayer wouldn't hurt either."

Here we go. Am I now going to get the religious talk? Jeff felt a tingling in his chest. If there was one thing he didn't need, it was to hear anything about God. The man upstairs had taken Jeff's mother, and Jeff didn't think he could ever forgive God for that. Truth was, he wasn't even sure there was a God.

If God's real, then He could have healed her from the ravages of cancer, Jeff thought. *If God is love, then why would He take a mother away from her young boys when they needed her so much? Dad needed her too.*

Jeff had never understood why, after his mother's death, his father had continued going to church, praying, and reading his Bible. Wasn't he angry about losing his wife?

Eric and Stan, though not as open about their faith, had kept going to church after Mom died. But not Jeff. The moment they'd lowered his mother's casket into the ground, he'd vowed never to pray again, pick up a Bible, or step one foot in church. He wanted nothing to do with God. Dad had tried to get Jeff to attend church many times over the years. But even as a boy, Jeff had refused, shouting that he'd run away from home if his father forced him to attend church or pray out loud at the table. His father must have known Jeff meant it, for he'd never forced him to do either of those things. Dad did, however, continue to pray at the table and talk about God. After Jeff married Rhonda and moved to Canton, his father had sent them religious birthday and Christmas cards. Jeff wondered if Dad thought he could wear him down and Jeff would eventually forgive God and start going to church like he had before Mom's death.

Jeff's fingers clenched into the palms of his hands, causing his nails to bite into his skin. *Well, if that's what he thinks, then he doesn't know me very well.*

"Do you still have the old marbles from your grandpa?" Dad asked, halting Jeff's contemplations.

"Yeah, sure. I keep them in a jar over there on my workbench." Jeff pointed in that direction. "Feel free to take a closer look if you want to."

His dad wandered over to the worktable, and Jeff followed. "I've learned a lot about marbles since I inherited these."

"Oh yeah? Like what?"

"Well, to begin with, no one really knows when the first marble was made or used in a game." Jeff reached into the jar and plucked out one of the older marbles from the nineteenth century. "This one is known as a 'Lutz.' See how the transparent glass has stripes of fillings around the center core that make it sparkle?"

Dad nodded.

"It was named after a New England glassmaker, but many believe it was made in Germany."

"That's interesting."

"There are other types of marbles with different kinds of swirls." Jeff pointed to another marble. "This is called a clambroth. It has striped swirls on a creamy background and was mostly produced in the United States at the turn of the century."

"You seem to know a lot about marbles."

"Yeah, I've studied up on them, and there's a lot more I could tell you, but we need to get busy painting that spare room, so why don't we head there now?"

"I'm willing, but I would like to see your backyard."

"How about we save that tour until after lunch? In fact, when the time comes, maybe we could eat lunch out on the patio."

Dad bobbed his head. "Sounds great to me. Fresh air and sunshine go well with food."

While Dad got his satchel and went to the guest bathroom to change into the work clothes he'd brought along, Jeff went to the master bath and put on a grubby pair of jeans and a light blue, stained T-shirt. He walked past the mirror in his room and stopped to take a second glance at his reflection. While what he wore wasn't the best, he thought his form looked pretty good. Then he opened his mouth wide. *Hmm. . .my teeth aren't as nice looking as my dad's though.* Jeff frowned. *Maybe I should do something to brighten my own smile.*

He closed his mouth with a snap of his teeth. *I wonder what is going on with my dad. Is there some reason he's driving a fancy car and has whitened his teeth?*

Jeff moved away from the mirror. *Guess I'd better make sure I have everything we'll need for painting laid out in the guest room.*

A short time later, Jeff and his father got to work.

"By the looks of those balloons painted on the wall, I'd have to say that this must have been a young child's bedroom for the previous owners," Dad commented as he stirred the beige-colored paint in the large bucket setting close to him.

Jeff offered a brief nod.

"If you would reconsider adopting a baby or even a toddler, the room could still be put to good use."

Jeff's face heated. "We've been through this before, Dad, and you know my reasons for not adopting."

"Yes, I remember. At first you said that you couldn't afford to adopt, but later, after you were making a decent living, you stated that you wanted a child who would be biologically connected to you and Rhonda."

Jeff merely shrugged in response. He really didn't want to talk about this. If Dad kept pressing, Jeff might end up blurting out the real reason he didn't want children, and then he'd be in for a big lecture. No, it was best that he kept his thoughts to himself—especially since he hadn't admitted the truth to Rhonda for fear of her reaction.

Jeff grabbed two paintbrushes and handed one to his father. "Let's change the subject, shall we?"

"Sure, no problem." Dad cleared his throat a couple of times, the way a person might do if they were about to make an announcement. "Remember when we spoke on the phone the other day, and I said there was something I wanted to tell you?" Dad dipped his brush into the paint can and began to paint his side of the room.

Jeff's brows furrowed as he turned to look more fully at his father. "You look so serious. Is something wrong?"

Dad shook his head. "Not wrong, but it's kind of a sensitive subject."

"Sensitive for who—you or me?"

"Maybe for both of us. Me in the telling and you in the hearing."

Jeff tipped his head. "What do you mean?"

"A few weeks ago, I logged onto the internet and joined a Christian dating site for people fifty-five and older."

Jeff nearly dropped his paintbrush. "Are you kidding?" *Now that explains the white teeth and fancy car. He's trying to make an impression on the opposite sex. I sure never expected my father would be interested in anyone but Mom. I'm not sure if I'm ready to see him with another woman—or even hear about his pursuit in finding someone compatible to date.*

"No, Son, I'm not kidding. There aren't any single women my age at the church I attend, so I decided—"

"Why, after all these years, would you want to get married again?"

"I didn't say anything about getting married. All I'm looking for is companionship right now. If something were to develop later, then—"

"Why don't you get a dog? They make good companions, you know."

"That would not be the same as a person-to-person friendship." Dad moved closer to Jeff and gave his arm a poke.

Jeff lifted his gaze to the ceiling to keep from rolling his eyes. "A dog won't make caustic remarks or give you the silent treatment if you say or do the wrong things."

Dad's forehead wrinkled. "Are you and Rhonda having marriage problems?"

Jeff was quick to shake his head. He had never let on to his dad or anyone but Russ that things weren't perfect in his marriage, and he wasn't about to admit it now. Besides, things had been going a little better between him and Rhonda since they'd moved to Walnut Creek—especially after Jeff gave her that bouquet of roses.

"Please take the worried look off your face," Jeff said as he resumed painting. "Everything's fine between me and my wife."

Chapter 13

After Rhonda put all the food on the picnic table, she took a seat beside Jeff, which put her across from his father.

"Would you two mind if I offered a blessing, or would you prefer to pray silently like some folks do?" Don asked.

Why does Jeff's dad think every time he has a meal it needs to be prayed over before we can eat? Rhonda held her tongue and looked at Jeff, hoping he would respond, because she wasn't about to tell his dad that he couldn't offer a prayer at their table.

"Umm. . .yeah, sure, Dad. Go ahead and pray if you want to." Jeff's tone sounded flat, but at least he hadn't said no, which would have been rude.

Although Rhonda didn't believe in prayer herself, she had no objections to others praying. To her way of thinking, offering prayers to God was a waste of time and about as useless as wishing on a star or hunting for a four-leaf clover. She'd tried praying when things first went sour for her parents. But no matter how hard Rhonda pleaded with God, her prayers had gone unanswered when Dad left Mom for another woman.

Pushing the painful memory aside, Rhonda lowered her head as Don began to pray.

"Heavenly Father, thank You for the meal set before us and for the hands that prepared it. Please bless this food to the needs of our bodies. Amen."

Rhonda was glad her father-in-law had kept his prayer short and did not mention her or Jeff. There had been times in the past when he'd said a lengthy prayer, asking God to bless and protect each of his family members.

If we're blessed, it's not God's doing, Rhonda thought as she passed the bowl of macaroni salad to Don. *The blessings we've received came about from hard work and the determination to succeed.*

"Here, Dad, have some cold fried chicken." Jeff passed the platter to his father. "I brought it home from the restaurant last night. There's also baked beans with bacon in that bowl with the foil. It's one of the customers' favorite sides at the restaurant. You should give it a try."

Rhonda took the foil off the beans and spooned some onto her plate.

Don nodded and forked a piece of chicken then handed the platter back to Jeff. "I'll try those baked beans and see how good they are too." He paused. "I guess having food to bring home is one of the fringe benefits of owning your own place to eat."

"Yep, but I don't bring food home for us every night. Rhonda and I both like to cook, so we prepare most of our meals here in our new kitchen."

Rhonda watched his father taste the beans. His eyebrows shot up as he smiled and commented on how tasty they were. She was pleased that their meal was good and hoped the conversation would be as well.

As Jeff's dad worked on his drumstick, he looked out into their yard. "This is some place you have here. With all this green grass, plus a beautiful pond, you'll probably be content to stay right here and never take a vacation."

Rhonda spoke up before Jeff could say anything. "It's a nice oasis, but I would still enjoy leaving the state of Ohio and going to the Bahamas or maybe one of the Hawaiian Islands sometime."

"Me too," Jeff agreed. "But running my business keeps me pretty tied down, so we're not likely to take any long vacations."

Her husband's comment didn't set well with Rhonda, but with Jeff's dad sitting there, she chose not to say anything. *Surely Jeff could take time away from his restaurant long enough to take me on a real vacation, which we haven't had in a long while.*

"You know, I bet Eric and Stan's kids would get a kick out of feeding the fish in your pond." Don looked over at Jeff. "During the time we spent painting the guest room this morning, didn't you mention that there were goldfish in the pond?"

"Yep." Jeff spooned some garlic dip onto his plate and added several potato chips.

"And with a nice big yard like this, the children would enjoy having so much space to run and play," Don added after he'd taken a drink of lemonade.

"Maybe later this summer, when we're more settled, we could have the whole family here for a get-together," Jeff responded.

"That's a great idea, Son. Everyone could bring something for a potluck picnic. You've certainly got the perfect place for that." He looked over at Jeff and smiled. "Let me know when you're ready to do it, and I'll spread the word."

The tightness in Rhonda's jaw and facial muscles caused her discomfort. *Why would Jeff have said that without talking to me first? A decision to have his family or mine over to our place is something we should discuss before extending an invitation.*

She took a deep breath to give herself a few seconds to think of what she wanted to say. "If we are able to make it happen, we can send out invitations," Rhonda spoke up. "I'll include a list of what each family should bring."

"Sounds like a plan." Don grinned at Rhonda. "My son's lucky to have married you. You're an organizer, just like my sweet Sharon was." His facial muscles slacked. "Even though it's been a good many years since she passed, I still miss her."

Rhonda glanced at Jeff to see if he would say something, but he kept quiet, and his focus remained on his unfinished plate of food.

"I've never lost a spouse, so I can't say that I understand how you feel, but I'm sure that losing your wife had to be difficult."

"You're right. And although the pain has lessened with time, it's never gone completely away." Don placed one hand over his heart. "The love I felt for Sharon will always stay with me."

Jeff's cheeks reddened, as though he'd been exposed to the sun too long. "Maybe now that you're putting both feet in the dating world again, you'll forget about Mom."

Don shook his head. "No, I won't, Jeff. But life goes on, so don't you think it's about time I started living again?"

Jeff lifted his shoulders in a brief shrug. "You're a grown man. You can do whatever you want."

Although Rhonda hadn't been aware that her father-in-law had started dating, she realized that he must have said something to Jeff about it before they'd come outside to eat lunch. It was obvious Jeff was unhappy about his dad's decision to start dating again.

Jeff's dad has been acting different than he normally does, Rhonda thought. *Like driving a sporty car here today and caring far more about his appearance than I remember him doing. And he's been whitening his teeth.*

Knowing they needed to get the conversation back onto smoother ground, Rhonda smiled at Don and said, "Thank you for helping Jeff paint the guest room—I've wanted it done since we first bought the place."

"You're welcome. Glad I could help, and I enjoyed the opportunity to visit with Jeff." Don offered Jeff what Rhonda thought looked like a hopeful expression. The poor man was obviously looking for some confirmation of his son's love and appreciation. If only Jeff would give an affirmative nod or say something positive. But Jeff just sat with a placid expression while he finished the food on his plate.

Rhonda had toyed with giving his leg a swift kick from under the table, but instead, she kept her composure and fiddled with the napkin in her lap. She'd thought things had been going fairly well between Jeff and his dad, but then the topic of his mother had been brought up. Jeff's obvious frustration had increased when he'd mentioned that his dad had begun dating.

Maybe he should have kept that news to himself or at least waited until his dad headed home to tell me. Rhonda pursed her lips. *How are we going to host a Davis family get-together if Jeff can't even be civil to his dad?*

~

"Ha! Ha! Ha! This is hilarious!"

Lois walked over to Orley, who sat behind the counter Monday morning, reading the paper. She gave his arm a poke. "What's so funny?"

"This. It's just plain laughable." He pointed to the "Dear Caroline" column.

She leaned a bit closer. "What does it say that you find so amusing?"

"Just listen to this: 'Dear Caroline: I have a pet pig that I let in the house. My mother is afraid of it. Should I put the pig outside when my mother comes to visit, or should I tell Mother she will either have to get over her fear of little piggy or stop coming to my house? Sincerely, In a Pig Dilemma.'"

Tears rolled down Orley's cheeks as he held his sides and rocked back and forth. "Can you imagine having a pet pig and letting it be in the house?"

Lois gave a shake of her head. "Well, I certainly couldn't, but—"

"And wait till ya hear what Dear Caroline said in response." He grabbed a tissue from the box on the counter and dried his face.

"What did she say?"

"'Dear In a Pig Dilemma, You may need to ask yourself this question: Who is more important to you—your mother or the pig?'" Orley reached under his reading glasses and wiped the moisture from beneath his eyes. "Why would anyone write to a complete stranger and ask such a ridiculous question? And why would Dear Caroline even bother to answer?"

"Well, maybe—"

"And who is this 'Dear Caroline' person that she thinks she has all the answers to people's problems?"

"Perhaps she—"

Orley closed the paper and slapped his hand on the countertop. "I can't believe the woman—if it is actually a woman who writes this column—gets paid to give advice to people who send her letters in care of the newspaper." He puffed out his chest a bit. "I sometimes give advice to people who come into our place of business and don't charge a penny."

Lois gave him another poke, this one on the middle of his back. "Go on with you now. The folks you give advice to haven't asked for it, and some may not appreciate your comments either."

"Jeff Davis, that young fellow who bought the old sled, seemed to appreciate it when he came by the store earlier this week. He mentioned that things have been strained in his marriage."

"What kind of advice did you give him?"

"I suggested that he buy his wife a nice gift or get her a pretty bouquet." Orley winked at Lois. "That's worked well whenever you've been put out with me."

"That's because you've always included an apology with it."

"Maybe Jeff did too." Orley leaned both elbows on the countertop. "Sure wish I could have been at their house when he gave his wife the flowers. I would've liked to have seen her reaction."

Lois clicked her tongue against the roof of her mouth. "That's because you're such a romantic at heart."

He slipped his arm around her waist. "That's absolutely true. I wish all married couples could be as happy together as we are."

She leaned her head against his shoulder. "We're very fortunate, jah?"

"Most definitely. But one of the reasons we're happily married is because we talk things through and don't keep secrets from each other."

Lois pointed to the antique clock on the wall across the room.

"Would you look at the time? It's past one o'clock, and we haven't had lunch. Should I go get our sandwiches and bring them up here so we can eat, or would you rather we took turns eating in the back room? Since it's been busy today, we probably shouldn't leave the main part of the shop unattended. One or both of us need to be here in case a customer comes in."

"You're right, so why don't you bring our lunches up here? Then we can read some more of the Dear Caroline column while we eat." He snickered.

Lois gave her husband a third poke before grabbing the newspaper and folding it up. "Enough about Dear Caroline. I'm sure there are plenty of other things we can find to talk about."

"All right, Fraa. While you go after our lunches, I'll sit here and think about what our next topic of conversation should be."

"You're so predictable."

"That's right, but you should keep a close eye on me, 'cause one of these days I might say or do something totally unpredictable." Orley gave Lois another wink.

She chuckled, gave him a hasty peck on the cheek, and headed for the back room. *How fortunate I was when he came into my life. I wouldn't trade my special man for anything in the world.*

Orley and Lois had no more than finished their lunch when she announced that she had an errand to run.

He frowned. "What, again? Who's gonna help me run this store if you're off doing who-knows-what kind of errand?"

"I'll only be making one stop, and I shouldn't be gone more than thirty minutes or so." She made a sweeping gesture with her arm. "Since the store is devoid of customers at the moment, you should be fine by yourself for a short while."

He folded his arms and gave an exaggerated huff. "Okay, but if we get flooded with customers while you're gone, I'll be a nervous wreck. We are going into the peak of tourist season, you know."

Lois gave his shoulder a tender pat. "I doubt many people will come in, but if it should happen, then you'll have to stick to business and forget about sticking your *naas* into other people's business while trying to solve their personal problems."

Orley grunted and touched the end of his nose. "Very funny. For your information, I do not stick my nose into anyone's business unless they open up and share their problems with me."

Lois gave him another pat. "I know, dear husband. I know, and I respect you for that." She picked up her purse and outer bonnet and hurried out the door.

Orley smiled, pulling his fingers through the ends of his long, full beard. *The best day of my life was when I met my sweet Lois. I wouldn't trade that dear woman for anything.*

Chapter 14

"Before you leave for work, there's something I'd like to talk to you about," Rhonda said as she and Jeff finished eating breakfast Monday morning.

He glanced up from the newspaper he'd been reading. "Sure, what's up?"

"I've been thinking about the way things went between you and your dad on Saturday."

Jeff gave no response. His concentration seemed to be on the paper again. Either that or he'd chosen to ignore her statement.

Rhonda tried again. "The way you talked to your father while we were eating lunch out back sounded disrespectful."

"You don't understand, do you?" The skin around Jeff's eyes tightened as he squinted.

"He accepted my mother's death as God's will, and even though Dad says he still loves Mom, he's looking—on the internet, no less—for another woman."

"I don't think it's wrong for him to seek love again, Jeff. After all—"

"Well, if he's gonna do it, then why mess around with an online matchmaking site? Probably more than half of the people who have signed up there are scammers."

"But if it's a Christian site—"

Jeff lifted his gaze toward the ceiling while shaking his head.

"Like that really matters. Some people call themselves Christians to give the impression that they're good people."

She looked at her well-groomed husband's clean-shaven face. "You're right. I can't argue with that. Even so, your dad is a grown man, capable of making his own decisions." Rhonda placed her hand on his arm. "Why don't you give him a call and apologize in case you hurt his feelings?"

"I'm not gonna apologize for saying something I believe is the truth. Besides, my dad isn't the type to carry grudges. He probably hasn't given much thought to the things I said."

"Maybe not, but in case he was upset, maybe you should call just to clear the air."

Jeff shoved the newspaper aside, drank the rest of his coffee, and stood. "I'm done with this conversation, and I need to get on the road. I'll see you this evening, Rhonda. I hope you enjoy your day off." He hurried from the room without giving her a kiss goodbye.

Rhonda remained at the table until she heard Jeff's vehicle leave the yard. Although she needed to unpack a few more boxes, she really needed to calm down and get her mind off Jeff and his stubborn attitude.

I think after I put the dishes in the dishwasher, I'm going to grab the newspaper and go out back to relax on one of the patio chairs for a while. Most of the time, my life is about work either here or at the hotel, so I deserve to take a break and enjoy the sunshine and fresh air.

Rhonda reclined on the chaise longue, listening to the sweet melody of the birds chirping as they flitted back and forth among the trees in their yard. The aroma of roses mingling with the light scent of clipped grass from the mowing Jeff had done yesterday was an added bonus. The only thing that disturbed the tranquility of it all was when a plane flew overhead.

She looked up and shielded her eyes from the glare of the sun. *I wonder where that plane is off to—maybe some of the passengers are on their way to a tropical place for a vacation.* Rhonda lowered her arm and heaved a sigh. *I wish Jeff and I could be taking a trip this summer or fall. Oh, well, at least we have this beautiful yard to enjoy.*

She'd almost forgotten the newspaper lying in her lap until a light breeze rustled the pages. Rhonda picked up the paper and scanned a few pages, and then her gaze fell on the Dear Caroline column. "Hmm. . . It might be interesting to read some of the letters and see what kind of a response Caroline offered."

After reading a few of the problems and complaints people had written about, Rhonda realized that she wasn't the only person facing situations they didn't know how to deal with. One letter spoke of a problem with a nosey neighbor who kept peeking over the fence and making snarky comments. Caroline's suggestion to the person who'd written was to either ask the neighbor nicely to refrain from spying on her or build a higher fence.

"Good answer," Rhonda murmured. "This Caroline, or whoever she is, must have a lot of wisdom to be giving such good advice."

She folded her hands beneath her chin and contemplated. *Think I might write a letter to Caroline and see what she has to say about Jeff's and my situation. In fact, I'm going to do it right now while I'm thinking about it.*

Rhonda got off the chaise longue and hurried inside to her desk. *"Dear Caroline,"* she wrote on a piece of lavender stationary. *"My husband and I are having marital problems."* She paused and lifted her pen, unsure of what to write next. It wasn't enough to say they were having problems with their marriage. Rhonda needed to be more specific.

She tapped her pen against the desktop. *Let's see now. . .what specific question should I ask Caroline? Okay, maybe I'll add this to my opening line: "I won't say it's all my husband's fault, although I think it mostly is. You see, he thinks he can say whatever he wants and is sometimes rude—like he was to his father the other day."*

Rhonda drew a line through her last sentence. *If I wrote that and Jeff would read the "Dear Caroline" column, he might realize it was me who sent the letter.*

Rhonda started again on another sheet of paper. *"Dear Caroline: My husband and I are having some marital problems and can't seem to agree on anything. When he doesn't want to talk about something, he retreats to another room and shuts me out. What can I do to get him to listen to me and be willing to talk through our problems? Unhappy Wife."*

Satisfied with her question, Rhonda folded the paper and slipped it inside an envelope. After writing the address of the newspaper on the front of the envelope and making it "in care of Dear Caroline," she sealed and stamped it but didn't include her return address. If the person who wrote the column did respond to Rhonda's question, it would be published sometime within the next few weeks.

And so I shall wait and try to be patient, Rhonda told herself. *I just hope Dear Caroline answers.*

Canton

When Jeff arrived at his restaurant, he found Russ washing the front windows.

"Where's Wally?" Jeff asked. "He's the one I hired to keep the restaurant clean, and that includes windows."

Russ glanced over his shoulder. "He called in sick, so I'll fill in for him today."

"Seriously? You're supposed to manage things here, not do the job of a janitor."

"I don't mind, Boss, really."

"Okay. Guess I'll be doing double duty too."

"We all appreciate it when you chip in. You're a great guy, Jeff."

"Thanks. Too bad my wife doesn't think so."

"What do you mean?"

Jeff took a seat and signaled for Russ to do the same. He spent the next fifteen minutes grumbling about his father's visit.

"I still can't believe, after all these years since my mom died, that my dad wants to start dating. The fact that he bought a convertible and has even whitened his teeth makes me wonder if Dad's lost it."

Russ chuckled. "Maybe he's in some sort of midlife crisis."

"Yeah, could be—only he's a little past midlife."

"Well, not to worry. Your dad will either give up on his quest or find the perfect woman."

Jeff frowned. What his manager had just said didn't set well with him. *I wish now I'd never said anything.*

He rose from his chair. "Well, it's time to get to work. The morning crowd will soon be pouring into the restaurant. I'll be in my office for the next hour or so. Give a holler if you need me."

Russ gave a nod and left his seat too. "Will do."

When Jeff entered his office, tucked away near the back of the restaurant, a thought entered his head. *Think I'll stop by Memory Keepers Antique Store on the way home this evening.* He picked up the remote to his television and clicked it on while taking a seat in the overstuffed office chair. "Ah, that feels better." Jeff relaxed into its soft cushioning and put his feet up on the desk. He surfed through the channels and then turned it off. "I don't have time for this. I need to look at my work list." He grabbed the paper, but before he started to read it, the Amish-owned antique shop reentered his thoughts. *Just being among all those old things might make me feel better, and it'll be nice to talk to Orley Troyer again.*

Walnut Creek

Orley watched from across the room as Lois talked with an elderly Amish woman from another church district. The way those two had their heads together made it appear as if they knew each other well and were good friends.

That's my sweet Lois, Orley mused. *She's friendly and outgoing and gets along with most people.* He gave his beard a little tug. *Of course, she says that about me too.*

Orley was about to rearrange some things he'd put on display earlier, when he spotted Jeff Davis entering the store.

"It's good to see you again." Orley approached the young man and shook his hand. "Where's your wife? I thought you were going to bring her along the next time you came in."

"I'd hoped to do that, but I got off work a short time ago and on a whim decided to stop here. Besides, Rhonda's not into antiques the way I am."

"Oh, I see." Orley gave his beard another tug. *Jeff seems kind of down in the dumps today. I wonder if everything's okay.*

"Speaking of Rhonda. . ." Jeff leaned against one of the tables where several old books had been displayed. "I gave her some flowers like you had suggested."

"Did she like them?"

"Yeah. I got her red roses, and she said she liked them, but now she's barely talking to me."

Orley tipped his head. "Oh? Why's that?"

"Well, it's like this. . ."

Orley listened as Jeff complained that his wife expected too much from him and often gave lengthy lectures whenever he did or said something she thought was wrong. "I oughta have the right to feel the way I do about certain things and say whatever I want in regard to those things without her getting on my case."

Orley said a quick silent prayer asking God to give him the right words to say. "You know, Jeff, there are times when we need to listen when our wives chastise us."

Jeff blinked. "You—you think so?"

Orley gave a decisive nod then glanced at Lois, where she still stood talking with Mary Schrock. "I'll admit I haven't always listened to my wife, but I've learned to give whatever she says my consideration, because she is often right."

Jeff reached around and rubbed both sides of his neck. "That might be true with Rhonda, as well, but not when it concerns my dad."

"Are you having some issues with your father?" Orley questioned.

"Yeah, but I won't bore you with my problems."

"I don't mind listening if you want to talk about it."

Jeff shook his head. "Not today." He glanced toward the front of the store, where two more people had come in. "You have other customers to look after, so I'll let you take care of business." Jeff turned in the opposite direction and wandered off to another area in the store.

Orley went to see if he could help the man and woman who'd come in, but they didn't stay long, saying they'd only come to look around.

When the couple left a short time later, Orley noticed Jeff looking at the plaque with the Bible verse on it from Psalm 46:10. Believing Jeff might be interested in purchasing the item, Orley stepped up to him and said: "If you're interested in buying that plaque you're looking at, I can offer you a good deal on it. How about half price?"

"Thanks anyway, but my wife and I are not into that kind of a decoration." Jeff was quick to set the plaque back on the table.

"The religious kind, you mean?"

"Yeah. We're not the churchgoing type of people."

Orley's brows drew together as he made strong eye contact with Jeff. "Do you believe in God?"

Jeff's gaze darted in another direction, as though he was unable to look Orley in the eye. Then, just as quick, a sheen of sweat broke out on his forehead. "Can we talk about something else? Religion, like politics, is not the best topic."

Orley would have liked Jeff to have answered his question about whether he believed in God, but he didn't want to push it, so he asked a different question. "Is there anything specific I can help you with today?"

"Not really." Jeff gestured to an area where several old household items had been displayed. "This may seem weird, but there's something about being around so many things from the past that makes me feel kind of settled inside."

"It doesn't seem strange to me," Orley said. "I always feel a sense of nostalgia when I am around old things here in Memory Keepers or at home, where we have some old items that were passed on to us from deceased relatives."

"I bet you don't have a bunch of antiques piled up in boxes inside a rented storage shed, the way I did before we moved to our new place that has a big garage."

Orley chuckled. "No, but I do have some boxes like that in my barn."

Jeff's facial muscles seemed to relax as he broke into a wide smile. "You know what, Mr. Troyer?"

Orley shook his head.

"After coming into this store and talking to you, I feel better than I have all day."

Orley placed his hand on Jeff's shoulder and gave it a squeeze. "I'm glad. Feel free to stop by anytime, and if you're out for a drive near our home on a Sunday afternoon, don't hesitate to stop and say hello."

"Thanks, I'll keep that in mind."

As Orley moved away from Jeff and up front toward the counter, where another customer now stood, he said a second prayer on Jeff's behalf. *Heavenly Father, Please give me more opportunities to speak with Jeff. And if You do, then I'll be asking for the right words to say to him, because I'm certain that he's facing some difficulties and needs a personal relationship with You.*

Chapter 15

It had been two weeks since Rhonda sent Dear Caroline a letter, and upon opening the newspaper during breakfast, she was pleased to discover that Caroline had responded.

"Dear Unhappy Wife," she silently read, *"It's a given that all married couples have disagreements. Some might argue about money, family problems, the best way to raise their children, or any number of things. No two people will see eye-to-eye all the time. But if disagreements happen often, it could threaten the strength of your marriage. If you and your husband are having serious marital problems and are unable to communicate and talk things through, then perhaps you should consider discussing your situation with a marriage counselor. It would be best if you could see the counselor together, but if your husband won't go, then you might benefit from going there alone."*

Rhonda put the paper down and massaged her throbbing temples. She had suggested counseling to Jeff when they first started having problems, but he'd given her a definite no, saying he would not discuss their problems with a stranger. Fortunately, neither of their families knew about the conflict in her and Jeff's marriage. Somehow, they'd managed to keep it a secret, and Rhonda hoped to keep it that way, because if either Jeff's father or her mother found out, they'd no doubt offer their unwanted advice on the subject.

Rhonda glanced across the kitchen table, where Jeff sat reading an antique collector's magazine. *Why would it be any different now if I suggested counseling? Besides, it's not up to me to solve the problems between Jeff and his dad. Between the craziness of my job at the hotel and dealing with other issues between me and Jeff, I have enough things to worry about, and I won't be going to see a counselor by myself.*

Rhonda folded the newspaper and laid it aside. *So much for asking Dear Caroline's advice. I might have been better off talking to some stranger on the street—anyone who would listen to what I had to say. Maybe they would have given me better advice.*

⁓

"Is everything all right?" Jeff looked across the table at Rhonda. "You haven't said more than a few words to me this morning."

"It's nothing. I just have a lot on my mind." She picked up her glass of tomato juice and took a drink.

Jeff didn't bother to ask what was on his wife's mind. If she'd been thinking about him and the situation with his dad, he didn't want to open the topic and rehash it again.

He took a sip of his steaming coffee and then bit into his toast spread heavily with peanut butter. *Maybe Rhonda isn't happy with me because I haven't gotten all the boxes unpacked in the garage. Those flowers I got her seemed to help, but if I gave her another bouquet this soon, she'd probably think something was up.*

Jeff continued to eat his breakfast while picturing how awesome the man cave would look with the antiques he still had in the garage, but the thoughts fleeted with Rhonda's brisk sigh.

"I dread going to work this morning." She set her juice glass down and placed both elbows on the table.

"How come?"

"Part of the hotel is still under renovation, and because of it, many areas are in disarray." Rhonda's nose wrinkled as she frowned. "I'll be glad when it's all completed and things get back to semi-normal."

"You sound a little overwhelmed."

"I am. Sometimes I wish I had a twin, because lately, some of my employees have been absent from work, which means there's more for me to do."

"I'm sure that adds stress to your day, and I'm sorry you have to deal with it." Jeff tilted his head. "Would you like me to bring something home from the restaurant this evening, so you don't have to cook supper?"

Her eyes brightened some. "I'd appreciate that. Thank you."

"No problem." *Good. At least she's speaking to me now.* He smiled at her. "Is there anything specific you'd like me to bring?"

Rhonda shook her head. "Whatever you choose is fine with me, especially if it's chicken."

He let out a chuckle and nodded. "Okay, great. I'll see what my head cook has planned for the special of the day, and if there's plenty of it left by the time I head for home, I'll bring some of that."

Jeff got up from the table, put his dishes in the sink, and leaned down to give Rhonda a kiss on the cheek. "I'm heading out now. I hope you have a good day."

"You too."

Jeff hesitated a moment, wondering if he should say anything more, but Rhonda had picked up the newspaper again, so he said goodbye and went out the door.

~

While Lois worked on her grocery list, Orley sat across the table from her reading the Dear Caroline column in the newspaper again.

"So many people with so many problems." He frowned. "I wonder how many readers of the Dear Caroline column actually take her advice."

Lois shrugged. "I suppose it all depends on whether they believe the things she says will help them or not."

"I suppose." Orley pointed to the newspaper. "One person Caroline responded to is having marital problems, and Caroline suggested professional counseling. It's a shame how many couples seem to be struggling in their marriage these days."

Lois glanced at Orley but said nothing.

His brow furrowed. "From the few things Jeff Davis has told

me, I believe that he and his wife are struggling in their marriage."

"That's a shame." Lois added a bit of cream to her coffee and gave it a few stirs.

"I think the biggest reason is that Jeff and Rhonda do not have a personal relationship with God."

Lois tipped her head. "How do you know that?"

"When Jeff was in the store the other day, he pretty much came right out and said so."

"How did you respond?"

"Well, noticing his curiosity in that old decorative item with the verse of scripture on it, I said, 'If you're interested in buying that plaque you're looking at, I can offer you a good deal on it. How about half price?'"

"How did Jeff respond to that?"

"He said, 'Thanks anyway, but my wife and I are not into that kind of a decoration.' Jeff was quick to set the plaque back on the table too." Orley gave his beard a tug. "He also said that he and Rhonda are not churchgoing people."

Lois pursed her lips. "That's a shame."

"Jah, and I then asked if he believed in God."

"What did he say?"

"He avoided my question and asked if we could talk about something else. So rather than push for an answer, I went in a different direction and asked if there was anything I could help him with."

"It's too bad he didn't want to discuss anything about God with you." Lois picked up her cup of coffee to take a drink, but then she set it back down. "But I suppose it was best not to push."

"I wish we could've talked about what might be troubling him. But it must be in the Lord's time, and apparently Jeff wasn't ready yet." Orley rapped on the tabletop with his knuckles. "The next thing Jeff said to me was that being in our store, around so many things from the past, made him feel kind of settled inside. I have to wonder if being in our store made him think of someone or something from his past, so seeing all the antiques brought him some measure of comfort."

"Do you think something from Jeff's past put a deep hurt in his heart?"

He shrugged. "Could be."

Lois clasped both hands under her chin. "Perhaps that young man is under conviction and therefore is trying to deny that God exists. Jeff needs to know that the only way he can find true happiness is to have a personal relationship with the Lord."

"Absolutely." Orley drank the last of his coffee. "I want to make it easy for Jeff to talk with me about God whenever he feels the need, but I won't force the issue. I feel that it's vital to reach out to Jeff, as well as others we meet, and share the love of God with them."

"You're right," Lois agreed. "As Christians, it's our duty to show them the way to salvation and a life of faith."

"As you stated, I shouldn't push," Orley said. "But I will continue to minister to Jeff as I see the need." He pushed his chair away from the table. "And now, my dear fraa. . ." He paused and glanced at the kitchen clock. "I believe it's time that we get our bicycles out and head over to the shop."

"All right. I'll be ready as soon as I rinse out our cups and put them in the sink." She smiled at Orley. "You never know who God might send our way on this bright, sunny day."

Canton

"I'm not feeling too well," Lori said when Rhonda joined her behind the hotel's reception desk. "Would you be able to fill in for me if I went to the break room and rested awhile?"

Rhonda leaned closer to Lori. "You're not having contractions, I hope."

"No, just some nausea and heartburn."

"Your shift will be over in two more hours anyway, so why don't you go home, where you can rest more comfortably?"

"But my replacement won't be here until close to the end of my shift, which would leave you here to manage things behind the desk on your own."

Rhonda patted Lori's shoulder. "There are only a few people with reservations for this afternoon, so I'll be fine."

Lori's lips parted, and she released a puff of air. "Thank you, Mrs. Davis. You're the best."

Rhonda smiled as Lori gathered her things and headed out the door. She envied the young woman's pregnancy, even though it meant sometimes not feeling well.

Rhonda's shoulders slumped as she stood behind the counter waiting for the next guests to check in. *If Jeff and I could have had a child, our lives would be complete, and we'd have peace in our home instead of quarreling so much of the time.*

Rhonda swallowed against the lump in her throat. She wasn't sure if Jeff truly wanted children. He had said that he did early on in their marriage, but as more time passed, and Rhonda didn't get pregnant, Jeff said he'd accepted the fact and figured maybe he and Rhonda weren't meant to have kids. He'd repeated that when she'd brought up the topic of adoption and added that he wouldn't feel comfortable raising a child who wasn't biologically theirs. This made no sense to Rhonda, for she could have easily loved and nurtured an adopted child. *If only Jeff could.*

Rhonda's self-pity increased when a young couple with a baby came through the front door and walked into the lobby. Their smiling faces and the sight of the fair-haired infant caused Rhonda to choke up. She moistened her lips and drew a couple of quick breaths, hoping she wouldn't give in to the tears pushing the back of her eyes. It certainly wouldn't appear professional if she allowed herself to cry.

"Hello. My name is Lewis McDowell, and we have a reservation," the young blond-haired man said when he stepped up to the counter.

The auburn-haired women beside him nodded. "I hope you have a crib available for our little girl. We forgot to bring her folding playpen when we left home this morning."

"It won't be a problem," Rhonda said. "We have a few cribs in our storage room, so I'll have one brought up to your room."

She processed the man's credit card and handed him two keycards. "Your room is on the third floor, and the elevator is down that hall a short way." Rhonda pointed in that direction. "Oh, and if you need a cart for your luggage, they're near the front door. Unfortunately, there is no one available to take your baggage up to your room."

"It's not a problem. I can manage," Mr. McDowell said before walking away.

Everyone from housekeeping had gone home, so Rhonda paged the maintenance man, but he didn't answer her call. She tried several more times and finally gave up. *Guess I'd better go get the crib myself.*

Rhonda hurried to the storage room, put the key card in, and stepped inside. When the door shut behind her, she grasped the handle, but the door did not open. It was then that she realized the strike plate and panic bar that could complete the electronic connection to the lock on the inside of the door were missing. Since the door worked electronically, turning the handle wouldn't do anything to help her get out of the cramped room.

Her heart began to pound as she drew a sharp intake of breath. *Oh no! I'm trapped in here! Now what am I going to do?*

Rhonda took a few more deep breaths and tried to think. *All I need to do is call someone to come and rescue me.*

Rhonda reached for her cell phone, which she normally kept in the pocket of whatever outfit she wore to work, but it wasn't there. That's when she remembered that she'd left it on the shelf under the welcome desk when she'd decided to come in here to get the crib herself.

Rhonda had always prided herself on having the key skills for hotel management, which included reliability, having stamina, and making good decisions. But since first coming to work here, she had never been locked in a room barely larger than a closet. At the moment, the prospect of being trapped in this stuffy small space for what could be a lengthy amount of time left Rhonda with nothing to do but pound on the door and scream.

Chapter 16

Rhonda continued to pummel the door and call for help. She'd been stuck in the storage room for over an hour, getting more frustrated and claustrophobic with each passing moment. The key card she'd used to get into the storage room was useless on the inside, so she'd put it in her skirt pocket. Her hope of getting out of the storage closet wasn't looking too good, but surely someone would hear her calls for help.

Rhonda wiped at the sweat on her forehead. *If anyone rescues me at this point, I'll give them a hug. I'm getting desperate, waiting to get out of this room, and oh, how I wish someone would hear my cries for help.*

Rhonda placed both arms behind her back, gripping one wrist with the other hand as she began to pace. *If I only had my cell phone with me and could call someone for help, I wouldn't be in this pickle. How could I have been so careless?*

The musty odor in the room had given her a headache, and the small size caused Rhonda to feel as if the walls were closing in on her. If she didn't get out soon, she feared she might faint or at the very least have a major panic attack.

Although Rhonda wasn't normally prone to anxiety attacks, she'd had a bad one when she'd been trapped in an elevator that had stalled a few years ago. At least there had been a call button inside the confined space, and thankfully she'd reached someone for help right away. But it had taken awhile for the repairman to arrive and get the elevator working again. By the time the door finally opened,

Rhonda was drenched in sweat, and her heart felt like it might explode. She had wanted to run someplace and hide, but there'd been nowhere to go. When the elevator walls had seemed to close in on her, Rhonda had become hysterical.

I can't let that happen again, she told herself. *I must keep control of my emotions and try to keep a clear head.*

Rhonda pounded on the door again for what seemed to be the hundredth time and jumped back when the door abruptly opened. She was so thrilled that she threw both arms around Bill, the desk clerk who had obviously come on duty and stood holding the door open. "Thank you! Thank you! I'm so glad I am freed."

Heat flushed Rhonda's face as she quickly released him and stepped back. Normally, she wouldn't have hugged a staff member, but in this case, who could blame her?

Bill cleared his throat and brushed at his shirt. "I—I wasn't expecting anyone to be in here—at least not till I heard pounding on the door. You surprised me in more ways than one. Are you all right, Mrs. Davis?"

"Yes. But the fact that this room access has issues doesn't set well with me." Rhonda drew in a deep breath and released it slowly. "I used a key card to get into the storage room, but after the door closed, I saw that the plate and panic bar were missing on the inside, so turning the handle did nothing, which meant there was no way to open the door." She stepped out into the hall to breathe in some fresh air. "That's when I realized I was trapped. And since I had foolishly left my cell phone behind the check-in counter, I couldn't call anyone for help."

"Good thing I showed up when I did then, huh?"

"Yes, most definitely. I was stuck in that room over an hour, and no amount of pounding or hollering for help rousted anyone until you came along. You're the hero of the hour, that's for sure." Rhonda felt so grateful that he'd opened the door, she could've given him another hug but thought it best not to do so. "I'm not sure how much longer I could've handled being locked inside there, so thank you, thank you for rescuing me."

His cheeks reddened. "No thanks needed, Mrs. Davis. I'm just glad you're okay."

"Me too. How'd you know to look for me in there?"

"A man who said he'd checked in earlier came down to the front desk, asking about a crib. He said you had told him and his wife that you were going to get one and have it brought up to their room. But they'd been waiting a long time, and you never showed up, so he came to me to ask for assistance."

Rhonda drew her fingers through the ends of her hair, tucking it behind her ears. "I'm glad you mentioned the crib just now. I felt so relieved to be out of the room that I forgot about that young couple's request."

"If you'll stand here and hold the door, I'll get the crib and take it up to them," Bill offered.

"Thank you. That would be much appreciated. I'll have to get someone here soon to fix the lock on this door so it doesn't happen to anyone else." Rhonda held the door open and watched as her employee picked up the crib and hauled it out of the room.

"I agree with you, Mrs. Davis. Being locked in this small area isn't a good thing, and it could have happened to any of us."

Rhonda let the door close behind her and walked with Bill to the elevator. "I will stay at the front desk while you're gone, and when you get back, I'll go up to that couple's room and extend my apologies. Oh, and one more thing," she was quick to add. "Until we can get the problem resolved, we'll need to make all the other hotel employees aware of the situation with this storage room so that none of them goes in without propping it open."

~

When Rhonda knocked on the couple's door a short time later, she heard the baby crying. Soon the door opened, and she was greeted by the child's father.

"I came to apologize for the delay in getting a crib up to your room." She gave a nervous laugh. "I am embarrassed to admit it, but

I got locked in the storage room, and it was over an hour before one of the hotel desk clerks came and rescued me."

"Oh, that's terrible," the woman said, joining her husband near the open door. She held the baby in her arms, patting the crying infant's back. "I'm sure that must have been frustrating."

"It was." Rhonda glanced at the crib that had been set in place near the king-sized bed and then she looked at the fussy baby. "I don't mean to be forward, but would it be all right if I held your baby?"

"Of course. Maybe you'll have better luck getting her to calm down than her father or I have had." The woman handed Rhonda the baby and asked if she would like to come inside.

Feeling a bit like an intruder yet eager to hold the young child, Rhonda entered the room and took a seat in the comfortable chair near the window. As she held the infant, she felt the little one's tears against her cheek. The aroma of baby lotion caused Rhonda's muscles to relax, and her nerves were soothed in the process. *After what I've just been through, this is like a tonic. I think mothers are truly blessed by their little ones.*

She patted the baby's back, like the child's mother had done, all the while gently rocking back and forth. Within minutes, the crying stopped and the baby's eyelids closed. Rhonda held the little one a while longer, until she felt certain the child had fallen asleep. Then she stood up slowly and placed the precious bundle into the crib.

"Thank you," the baby's mother whispered. "You must have children of your own, for you certainly have a mother's touch."

Rhonda slowly shook her head. "My husband and I have not been blessed with children." Before the man or woman could comment, she hurried over to the door. "I need to get back downstairs now, but don't hesitate to call the front desk if you need anything."

"Thanks, we will." The man opened the door for Rhonda, and she stepped out. When the door shut behind her, she walked slowly down the hall toward the elevator. Holding the couple's baby had brought back memories of how she had felt when her sister's girls were babies and she'd held them in her arms. Although it had been a painful reminder that she and Jeff had no children of their own,

Rhonda had cuddled Gwen's babies as often as she could.

I can't think about that right now, she chided herself. *I need to return to my office and get some paperwork done before it's time to go home.*

The thought of returning to her and Jeff's sanctuary gave Rhonda some measure of comfort. *We may not have any children, but the house Jeff and I live in is a lot nicer than Gwen and Scott's place.*

Rhonda stepped into the elevator and pushed the button for the first floor. *Who am I kidding? I'd sooner live in a humble dwelling with one child than be childless and live in a palace.*

~

Walnut Creek

When Jeff entered the house that evening, he found Rhonda stretched out and asleep on the living-room couch. It wasn't like his wife to take a nap this late in the day. He figured she must have had a rough day at the hotel and had come home feeling exhausted, which was a common occurrence for Rhonda. It seemed like things were always hectic at the hotel. He often wondered how she functioned so well as the manager, dealing with so many stressful situations and events.

Of course, my job can be demanding and hectic, Jeff reasoned. *In addition to supervising my employees, I assist in the planning and managing of menus, oversee inventory, take care of finances, promote the restaurant, and develop business strategies.* He thumped the top of his head. *Sometimes it feels like I'm going in a hundred directions and my noggin is about to explode.*

Careful not to wake Rhonda, Jeff quietly made his way to the kitchen with the meat loaf and mashed potatoes he'd brought home from the restaurant. He then turned the oven on low and put the food in to stay warm while he made a leafy tossed salad to go with the main dish.

I sure wish I had time to grow a big garden. If I could be around here more, I'd be able to get a lot of things done. Jeff took out a cucumber, tomato, and some red cabbage to add to the salad. *Maybe I should give Russ more authority at the restaurant so I can be at home more hours.* He took out a sharp knife to cut up the veggies. *Of course, that would mean I'd have to hire someone else to take over some of Russ's responsibilities. Yeah, I'll definitely give it some thought.*

Jeff washed and sliced the veggies to begin the process of making the salad. *Maybe I can talk Rhonda into working fewer hours at the hotel too. I bet things would go better between us if we spent more time together, like we did when we were newlyweds. Boy, I sure miss those carefree days.*

He glanced out the kitchen window and smiled when two finches landed on the feeder he'd put up over the weekend. *I would like it if Rhonda and I had fewer hours at work and more time to spend at home doing things together.*

Jeff's musings were set aside when Rhonda entered the kitchen and joined him at the window. "What are you looking at?" She yawned and rubbed her eyes.

"Just watching the birds and wishing we could both spend more time at home."

"That's a nice thought, Jeff, but clearly not possible since we are up to our ears in debt with this house. And I'm beginning to think our townhouse is never going to sell."

"It will sell, Rhonda. The right buyer just hasn't come along."

"I wish I had your optimism." When she looked at Jeff, he saw in her eyes the depth of her fatigue.

"Rough day at work?" he asked. "Is that why you were sleeping on the couch when I got home?"

"Yes. I'll tell you about it while we're eating supper." She glanced at the stove. "Speaking of which. . .what's that delicious aroma coming from the oven?"

"Meat loaf and mashed potatoes—my chef's special today." He gestured to the wooden bowl on the counter. "I'm making a nice tossed salad to go with it."

Rhonda smiled, although it didn't quite reach her eyes. "That was thoughtful of you."

Jeff slipped his arm around her waist. "I hate it when we argue, and I've been thinking about what you said to me this morning concerning my dad."

"Oh?"

"I'm gonna give him a call after supper and apologize for anything I may have said that might have hurt his feelings while he was here."

"I'm glad."

"I'm still not okay with the idea of him looking for a woman to date—especially via the internet."

"You never know, Jeff. It could work out."

He shrugged and returned to his salad-making duties. "We'll see."

"Do you think we should make plans to have your dad and the rest of your family over for a picnic soon?"

"I suppose. I'll bring it up to Dad while we're on the phone."

"When would you want to do it?"

"How about the Fourth of July? That'll give us a few weeks to make our plans for the event."

"Okay." Rhonda opened the cupboard door and took out two plates and two tall glasses. After setting them on the table, she got their silverware. "Would you be okay if I invited my family too? If we don't include them, my sister will probably end up dropping by here unannounced sometime soon, the way Mom did." Rhonda pressed her lips together in a grimace. "I'd rather host one big family get-together than have people showing up here at inopportune times."

"Agreed." Jeff grabbed a couple of pot holders and removed the meat loaf and potatoes from the oven. "Since that's settled, we can eat, and you can share with me about your day. Once we're done with our meal, we can both call our parents and extend the invitation."

After Jeff sat down, and Rhonda had taken a seat, he leaned slightly forward and massaged his forehead. *Sure hope we're not making a mistake having both of our families here on the same day.*

Chapter 17

"Are you ready to go yard-saling with me?" Orley asked Lois the morning of the last Saturday in June.

She looked up from the letter she'd been writing and frowned. "I don't understand why you'd want to close Memory Keepers on a day when we're usually quite busy to go traipsing all over town from one yard sale to another."

"Well, for one thing, my youngest sister, Martha, is having a yard sale today, and I told her we would probably stop by. Also, whenever we've gone yard-saling, we have always come back with something we can fix up or sell as is in our antique store. And if we go early, we're more likely to get the best deals." Orley's words were rushed as he grabbed his straw hat off the wall peg in the kitchen.

"Not only that, but stopping at yard sales gives us a chance to visit with people we might never have met. And you never know whose lives we might touch." He picked up the newspaper and held it out to her. "There are a lot of good ones listed today, so what do you say? Should we go by horse and buggy, hire a driver, or ride our bikes?"

Lois saw the determined look on her husband's face and figured he was not going to give up the idea of checking out some yard sales today. Since she had no desire to be at the antique store by herself, she decided she might as well go with Orley on his treasure hunt.

"I'll go with you, Husband, but let's take our bikes. It'll be good exercise, and we won't have to pay a driver or take the time to hitch our *gaul* to the carriage."

"Good thinking." Orley bobbed his head. "And if we find anything too big to put in our bike baskets or the cart I'll hook up to the back of my bicycle, we can call a driver to pick up any larger items."

"All right," Lois agreed. "I'll get my purse and outer bonnet, and we can be on our way."

~

"I don't know why I agreed to do this today," Rhonda complained as she and Jeff left one yard sale and headed for another. "With all the things that need to be done at our place, we shouldn't be out looking at other's people's junk."

"Well, you know what they say. One man's junk is another man's treasure."

"Right." She folded both arms across her chest and stared straight ahead. *I am already dreading this silly outing. Knowing my husband, if he sees an antique or some collectible, he'll want to buy it.* Rhonda's back stiffened. *I'll have to watch Jeff like a kid and try to talk him out of buying whatever old thing he finds. As it is, my husband still hasn't sold any of his own antiques to help with our finances like I've asked him to do. And here we go again possibly adding more junk to an existing problem.*

"Look at it this way," Jeff continued, "if we were at home this morning, you'd probably be inside the house doing laundry or cleaning, and I'd either be in the garage or outside mowing the lawn and pulling weeds." Jeff reached across the front seat in his SUV and gave Rhonda's arm a gentle squeeze. "This way we're getting some together time, which I like."

Rhonda enjoyed being with Jeff too—when they weren't quarreling.

"Okay, but let's not stay out too long or go to many more sales. When we get home, I'll help you with the yard work, which means we'll be together while getting something done."

"Just a few more places, and then I'll take you out to lunch.

After that, we'll go home and spend a good part of the afternoon working in our beautiful yard."

So far Jeff hadn't found anything he seemed interested in. Rhonda was thankful, and she hoped the place they went next wouldn't have anything eye-catching either. She had to admit that the kinds of things people sold at yard sales were interesting. Some of the items still had original price tags on them, indicating they'd never been used.

Why would a person buy furniture, clothing, or appliances and not use them? she wondered. It seemed like a waste of money. Rhonda thought about her mother and how she had always been frugal, seldom wasting money on unnecessary things. Of course, Rhonda's father had been the opposite—spending money whenever he had a whim.

"We don't need to go out for lunch, Jeff." She uncrossed her arms. "Let's save the money, and I can fix us a salad or sandwich when we get home."

"No way! We rarely go out to eat anymore. Besides, there's that Amish-style restaurant not far from our home that we still haven't tried. I hear they serve pretty good food." He looked over at Rhonda and winked. "It's always good to keep a check on the competition."

She poked his arm. "Yeah, right, Jeff. Your restaurant's in Canton, and it doesn't serve Amish food."

"No, but we do offer home-style cooking, and I might get a few ideas for some things we could add to the menu at the Red Barn Café."

"Okay, fine," Rhonda conceded. "We can go out to lunch when we're done yard-saling."

"Wow, look at all the great stuff they have for sale here." Jeff made a sweeping gesture with his arm. "I bet there are some antiques and collectibles too."

Rhonda moaned and shook her head. "You bought some old marbles at the last yard sale we stopped at, so please don't get carried away here."

"Who said anything about getting carried away?" Jeff's eyes

appeared wide and rounded as he licked his lips in anticipation.

Rhonda held her ground. "I mean it, Jeff. We're on a tight budget, and we can't afford to spend money on unnecessary things."

He put his hand on the small of her back and gave it a few taps. "Don't worry. I'm just gonna take a look and see what's available."

Yeah, right. Rhonda figured she'd better stick close to her husband or he would end up buying some antique or collectible that he most certainly didn't need. "Let's start over on the right side of the yard." She clasped his hand.

He hesitated but finally went along. As they approached one of the tables, Jeff halted. "Look over there." He pointed across the yard. "That's Orley and Lois Troyer."

"So it is." Although Rhonda had only met them the one time when she and Jeff stopped at the Troyers' home, she recognized the Amish couple. "They're probably on the lookout for things they can buy at a reasonable price and resell in their antique store."

"Let's go over there and say hello." Jeff let go of Rhonda's hand and turned in that direction.

"Wait. Maybe we shouldn't bother them right now. They seem to be talking to another Amish couple."

"We can just meander over that way, and I'll wait to speak to them until they end their conversation with the other couple." Jeff took hold of Rhonda's hand again and started moving in the Troyers' direction. Rhonda had no choice but to go with him.

As they approached the Troyers, the other Amish couple moved off in another direction. Orley looked over at Jeff and Rhonda and smiled. "Well, hello there, you two. Looks like Lois and I aren't the only ones out yard-saling today." He stepped forward and shook Jeff's hand.

Jeff grinned back at him. "Yep, but this will be the last one we stop at, because when we leave here, I'm taking my wife out to lunch."

"How good it is to see you both." Lois greeted Rhonda with a hug, which took her by surprise. She wasn't used to hugging people she barely knew.

"Umm. . .yes, it's nice to see you too." Rhonda stepped back, surprised by the warmth and comfort she'd felt from Lois's greeting. She still couldn't get over how plain Lois and Orley dressed. It was funny how simple the Amish seemed, having no electricity in their homes or a car to drive. Rhonda had heard from Jeff that they didn't have televisions either. She glanced at her husband. *The way he watches TV in his man cave all the time, I think I could welcome not having that electronic inconvenience.*

"Say, Jeff, there are some nice-looking collectibles on that table over there." Orley gave his beard a quick tug. "Why don't the two of us check it out and let our wives visit for a while?"

Jeff hurried off with Orley.

Rhonda pinched the skin between her thumb and forefinger, unsure of what to say. It wasn't like she and this Amish woman had anything in common, so there wasn't much to talk about. And now that Jeff had run off with Orley, there was no telling what he might buy. As an antique dealer, Mr. Troyer might be a bad influence on her husband.

"How have you been?" Lois asked. "Are you and Jeff getting settled into your new home?"

"For the most part, but there are still some boxes in the garage we haven't gone through." Rhonda glanced across the way to see where Jeff and Orley had gone and cringed inwardly when she saw her husband pick up what looked like some sort of vintage tool. She wanted so badly to go over and check on things but didn't want to be rude to Lois.

"Jeff mentioned that you work at a hotel in Canton. I imagine that keeps you pretty busy."

Rhonda turned to face Lois again. "Yes, it does." She was on the verge of mentioning how stressful her job could be, when two young children—a girl and a boy—ran past, each with a toy in their hands. Their laughter rang out, and Rhonda felt compelled to watch them. On the other hand, it was one more reminder that she and Jeff would never have any kids of their own. She looked at Lois and then Orley. *They have no children either. I suppose in that way, she and I do have something in common. But would Lois mind if I brought up that sensitive topic?*

"Those children seem to be having a good time," Lois said. "I've always enjoyed watching my nieces and nephews when they run and play. In fact, Orley and I saw some of them earlier today when we stopped by to check out my sister's yard sale."

"Do you miss not having children of your own?" Rhonda questioned.

Lois grew quiet for a minute, as she pressed her lips together and looked down. Then, just as quick, she looked up at Rhonda and smiled. "My husband and I have learned to take pleasure in spending time with other people's children. We also enjoy the quality time we have together as husband and wife."

"I see." Rhonda thought about her own nieces and nephews and wondered how things would go on the Fourth of July during their combined family get-together. Lois's statement made Rhonda wonder if she could find joy in spending time with her sister's daughters, as well as her brother and sister-in-law's children. She also questioned why spending time with Jeff had never been enough for her. It wasn't that she didn't love him. She just felt incomplete without a family to care for and dote over, the way Gwen did with her two children.

All I can do is try to enjoy my nieces and nephews, Rhonda told herself. *It would be better than spending the Fourth feeling sorry for myself.*

⁓

"Wow, would you look at that?" Orley pointed to a vintage oil lamp made of thick glass with a cranberry red hue. "I've done my research on oil lamps, and I'm 100 percent sure that this one was made in the mid-1800s."

Jeff studied the lamp for several seconds. "It's beautiful, but how do you know it's not a newer lamp made to look old?"

"For one thing, it doesn't have a base that is glued to the font, which is another piece of glass. They were fused together while the glass was still hot." Orley fingered the base of the lamp. "A newer one would most likely be glued together."

"That's interesting. As you can probably tell, I don't know much about antique lamps other than that I assume they burned kerosene."

"That's true, but at one time they used animal oils. Then in the 1800s, kerosene replaced the oils from animals." Orley held the lamp up toward the sunlight, looking it over thoroughly. "The price isn't bad, and if I buy it, I'm sure I could turn a profit."

"I'll bet you could too." Jeff's gaze went to several pieces of vintage jewelry. One in particular caught his eye. It was an enamel daisy pin priced at ten dollars, although he was sure it was worth more than that. "I think Rhonda might like that," he said, pointing to the piece of jewelry.

"Then why don't you get it for her?"

Jeff drew in his lower lip as he weighed the issue. "I'd like to, but she might say no if I show it to her."

"Maybe you should buy the pin and surprise her with it." Orley grinned. "Most women like surprises—at least the good kind."

"You know, now that I think about it, our wedding anniversary is coming up in September, and the pin might make a nice gift for Rhonda." Jeff gave a decisive nod. "While she's over there talking with Lois, I'm going to go pay for the item."

"I'll go with you," Orley said. "And I'm definitely getting this old lamp."

Jeff picked up the daisy pin and looked around. This yard sale was a good-sized one compared to the others they'd been to today. People were looking over the goods, and some carried different items with them to purchase. Thankfully, no one was up at the cashier at the moment, so he and Orley could be waited on quickly. *I would sure like to keep this pretty pin a surprise for Rhonda.* Jeff glanced Rhonda's way to be sure she wasn't watching, and once he was certain that Lois had his wife's full attention, he headed over to the table near the garage door to pay for the item. *When we get home, I'll need to find a good place to hide the pin until our anniversary.* He scratched his chin. *It just needs to be someplace where I don't forget it.*

Chapter 18

"I hope we didn't make a mistake by inviting both your family and mine to celebrate the Fourth of July with us today," Jeff said as he and Rhonda set up folding tables in their backyard.

Rhonda had been having some reservations about the day's event too. She wanted to have everything perfect, but so far, her planning had been pretty much guesswork. "Should we have the tables lined up in one row so we're all sitting together, or should they be nearby each other but separate?" She stood with one hand on her hip.

Jeff slowed his work. "You seem to be overthinking this."

"I want everything to go as smoothly as possible, and I'm hoping we will all have a pleasant day." Rhonda reached back to make sure her ponytail was secure. "I hope we have enough folding chairs. I'm only seeing fourteen out here."

"The others are still in the garage, and there are four more leaning up against the wall by the door going into the house."

Rhonda looked at her soiled hands. "All the chairs still need to be wiped down; they're quite dusty."

"Don't worry, honey. I'll stop what I'm doing here and go grab the remaining chairs and a rag for cleaning them."

"Thank you." Rhonda watched as Jeff headed inside. *I wish we hadn't had to dip into our spare money to buy these three tables for this Fourth of July gathering. It will set us back even further than we need to be with the big debt we're living with right now. It probably would have been cheaper in the long run if we'd just rented some tables.* She slid a few of the folding chairs near one of the new tables and stood back to get a good look.

A short time later, Jeff came out with the last of the chairs and a rag dangling from his back pocket. "That's all of them, so we can start wiping off each chair now."

Rhonda pointed at what she'd just set up. "Do you think these chairs will look okay with the new tables?"

Jeff shrugged his shoulders. "I don't see why not."

"They don't seem to go together that well."

"I believe you're overthinking it again. No one is going to care about whether the chairs perfectly match the tables. Let's just get this all set up and be done with it."

If everyone they'd invited came today, there would be a total of eighteen people. That could create a lot of mayhem, especially with eight children running around. Rhonda could see one of the children falling into the pond and getting wet. Or a couple of kids might get carried away and overfeed the fish, leaving waterlogged food floating all over the surface of the water.

I shouldn't think about things like that happening on such a nice day. I'm sure the children's parents will keep a close eye on their kids. She set up the next folding chair and tried to shake off any bad vibes.

Rhonda looked over at Jeff. "The only time our families have ever been together was the day of our wedding, and that was briefly, so they are basically strangers to one another." She rubbed the small of her back, where a kink was trying to form. "I wonder if our two families will even have anything to say to each other. It would be awkward if nobody did much talking."

"Let's not borrow trouble, Rhonda. It will work out fine." Jeff paused from what he was doing to wipe the sweat from his forehead. "Sure is a hot one today. Makes me wish we had a swimming pool instead of a pond full of fancy-looking fish."

Using the handkerchief he'd pulled from his short's pocket, he gave his forehead another swipe. "Maybe when the townhouse finally sells, we can have a pool put in. Think how nice that would be during the hot summer months."

"With our jobs, we're gone most of the time, so it wouldn't be worth it to have a pool we wouldn't use regularly." Rhonda grimaced as the muscle in her back tightened a bit more. Since they'd been shorthanded at the hotel again yesterday, she had ended up having to help haul some boxes of bedding into some of the rooms that had recently been renovated. Rhonda figured the unwanted sensations in her back had something to do with yesterday. She hoped it wouldn't go out on her today, of all times.

"You okay? You look like you might be in pain." Jeff stood from his squatting position and came over to stand beside Rhonda.

"My back's acting up a bit, and I hope it's nothing to worry about. Once we get the rest of these tables set up, I can sit down and rest awhile."

"Go ahead and take a break now. There's just one table left, and I can finish it." Jeff pointed to a chaise longue. "I'll get an ice pack from the freezer, and you can stretch out for a bit. Our company won't be here for two more hours, so you have enough time to rest your back."

"Okay, but if I fall asleep, please wake me in plenty of time before they get here."

"Sure thing, honey." Jeff kissed her cheek. "After I get your ice pack, I'll set out the paper plates and plastic utensils we'll use for our afternoon meal and make sure the frozen ground beef patties have thawed sufficiently."

Although their guests had volunteered to bring something to contribute to their meal, Jeff had insisted that he and Rhonda would supply all the food. Fortunately, the only cooking involved barbecuing the burgers and hot dogs. Jeff had brought potato and macaroni salads home from the restaurant last night, and Rhonda had picked up several bags of chips at the grocery store. For dessert, they would serve ice cream and cookies, so there really wasn't a lot of work involved.

Rhonda smiled. "Thank you, Jeff, for being so helpful."

"No problem," he said before going into the house.

Rhonda was pleased that things had been going better between them lately. It seemed like Jeff had been trying harder to please her. *Perhaps there's some hope for our marriage after all*, she thought as she reclined on the chaise lounge. *Maybe Jeff has figured out that he needs to be more attentive to my needs.*

~

After Jeff got out the paper plates and plastic utensils, he opened the back door to see how Rhonda was doing. He'd given her an ice pack fifteen minutes ago and hoped it was helping.

Seeing her eyes were closed and that she wore a peaceful expression, Jeff decided not to disturb her. After her day at the hotel yesterday, his wife deserved a little downtime. He hoped Rhonda's back would feel better by the time everyone arrived.

Jeff closed the door quietly and went back to the kitchen. When he looked at the clock and saw they had ninety minutes to go until their guests arrived, he decided to head down the hall to his man cave and see what was on TV.

Although Jeff wouldn't have admitted it to Rhonda, he too had a few misgivings about having his family here to visit and hoped everything would go well. His and Rhonda's old place hadn't been set up well for entertaining, and get-togethers were always at Dad's or one of his brothers' homes, so this would be a new experience for them.

Jeff pulled his fingers through the back of his thick hair and puffed out his chest. *I bet my brothers will be envious when I show them my private oasis. If Eric and Stan lived closer, they'd probably be over here all the time.* He frowned. *I doubt Rhonda would approve of that. And truthfully, I probably wouldn't appreciate it either, because my brothers and I would most likely be arguing over what program we wanted to watch on my large-screen TV.*

After Jeff entered his man cave and took a seat in his recliner, he waited a bit to turn on the TV, reflecting instead on the relationship he had with his brothers. Eric, being two years older than Jeff, had always tried to be the leader, telling his younger brothers what to do. Jeff had tried to stand his ground, but Stan, who was two years younger than Jeff, was more compliant and went along with whatever

Eric said. Consequently, some of the things Jeff and his brothers did as boys had gotten all three of them in trouble with their parents.

Jeff leaned his head back and closed his eyes. He dozed off for a while, and when he came fully awake, an image of his mother came to mind. She'd been a kind, soft-spoken woman and hadn't deserved to die when her boys weren't even fully raised. Eric had been fourteen; Jeff, twelve; and Stan, ten. Although Jeff's dad had done his best to see to Jeff and his brothers' needs, it hadn't filled the empty spot in their home left by his mother's death. Even now, twenty-three years later, Jeff missed his mother's gentle spirit. He'd never heard her say an unkind word about anyone.

The day of Mom's funeral, Jeff had heard several people say that Sharon Davis had always set a Christian example for her family as well as everyone else who knew her. The minister had stated during the eulogy that Jeff's mother loved the Lord and had served Him well.

Jeff's jaw clenched. *Then why didn't God make her well so she could continue to serve Him?*

The doorbell rang, and Jeff nearly catapulted out of his chair. Glancing at his watch, he grimaced. *Oh, no—they're here! How could I have lost track of the time?*

Jeff rushed out of the room and down the hall. He had to rouse Rhonda before he opened the door to their company. *Oh, boy—I bet she's gonna be mad.*

~

"Honey, wake up. Some of our guests are at the front door."

Rhonda's eyes flew open, and she jerked her head. "They came early?"

"No, they showed up on time. Sorry, Rhonda, but I messed up and didn't keep an eye on my watch."

Rhonda got off the lounger, being mindful of her back. At the moment, it felt better than when she'd lain down, and she wanted to keep it that way. "I need to go check my appearance. Would you please answer the door?"

"Okay, sure. . .no problem." Jeff took the ice pack from her, which was now quite warm. "I'll drop this off in the kitchen and then go see which of our family members is waiting on the front porch."

"Please hurry, Jeff. If you leave them standing there too long, they might think we're not home."

"I'm sure no one will believe that since we specifically invited them here today."

Rhonda went inside and made her way down the hall to their room. Her clothes were wrinkled, and she felt a wet spot on the back of her shorts where the ice inside the cold pack had melted.

Her back felt a bit better, and she hurriedly undressed and put on a clean, rose-colored tank top with a pair of beige capris. Then she touched up her makeup and redid her ponytail. It was time to greet her guests.

A few minutes later, she saw Jeff in the entryway talking with his father and two brothers. Beside them stood Eric's wife, Monica, and their children, Susan, Billy, and Steve. Stan's wife, Connie, along with their kids, Tim, Debbie, and Nina were also there.

Looking at the size of this group, crowded in the hall and all talking at once, Rhonda was glad none of her family had arrived yet. It was bound to become even more hectic when they got here.

Once everyone had been sufficiently greeted, Jeff's dad offered to take the kids out back, while Jeff gave his brothers and their wives a tour of the house. Rhonda appreciated Don's suggestion but cautioned him to keep an eye on the children because of the pond.

"No worries," he was quick to say. "I'll make sure none of my grandkids fall in."

Soon after Jeff headed down the hall to give his brothers and sisters-in-law the house tour, Don and the kids went out the back door. Rhonda was tempted to go with them, but someone needed to stay close to the front door to let her family in when they arrived.

Her back had begun to knot up again, so she took a seat on the bench in the entryway. A short time later, Rhonda heard a vehicle pull in. Opening the door, she saw Gwen and her husband, Scott, exit the front seat of their van. Then the back doors opened, and Rhonda's mother, along with Gwen and Scott's daughters, Kimberly and Megan, ages nine and eleven, got out.

Rhonda waited until they stepped onto the front porch to greet them. "Welcome. It's nice to see all of you." She looked down at the girls. "You two have sure grown since the last time I saw you."

They both giggled and nodded.

Gwen gave Rhonda a hug, then she turned to their mother and said, "You were right, Mom, this place is a palace."

"I'd hardly call it that, but our new home is pretty good-sized." Rhonda hugged her mother then shook Scott's hand. "Come on in everyone, and I'll show you around."

After they'd entered the house, Rhonda told the girls that Jeff's nieces and nephews were out back with his father. "Maybe you'd like to go out there while I show your parents the rest of the house."

"I wanna see it too." Megan's lower lip protruded.

"You girls can see it later," their father said. "Right now, I think you should go outside and say hello to the other kids."

"Okay, Daddy," the girls said in unison.

"I'll take them out back," Rhonda's mother spoke up. "Since I've been there before, I know the way."

"Thanks, Mom." Gwen gave a wide smile.

After Mom ushered the girls out the back door, Rhonda led the way down the hall. When they entered Jeff's man cave, where he and his brothers and sisters-in-law had gone, Scott gave a whistle. "Wow, the lucky dog. I'm so jealous."

Rhonda was about to comment, when Gwen leaned closer to her and whispered, "Did Mom tell you what she's been up to lately?"

Rhonda shook her head.

"You're not going to believe this, but she's recently decided to. . ."

Gwen's sentence was cut short when Megan came running into the room. "Mommy! Daddy! Come quick! Kimberly fell in the pond, and I think she's drowning!"

Gwen and Scott raced out of the room, and with her heart pounding, Rhonda followed. She couldn't even comprehend how her sister and brother-in-law would feel if their little girl drowned.

Chapter 19

Rhonda's back tightened even more, and her heart continued to pound as she dashed out the back door behind her sister and brother-in-law. To her surprise, there were two people in the pond — Megan and Jeff's father. Holding the waterlogged girl around her waist, Don moved toward the edge of the pond. Meanwhile, Rhonda's mother stood by with her hands cupped around her mouth, shouting directions at him. By the time everyone reached the pond, Megan and Don were out of the water.

Gwen rushed forward and hugged her wet child. "Are you all right, my darling girl?"

"I'm fine, Mommy. Just really wet is all."

"What were you doing in the pond? Weren't you warned to stay away from there?" Scott bent down so he was eye level with his daughter.

"I leaned forward to look at the fish, and then the next thing I knew, I was in the water with 'em." Her teeth chattered as she briskly rubbed her arms.

"Let's get you inside and out of those wet clothes." Rhonda took hold of the young girl's hand.

"I didn't bring either of the girls a change of clothes today," Gwen was quick to say. "But now I wish I had."

"It's okay," Rhonda responded. "I'm sure I can find something she can wear while her clothes are being washed and dried."

"My clothes aren't dirty; they're just wet." Megan lifted her chin and looked up at Rhonda with a determined expression.

"The pond water is dirty, so your clothes aren't clean now." Rhonda turned her attention to Jeff's dad. "I'm sure Jeff has something you can wear while your clothes are being washed and dried."

Don looked at Jeff and jiggled his brows. "I don't know. . . I've been working out at the gym lately and getting in shape, so your clothes might be too big for me."

Jeff's cheeks reddened. "Very funny, Dad."

Rhonda held her breath and waited for her father-in-law's response. She felt sure Don was only kidding and hoped no tension would develop between Jeff and his dad.

Don poked Jeff's arm and said, "Just kidding, Son. I do think, however, that I can probably fit into a pair of your shorts."

"Okay then, follow me." Jeff headed back to the house, and his father followed. Rhonda and Gwen, with Megan in tow, went in behind them.

When Rhonda stepped inside, she paused at the door and hollered back to those still outside, "Relax and enjoy yourselves. We'll be back soon, and then Jeff will get the grill heated so we can cook the meat and eat."

After putting the clothes in the washer, Rhonda provided Megan with a T-shirt and her terry cloth robe. They were too big for the young girl, but at least her body was covered. Jeff loaned his dad a button-down shirt and a pair of his shorts, so at least no one would have to sit through their meal wearing wet clothes.

Jeff noticed that his wife seemed agitated as she flitted around, asking several times if Megan was okay. He hoped the incident wouldn't get her down since she wanted this whole family gathering to go well. He also was concerned that the tension might make his wife's back worse.

When they returned to the patio, everyone found a seat to visit while Jeff got the grill going. Jeff's brother, Stan, offered to help, but Jeff said he could manage and told Stan to relax and enjoy himself.

Jeff looked around his barbecue grill for the tool to clean off the grilling surface.

Rhonda came over to him and tilted her head. "What are you looking for?"

"I found it." He held up the nasty-looking scraper.

She grimaced. "Is that all you have to clean the grill with?"

"Yeah, and there's nothing wrong with it." Jeff smiled and in a low voice he asked, "How are you doing?"

"Okay. At least my back seems to be holding out."

He winked and began scraping at the grill. "I'm glad."

"I'll go inside and grab the rolls." She turned and headed into the house.

Jeff paused his cleaning and closed the lid on the grill. The temperature gauge climbed higher, as he set his tool down and went inside to get the meats. When Jeff returned, he was pleased to see that their guests looked content as they chatted with each other.

While the hot dogs and ground beef patties cooked, Jeff looked out at the beautiful yard. The grass had been freshly cut, and there wasn't a weed in sight. He felt kind of puffed up being able to show his family his and Rhonda's new home. Jeff hoped it was an indication to them—especially Stan—that as a business owner, he'd become successful. It probably shouldn't matter what anyone thought, but Jeff needed the reassurance that he had made something of himself.

Shaking his thoughts aside, Jeff concentrated on cooking the beef patties and hot dogs, while Rhonda took care of setting out the chips, condiments, and eating utensils. The salads and other cold items wouldn't be taken from the refrigerator until the meat had finished cooking.

Half an hour later, everyone took their seats at the tables. Although Jeff wasn't thrilled about it, he wasn't surprised when his dad asked if he could offer a prayer before they began eating.

"Sure, Dad." Jeff nodded. What else could he say? His father was a churchgoer, and so were Stan and Eric, not to mention that Rhonda's mother had told her previously that she'd begun attending church with Gwen and her family. There was no question about it: Jeff and Rhonda were outnumbered when it came to their non-religious beliefs.

When everyone bowed their heads, Jeff did the same. Instead of praying, he allowed his mind to wander. *Sure am glad Megan didn't drown. No doubt Rhonda and I would have gotten the blame for not having a fence around the pond, and of course, we'd have felt guilty about it. And who knows—Rhonda's sister and her husband might have filed a lawsuit against us.*

He shifted uneasily on his folding chair. *I'm surprised no one from either of our families made any comments about the lack of a fence.*

Since the front of their property had an iron gate that usually remained closed when they were home, Jeff hadn't seen the need to put a fence around the pond. Apparently, neither had the previous owners.

Things are different now, Jeff told himself. *If we continue to have family with young children over or in the event that some neighbor kids should wander onto our property, we need to be proactive in protecting anyone from the potential of drowning in our pond.*

Jeff made a mental note to see about the cost of getting a fence put up. He grimaced. *Rhonda and I are away from home a good deal of the time because of our jobs. If we aren't here and the gate is closed, no deliveries would ever get made. Maybe it's a good thing we don't have any kids of our own*, he reasoned. *Then we'd really have to be worried about the pond.*

When an elbow connected to his ribs, Jeff's eyes snapped open. He looked at Rhonda, sitting beside him, and saw that her eyes were open too, as were the others who sat at the tables.

"Did you have a lot to tell God about, Uncle Jeff?" The question came from Eric's youngest son, Jerry, who was six.

Jeff's face warmed. "Uh, yeah. . .I guess." He got up, grabbed the pan of hot dogs and burgers, and took them over to the serving table, where all the other food had been placed. Pointing to the table, Jeff hollered, "Come on, everyone, it's time to fill your plates!"

When the people sitting at the first table got up, Jeff saw his dad look over at Rhonda's mother and heard him say, "If you'd like to sit tight, I'd be happy to get your food, June."

She shook her head, barely making eye contact with him. "Thanks anyway, but I'm kind of a fussy eater, so I'd better do my own choosing."

Fussy eater? This was the first time Jeff had heard his mother-in-law say anything like that. *Maybe June's too independent to let anyone wait on her—especially someone she barely knows. Or maybe she doesn't care for my dad. From the way she hollered at him when Megan was in the pond, I'd have to say that's probably the case.*

After both of their families had filled their plates, Jeff and Rhonda went over to the serving table. "I wonder if everyone will go home after they eat," he whispered to her. "Or should we invite them to stay longer and set out some outdoor games to play?"

"You know, we still have dessert to serve our guests."

"Oh, yeah, I almost forgot about that."

"Instead of playing outdoor games, maybe we should invite everyone into your man cave to watch a family-oriented DVD on your large-screen TV," she suggested. "It might be less stressful than worrying about one of the other kids getting too close to the pond."

Jeff bobbed his head. "Good point. I'll extend the invitation after everyone is done eating. And in addition to serving ice cream and cookies, I'll offer to pop a big batch of buttery popcorn."

"Whew! I don't know about you, but I'm exhausted." Jeff flopped onto the living-room couch beside Rhonda. "Our company stayed longer than I expected."

She nodded and rubbed her stomach. "I definitely ate way more than I should have today. The food was so good. Everyone seemed to enjoy themselves, and I can't believe we all sat through two movies. There was only a little ice cream left over, but those cookies we served were devoured. And who knows how much popcorn and soda pop you served?"

Jeff chuckled and gave his middle a pat. "I agree, the meal was tasty, and I got carried away and ate more than I should have." He reached for her hand. "I'm glad my man cave is big enough to accommodate them all, but we couldn't have done it without bringing in several folding chairs. Makes me wonder if we ought to buy a few more recliners or even a sectional."

"That's not necessary," Rhonda said, following a yawn. "We probably won't have that many people here all at one time very often."

"True. Except for Megan falling in the pond, I believe things went pretty well today."

"I suppose, but that accident really scared me." Rhonda's voice lowered to a near whisper. "I shudder to think of what could have happened if your dad had not jumped in and rescued her."

"If we have another family get-together here this summer, it should probably be with just one of our families at a time. Things were pretty hectic today, and it was hard to visit one-on-one with anybody."

"I agree, but I'm not sure I'll be up to another get-together this summer—with your family or mine." Rhonda reached around and massaged her lower back. "It was a bit too much for me."

"I'm sorry. How's your back holding up?" Jeff asked. "Did the stress of today make it worse?"

"A couple of times, like during the pond incident, it started to spasm, but it seemed to work itself out." She winced. "At least until now."

"Would you like me to massage it for you? Or how about taking a warm bath with Epsom salts? I'd be happy to fill the tub for you."

"A relaxing bath does sound nice. Thanks for offering."

He pulled her close and rubbed the small of her back for a few seconds. "I'll get the water running right now."

When Jeff left the room, Rhonda followed him down the hall. She heard the water running in the tub and took a seat on the edge of their bed to wait until Jeff told her it was ready.

Maybe I should write a letter to the Dear Caroline column again and let her know that she was wrong. My husband and I don't need counseling, because things are getting better between us now that he's being more attentive.

Once Jeff had the tub filled, Rhonda went into the bathroom to prepare for her bath. After stepping into the tub of warm water, she felt herself begin to relax.

I wonder what Gwen was going to tell me about Mom before Kimberly rushed in to tell us Megan had fallen into the pond. In all the excitement, I forgot to bring the topic up before everyone went home. The next time Gwen and I talk, I'll ask her about it.

Chapter 20

Rhonda stood on the porch, holding the remote that opened and closed their front gate, while watching her husband pull his SUV out of the yard. She wished her day off could be easy, with nothing to do but relax in the chaise longue out back. The outside temperature was pleasantly warm, without a cloud in the sky.

What a bummer to waste such a beautiful day stuck indoors working, but I have an agenda to follow. Rhonda leaned against the doorjamb and looked down at her feet. *My toenails could sure use some fresh polish, but those dumb boxes in the garage won't take care of themselves.*

Rhonda looked up and watched her husband give a wave as he pulled his rig onto the street. When he was out of sight, she clicked the button that closed the gate. It had been three weeks since their family get-together, and the decision Rhonda and Jeff had made two weeks ago was to put a large waterproof tote box outside of their front gate for any packages that might be delivered. Thankfully, their mailbox was the locking kind, and it also sat outside the front gate.

After much discussion, Rhonda and Jeff had agreed that they couldn't afford to put up a fence around the pond at this time. Besides, Rhonda didn't like the idea of having one there. It would take away from the pleasant look of the pond and waterfalls. This meant if they did have company with small children, they would need to watch carefully, making sure none of them got close to the pond unless an adult was nearby.

We probably shouldn't have bought this house, Rhonda thought as she opened the front door and went inside. *It's really too big for just the two of us, and since our townhouse still hasn't sold, I'm more concerned about our finances than ever.*

She placed the gate remote on the table in the entryway. *The sensible thing would be to move back into the townhouse and put this place on the market. Though that would be difficult to do, because Jeff and I like it here so much. No, there's got to be some other way.*

Last night, Rhonda had pleaded with Jeff to sell some of his antiques that were valuable and put the money in their savings. He'd refused and suggested instead that they should lower the price of the townhouse. Rhonda's response was that they had already lowered it once, and if they continued to lower the price, they wouldn't break even, let alone make a profit. The subject came up again at breakfast this morning, and Jeff had left for work with nothing resolved. She wondered if they would ever truly get their marriage back on track. Jeff had been more attentive lately, which helped, but this topic seemed to make him more stubborn than a mule.

I need answers, and I'm running out of ideas. My husband doesn't seem worried about our financial situation.

Rhonda made her way to the kitchen to fix a cup of tea. "One step forward and two back. Maybe there's no hope for us at all."

She took a seat at the kitchen table with her cup of tea while she went through yesterday's mail and read the newspaper. "Nothing but bills and a few junk catalogs," she muttered. "Sure don't need those."

Rhonda had vowed not to buy anything they didn't need until their townhouse sold and they could pay off the mortgage on their new place, which would leave them free of any major debt. But with their anniversary coming up, she would make an exception and get her husband a gift.

She heaved a sigh. *If I had known that we'd be in this position right now, I never would have agreed to buy this place. We both thought this endeavor might help our marriage, but we sure called it wrong. When the topic of money comes up, we end up in an argument every time.*

How often had she been over this? She'd said it to herself so many times, not to mention all the discussions that had occurred between her and Jeff. The way his face would tighten whenever she brought up the subject of money let Rhonda know it was not something her husband wanted to discuss.

She doodled on the envelope flap from a utility bill, making a frowny face. *My husband's pride has always gotten in the way of his making good decisions, and I'm just as guilty for going along with it.*

Rhonda tapped her pen and drew another upside-down smile. *I need to think of some ways to make extra money so we can pay off some credit card bills and add some to our savings account. If Jeff would be willing to sell some of his collectibles and other things he doesn't need, we could have a yard sale.*

Rhonda's lips pressed together as she gave a shake of her head. *Hosting a yard sale entails a lot of work, and neither of us has the time for that. Besides, it's doubtful that I could talk Jeff into parting with much of anything.*

Rhonda rested both arms on the table and blew out a puff of air. *If I'd seen that side of him when we were dating in college, I would have run the other way.*

She gave a soft shake of her head. *Who am I kidding? I was drawn to Jeff's outgoing personality and all the compliments and gifts he showered me with. Even if I had known about his compulsion to collect old things, I probably would have looked the other way.*

Rhonda closed her eyes and reflected on the fun times she and Jeff had shared during their two years of dating before he'd asked her to marry him. Even though he'd said she could take time to think it over, Rhonda had given him her answer right away. She'd fallen deeply in love with Jeff and couldn't wait to be his wife. Now, nearly thirteen years later, Rhonda was filled with doubts. Perhaps if she'd waited and dated more men, she would have found someone to whom she was better suited.

Desperately needing to clear her mind of these thoughts, Rhonda opened the newspaper to the Dear Caroline column.

Maybe reading about some other people's problems would make her situation seem minor.

"Dear Caroline," the first one read. "My sister hasn't spoken to me for the last five years. We had an argument after our father died about who would get his guitar and harmonica. It was clearly stated in his will that he wanted my son, who plays in a band, to have both of his musical instruments. My sister didn't think it was fair for Dad to choose my son over hers—never mind that her son isn't interested in music at all. The discussion led to us parting ways. When I tried calling her a few months later, she hung up on me, but not before she said a few choice words and made it clear that she wanted nothing more to do with me. I've tried calling her a couple of other times, but she refuses to talk to me. Is there anything I can do to restore the relationship with my sister? Frustrated and Deeply Hurt."

Eager to know what Caroline's response was, Rhonda read on.

"Dear Frustrated and Deeply Hurt: Since your sister won't take any of your calls, you might consider writing her a letter or asking another family member to talk to your sister on your behalf. Perhaps an impartial person might be able to help the two of you work things out. If, however, your sister is still unwilling, you may have to respect her wishes and move on with your life without a resolution."

"Guess I'm not the only one with unresolved problems." Rhonda set the paper aside and stood. It was time to quit stalling and get something practical done.

Shortly after noon, Rhonda wandered out to the garage to empty a few more boxes. These had been in the storage unit they'd rented while living in the townhouse, and she had no idea what was in any of them.

"Probably more of Jeff's collectibles he didn't want me to know about." Her knuckles whitened when she tore open the lid and saw two glass oil lamps. "Why does my husband have to be so eccentric when it comes to his hobby? With all the stuff he's collected, he could start his own antique store."

Rhonda's forehead wrinkled as she studied the intricate lamps. She could only imagine how much money they must have cost. Was it any wonder they had so little left in their savings account?

"This has gone on long enough," Rhonda grumbled. "If Jeff won't sell some of his things, then maybe I will. There are so many items in these boxes, I doubt he would miss one or two."

Rhonda stood in front of Memory Keepers, wondering if she should go in. She'd come here with the idea of asking if they would buy the ornate oil lamp she'd placed in the trunk of her car, but now Rhonda had second thoughts. If she left the lamp here to be sold on consignment or even sold it outright to the Troyers, what would happen if Jeff came in and saw it sitting there?

A warm breeze came up, blowing several strands of Rhonda's hair to one side, and she pushed them back in place with her hand.

Suddenly, a thought came to mind, and she smiled. *I won't take the lamp inside or see if they will buy it. Instead, I'll ask them not to sell Jeff anything else if he comes into their store.*

Lois got out a dust rag to clean an empty shelf that Orley would be putting some newly acquired items on soon. Their busy morning had stretched into the noon hour, with more customers coming in than normal. Although they'd made several sales, Lois hoped things would slow down a bit for the rest of the afternoon so she could get some paperwork done.

She glanced toward the front of the store, where Orley stood behind the register, waiting on a customer. He seemed in his element here, always smiling and chatting with the people who visited their store. Her husband was definitely an extrovert, whereas Lois kept to herself a bit more. Of course, at times she was quite talkative, especially when she suspected someone was hurting emotionally and needed to talk.

The bell above the door jangled, and Lois glanced in that direction.

She was surprised to see Rhonda Davis enter the store. Lois looked past the young woman to see if Jeff was with her but saw no sign of him.

Since Orley was still busy with his customer, Lois set the dust rag aside and went over to greet Rhonda. "Good afternoon." She smiled and gave the young woman a hug. "What brings you into our store today? Did you come to buy something for your husband?"

Rhonda's hand movements appeared flighty as she fiddled with the straps on her purse. "No, I. . .uh. . .came to ask you a favor."

"Of course. What is it you would like me to do?"

Rhonda shifted her purse to the other arm and lowered her voice. "If my husband comes in here again and wants to buy something, would you and your husband kindly refuse to sell it to him?"

Lois's eyes widened. She'd never had a request such as this and wasn't sure how best to respond.

"I know it might seem like a strange thing to ask, but there's a reason for it."

Lois leaned closer and listened as Rhonda explained that the home they'd left in Canton several months ago had not sold yet, and money was tight.

"And so," Rhonda continued, "we can't afford for him to be coming in here buying antiques he does not need."

"Orley and I cannot force any customer who comes into our store to leave without buying anything, but we can certainly try to dissuade him."

Rhonda pressed a palm to her chest. "Thank you. I appreciate your help with this."

Before Lois could offer a response, the young woman said, "I'd better head out now. I need to go home and get supper started before Jeff gets home from work." She turned and was out the door before Lois could form the word *goodbye*.

Lois's mind raced as she struggled with doubt. *I certainly hope I said the right thing to Rhonda. I also hope that Orley and I can talk Jeff out of buying anything if he does show up here again.*

Chapter 21

"Our driver's here. Are you about ready to head out?" Orley asked Lois from the front door.

She nodded. "I'll get my outer bonnet and be right there."

"Sounds good. I'm going out to the barn to make sure I closed the horse's stall door, then I'll join you in Rick's van."

"Okay. I'll be in the backseat waiting for you."

Orley left the house, and Lois went to get her bonnet. After putting it on over her white head covering, she stepped into the living room to get her purse. She had previously placed it on the small table next to her rocking chair, but to her surprise, it was not there now.

She looked around the room and rubbed her forehead. *I can't go without my purse. It has the money in it that we'll need for our shopping trip to Millersburg. I'll look in a few other rooms for it, but first I'd better run outside and let Orley and our driver know that I am going to be a few more minutes.*

Lois opened the front door and stepped onto the porch. *Now that's strange. There's no van in sight. I wonder if Rick drove around back, thinking I'd be coming out that door.*

Lois hurried through the kitchen and spotted her handbag sitting on the table. *At least I found my purse; now I just need to find out where those men are.* She grabbed the purse on her way to the back door and stepped out. "This doesn't make sense. There's no van here either. Did they leave without me?" She grimaced. "For goodness' sake, why would they do that? Orley knows there were some things I needed to shop for." Lois patted her purse. "I have the money right here."

Feeling a bit put out, she took off her black bonnet and placed it on the kitchen table. It was strange to be forgotten when she and Orley had talked during breakfast about going to Millersburg.

Lois stood there, looking out the window in hopes that the van would roll back into the yard to pick her up. But the longer she waited for the vehicle to return, the more the anticipation of that happening faded. *I really wanted to go with him and have some fun shopping today, but since it looks like I'll be stuck here all morning, I may as well get something done.*

Lois went to her sewing room and opened the middle drawer of her desk. *Think I'll catch up on my letter writing, and then maybe I'll bake some bacon-cheese muffins.*

After Lois finished writing the first letter to her once-widowed father, who had remarried twenty years ago and lived in Pennsylvania, her thoughts went to the visit she'd had from Rhonda yesterday. After the young woman left the antique store, Lois had waited to tell Orley about Rhonda's request until he'd finished with his customer. He had been as surprised as she was about the situation but agreed that if Jeff came in looking to buy something, he would try to talk him out of it. Of course, Lois knew, from being married to a determined man, that if Jeff really wanted to buy one of the antiques in their shop, there would be nothing she or Orley could say or do to dissuade him.

Shaking her concerns aside, Lois returned to her letter writing.

A short time later, after she'd finished the last one and was about to head for the kitchen to fix a cup of tea, Lois heard a horn honk in the front yard. She hurried to look out the living-room window and was surprised to see her husband get out of Rick's van and approach the house.

Lois opened the door and greeted him on the porch, but before she could say anything, Orley spoke first. "I'm sorry we left you behind. You'd said you'd be right out, and when I came out of the barn, I assumed you'd gotten into the back of the van." He paused and swiped at the trickle of sweat running down his forehead. "When I took my seat in the front of the van, I never thought to look in the back. Then Rick started talkin' to me and away we went. We were halfway to Millersburg when I turned in my seat to ask you a question. Imagine my surprise when I realized you weren't there." A crimson flush swept across his cheeks. "I feel like a *dummkopp*. Will you forgive me, Lois?"

She stepped forward and gave him a hug, unmindful of whether Rick might be watching them from the van. "You are not a dunce, and of course I forgive you, dear husband. Next time, however, please make sure that I'm with you before you let our driver take off."

Orley thumped his forehead. "I guarantee it will not happen again."

Canton

Rhonda sat at her desk, going over the checklist of things that had been done in the hotel's renovation so far. Only half of the rooms were finished, but the lobby had been completely refurbished, which made it more appealing when guests checked in. Some of the older rooms were decent enough and could still be rented, but most were in the process of being repainted or having tile replaced in the bathrooms, so they were not available to guests right now. That meant less money coming in; but once the renovations were completed, the entire hotel would be more appealing, and they would hopefully make up the difference in income with more reservations from people booking rooms.

Rhonda reached around to rub a spot on her back where a

muscle wanted to spasm. *I wish there was something I could do about Jeff's and my personal finances. It would help if I could talk him into selling some of his antiques.*

Rhonda reflected on how she had stopped by the Troyers' antique store yesterday. She hoped Lois had remembered to tell her husband about the request to discourage Jeff from buying any antiques. Hopefully, the Amish couple would honor that appeal.

She doodled on the edge of her paperwork. *I'm glad I made it home before Jeff did and was able to put the fancy kerosene lamp back in the box where I found it. I hate to think of what he would have said if he'd discovered the lamp was missing and questioned me about it. Of course, he would have been more upset if I'd actually sold the antique without his knowledge or permission.*

Rhonda often felt as if she were walking on eggshells around her husband when she tried to discuss their finances. Since she and Jeff had been getting along better for a while, she didn't want to do anything that might make things worse. But keeping quiet on the topic of money only meant prolonging their problem, and it almost drove her crazy. *What can I do? I wish I had some answers.*

Her desk phone rang, ending Rhonda's contemplations. When she picked up the receiver and heard Susan's voice from the corporate office, she cringed. Whenever there was something unpleasant to relate, it was usually Susan who called. She was good at what she did, and perhaps that was why she'd been hired for the job, but Susan could also come off as demanding and rude.

"Good morning, Susan. How are you?" Rhonda tried to keep her tone pleasant and upbeat.

"I'd be doing a lot better if the most recent reviews written about our hotel were not so negative."

Rhonda could almost visualize Susan's wrinkled forehead and squinted eyes. "Which reviews are you referring to?"

"The ones that were posted yesterday."

"I wasn't here then. It was my day off."

"You could have checked them from home. You do have a computer there, right?"

"Well, yes, but—"

"For heaven's sake, haven't you looked at them today?"

"No, actually, I've been working on—"

"Need I remind you that part of your job is reading the reviews and responding to them promptly?"

"I am aware of that, but as you know, I have many other responsibilities here."

"Regardless, you are supposed to check for reviews first thing every morning and respond to them in a timely manner." There was a pause, then Susan spoke again. "If you'll get on your computer right now and go to the page that lists reviews of our hotel, you will see a very negative complaint about the hot tub not working. I want you to see that it gets fixed right away. Is that understood?"

Rhonda's body heat rose as she went online and to the page Susan had directed her to. "Yes, I see that review, but it makes no sense because we don't have a hot tub at this hotel." *You should know that, Susan.* "Maybe the person who posted the review stayed at some other hotel and got it mixed up with ours."

"I don't care if they did mix it up. The review is under our hotel listing, and it needs to be dealt with right away."

"Okay, Susan, I'll take care of it."

"And remember that you need to respond positively to any and all reviews—even those that are negative."

Rhonda's pulse quickened as her muscles quivered. She felt like a child being told what to do. *Doesn't Susan believe I'm a responsible person who can think for herself? Maybe I should remind her that I do have a bachelor's degree in hotel management and one in marketing.*

"I've always responded correctly whenever we've gotten positive or negative reviews, Susan, and I will continue to do so," Rhonda said.

"Good. And don't forget to check for reviews regularly."

"I will. Is there anything else you wish to speak with me about?"

"That's all for now. You'll be hearing from me if there are any other problems, though. Goodbye, Rhonda."

When Rhonda hung up the phone, she stared at the computer

screen with her teeth and fingers clenched. She wished those who worked at the corporate office—especially Susan—would be a little kinder and more understanding.

Rhonda had worked for another hotel before taking this job, and no one from the head office had ever spoken to her so harshly or condescendingly. She wished she could either quit her job here and find something closer to home or, better yet, stop working all together and make her career as a homemaker.

Rhonda bit down on her bottom lip so hard that she tasted blood. *If Jeff and I had even one child and we weren't in debt up to our necks, I could stay home and be a full-time mother.*

Tears pricked the back of her eyes. *But with Jeff refusing to adopt and our finances being so tight, there is no way I can stop working right now.*

Walnut Creek

Jeff entered the house and placed his car keys on the narrow table in the entryway. He'd had a busy day at the restaurant and was glad to be home where he could unwind.

Rhonda had called earlier to tell him that she would be working a few hours later than usual today. Some new tables and chairs had been delivered to the hotel for the breakfast room, and she needed to make sure they were set up correctly.

"I believe my wife's job is more stressful than mine," Jeff said to his reflection in the mirror above the entry table. "Too bad neither of us is old enough to retire. It would be nice to stay home all the time and enjoy our place here."

He stroked the stubble on his chin, realizing for the first time all day that he'd forgotten to shave this morning. "Guess I'd better take care of that before Rhonda gets home. She wouldn't appreciate a kiss from a prickly pear."

Jeff headed down the hall to their bedroom. When he stepped

into the master bath and picked up his shaver, a thought popped into his head. *Since Rhonda's not here, I should get out that daisy pin I bought for her at that yard sale awhile back. I'll put it in a nice box and wrap it in some of that fancy paper Rhonda keeps in one of the guest room closets, along with some craft items she rarely finds time to use.*

After Jeff finished shaving, he went to his closet to change into a pair of shorts and a T-shirt. It felt good to lounge around in comfortable clothes when he was at home.

"Okay now, where did I put that daisy pin? Did I hide it in one of my dresser drawers?"

He opened each one and rummaged through the clothes, but there was no sign of the pin. He scrunched up his face then relaxed it, trying to remain calm. *It hasn't been that long since I brought the piece of jewelry home. I ought to remember where I put it.*

Jeff walked to the front door. *I'll try retracing my steps from that day. I just need to recall where I'd feel the surest of a place that Rhonda wouldn't find the pin.*

He went back to the walk-in closet and looked through some shoe boxes on the top shelf of his side. Nothing there but shoes, and some boxes were empty. Jeff didn't know why he'd saved the ones with nothing in them, but he didn't want to take the time to discard those boxes now.

Hmm. . .I'm still not remembering where I hid her gift. His shoulders slumped as he stared at his top shelf in the closet. *This isn't good at all. How can I be so absentminded or careless? Rhonda could arrive home any minute, and I wouldn't feel good about spoiling her surprise. Since our anniversary is a week away, if I can't find that pin, I'll need to buy Rhonda something else,* Jeff told himself.

Jeff remembered seeing several pieces of vintage jewelry for sale at Memory Keepers, so if he couldn't locate the daisy pin, he would stop by the Troyers' store within the next few days. Hopefully, he'd be able to find something there that Rhonda might like. Otherwise, he'd have to come up with a gift for her that didn't include vintage jewelry.

Chapter 22

It was down to the wire. Jeff and Rhonda's thirteenth anniversary had arrived, and he still hadn't found the vintage daisy pin he'd planned to give her. He had called Russ this morning to let him know that he wouldn't be at the restaurant when it first opened and might not arrive until closer to noon. He'd wished his wife a happy anniversary and reminded her that they had dinner reservations at the Chalet in the Valley restaurant for seven o'clock that evening. Jeff had also given Rhonda a kiss before she headed out the door for work half an hour ago. Since that time, he'd searched for the pin again but had finally given up and was now heading down the road toward the Troyers' Memory Keepers.

Jeff looked forward to this evening and the meal he and Rhonda would share. Although the restaurant's address was in Millersburg, the building was actually closer to the quaint village of Charm and overlooked the Doughty Valley. Jeff hoped things would go well tonight and that he and Rhonda would have a memorable evening.

A short time later, Jeff pulled up in front of Memory Keepers. When he entered the building and saw Orley sitting on a stool behind the front counter, he gave a wave and went directly to the spot where he'd last seen the vintage jewelry. But the items he'd hoped for were not there. Thinking they might have been moved, Jeff looked at the nearby tables but saw nothing there either. After a few minutes of moving things around and checking more places, he stepped up to Orley and asked if they still had some vintage jewelry in the store.

The pleasant Amish man shook his head. "Sorry, but we sold the last few pieces yesterday."

Jeff felt sweat leaching out of him from the frustration he felt and sagged against his side of the counter. "That's a disappointment. I had hoped to buy my wife a special piece of jewelry from what I'd seen in here before. Our anniversary is today, and I want to give her a nice gift when we go out to dinner this evening."

Orley's eyebrows rose slightly as he leaned both elbows on the counter. "I thought you were going to give Rhonda that antique daisy pin you found at the yard sale the four of us attended."

"I had planned to, but now I can't remember where I put it." Jeff drew in a quick breath. "Guess now I'll have to give Rhonda something else."

"Does it have to be vintage?" Orley questioned.

Jeff shrugged. "I suppose not, but since she likes daisies, I thought. . ."

"You might find something nice in one of the gift shops here in Walnut Creek or the village of Berlin." Orley drummed his fingertips on the countertop. "With all those stores catering to the tourists, you're bound to find something to choose from."

"Yeah, I guess." Jeff glanced around, allowing his gaze to roam over the various tables, shelves, and cabinets filled with numerous antiquated items. "Have you gotten anything new in the store lately?"

Orley rubbed the bridge of his nose before nodding. "Just some bigger pieces of antique furniture. Nothing you'd be interested in, I'm sure."

"You're right. We've already got enough furniture in our house." Jeff pulled his fingers through the back of his hair. "Since our new place is bigger than our old one, we had to buy a few extra chairs for the living room after we moved in. We also purchased a pull-out sofa for the second guest room to accommodate extra overnight guests, should we have any. Our townhouse in Canton had a spare bedroom, so fortunately we already had furniture to put in the other guest room at our new place."

"I assume your townhouse still hasn't sold?"

"No, and I'm beginning to wonder if it ever will."

Orley stepped around from the register and placed his hand on Jeff's shoulder. "I can understand your feelings of discouragement, but you can't give in to despair or let negative thoughts overtake you."

That's easy for you to say. You're not the one in my predicament. Jeff didn't voice his thoughts. Instead, he forced a smile and said, "I'd better get going and see if I can find something for Rhonda at one of shops in Berlin before I head to my restaurant in Canton."

He was almost to the front door when Orley called out to him. "Wait a minute, Jeff. There's something I'd like to give you and Rhonda for your anniversary."

Jeff turned around to face the bearded man. "I appreciate the thought, but there's no need for that."

"Please don't say no. I'd really like to give you something, and I'm sure if my wife wasn't in the backroom doing some paperwork, she'd agree with me." Orley walked over to one of the tables in the center of the room, picked up something Jeff couldn't distinguish, and placed it in a small box he'd taken from under the table. Then Orley came back to where Jeff stood and handed it to him. "Happy anniversary. Perhaps you and your wife can open this tonight, either before or after you go out for supper."

A warm flush crept across Jeff's cheeks. "Thank you." Gripping the box in his hands, he hurried out the door. *That surely was unexpected.*

———

Canton

"I'm surprised you're still here," Lori said when Rhonda met her in the hotel's downstairs hallway at four o'clock that afternoon.

"Why wouldn't I be?" Rhonda asked.

"With today being your wedding anniversary and figuring you and your husband would have made plans for this evening, I assumed you'd be getting off work early this evening." Lori brushed a loose curl aside and smiled.

Rhonda shook her head. "I got here a little later than normal this morning so I could pick up something I had ordered for Jeff at the jewelry store. Now I have to make up the time I lost." She glanced at her watch. "I'll be leaving by five, which should give me plenty of time to get home, change into something nicer, and still make our seven o'clock dinner reservations."

"Where are you going to eat? I assume it's not Jeff's restaurant?"

Rhonda shook her head. "I don't know where it is, but Jeff said it's someplace close to home and has a very nice atmosphere."

Lori smiled. "I'll be eager to hear about your evening, and I hope you and Jeff have a wonderful anniversary."

"Thank you, Lori. I hope so too."

Rhonda watched her ever-pleasant employee amble toward the front desk as a couple came in through the front entrance with their suitcases in tow. Rhonda listened to Lori greet them with a cheerful tone. Even though at times the young woman complained of some discomfort from her pregnancy, she nearly always seemed to be in good spirits. Lori had said once that despite the distresses that went with being pregnant, it was worth it and that she couldn't wait to be a mother to her precious baby.

Rhonda bit the inside of her lip. *If only I could be in her shoes.*

~

Walnut Creek

"You look beautiful in that color," Jeff said when Rhonda stepped out of their master bathroom wearing a pale yellow dress with white trim around the collar.

"Thanks.

Jeff liked to see his wife dressed up, but even more than that, he loved to spend quality time with her. He watched her go to the closet and pick out two pairs of shoes—a white pair of heels and black flats.

"Which shoes should I wear?" Rhonda turned toward him.

He shrugged. "Either one looks fine to me."

Rhonda slid on the heels and stood in front of the full-length mirror. "I should probably go with these. What do you think?"

"They look nice, but wouldn't the others be more comfortable?"

"Yes, that's true." She removed them and slipped on her leather flats, gazing back at the mirror. "These are dressy enough, and they are more comfortable on my feet."

Rhonda put the white ones away in their closet. Then she stood in front of the mirror fussing with her hair a bit before walking over to Jeff. "I'm ready to go."

"Okay, but before we leave, I'd like to give you something." *Sure wish I could have found that dainty daisy pin. It would have looked great on Rhonda's yellow dress.* Jeff handed her a peach-colored gift bag. "This isn't what I'd originally planned to give you, but I hope you'll like it just the same. Happy anniversary, honey."

Rhonda opened the bag, and when she reached inside, a smile spread across her lovely face. "A picture-framed alarm clock. What a clever idea. And you even thought to put one of our wedding pictures in it. Thank you, Jeff."

"I'm glad you like it." He felt a head-to-toe release of all tension.

She placed his gift on her nightstand and stepped over to her side of the dresser. "Now it's your turn." Rhonda opened her top dresser drawer and took out a gift box with a green bow stuck to the top. "I ordered this for you from the jewelry store in Canton. I hope you like it."

Jeff lifted the lid off the box and grinned when he withdrew a wristwatch. "Wow, honey, this is great. I especially like that it has the logo for my favorite football team in the center of the watch. This will be fun to wear on game days."

Her gaze remained fixed on him as he set the time and put the watch on his left arm. "It cost a little more than some of the other watches I looked it, but I've been saving up to get it, so I hope you like it."

"I love it, and I love you even more." Jeff bent his head and gave her a lingering kiss. When they broke away from each other, he looked at the watch again. "We'd better go or we're gonna miss our reservations."

"Okay. I just want to check my makeup and get my purse, and then I'll meet you in the car."

"Sounds good, and if you have no objections, we'll take your sporty car tonight. It's classier looking and a lot more fun to drive than my SUV."

Rhonda offered him another pleasant smile and nodded before going over to her makeup table.

Jeff whistled as he headed out the door with a spring in his step. He hoped the rest of their evening would go as well as the beginning had.

Millersburg

"This restaurant is so quaint and lovely." Rhonda smiled at Jeff from across the table. "It's like a hidden gem here in the heart of Amish country."

He nodded. "You're right. I chose this place because it offers Swiss, Austrian, and American cooking, which gives us a varied menu to choose from. The atmosphere is also nice."

"I agree." Rhonda studied the rich wooden decor throughout the dining room. It had a warm, cozy feeling and made her feel as if she were in another country. "Those spunky goats we saw in the fenced-in area outside the restaurant when we arrived were pretty cute too."

"Yeah." Jeff chuckled. "I really got a kick out of the biggest one and the way he sat up there on the hill, like he was a king overlooking his domain."

She laughed. "That was pretty funny."

"Do you know what you're going to order?" Jeff pointed to Rhonda's menu.

She pressed her lips together and studied the entrées. "Nearly everything listed here appeals, but I think I'll go with the chicken schnitzel. It comes with either asparagus or broccoli and one side."

"Which of the sides sounds good to you?"

"Think I'll try the hot German potato salad. I've never had it served that way before. What are you going to order, Jeff?"

"I'm goin' with the Reuben schnitzel, topped with sauerkraut and Guggisberg Swiss cheese. It's also served with broccoli or asparagus, covered with hollandaise sauce. For my side, I'll get either the mashed potatoes and gravy or some applesauce."

"There are a lot of carbs in mashed potatoes, and the gravy would also be fattening."

Watching Jeff's face tighten as he rubbed the back of his neck caused Rhonda to wish she hadn't said anything negative about the potatoes and gravy. "I—I didn't mean to imply that you need to watch your weight, I just thought. . ." *I suppose I shouldn't have thrown cold water on his choice for this evening's meal. It's not like he normally eats like that. Tonight's a special occasion for us.*

Their waitress, wearing a Bavarian-style dress, arrived at their table and asked if they had any questions about the menu.

"No questions on my part," Jeff was quick to say. "I think we're both ready to order." He looked at Rhonda. "Why don't you go first?"

Rhonda told the young woman what she wanted, and then Jeff placed his order. After the waitress left, they sat quietly, drinking their water. When Rhonda couldn't stand the silence any longer, she said, "Are you upset with me, Jeff, for reminding you about the carbs in the potatoes?"

"No. You were right. I don't need the extra carbs, and I'm sure I'll enjoy the applesauce."

"Okay. I just don't want to spoil your evening."

"Don't worry—you haven't. And unless the food is either cold or not cooked to our liking, the meal won't be spoiled either."

~

"That sure was a good dinner. I enjoyed every bite of food on my plate." Rhonda reached across the leather seat of the sports car and placed her hand on Jeff's arm.

"Mine was good too," he agreed as he shifted it into fifth gear, being careful to keep his eyes on the road. Now that the sun had set and they were driving on a curvy road, Jeff needed to give driving his full attention.

Jeff felt like he owned the road, shifting with pleasure and having all the vehicle's power at his fingertips. His SUV had an automatic transmission, which he didn't mind, but Rhonda's sporty-looking vehicle was more fun to drive.

Rhonda turned on the radio, and the pleasant music was no distraction at all. In fact, Jeff felt quite content and relaxed. In addition to the tasty meal they'd eaten, the conversation at the table between him and Rhonda had been pleasant and upbeat. Neither of them had mentioned their jobs or said anything negative to the other. Jeff was convinced that their marriage had gotten back on track and without much effort from either of them.

We have hit a few bumps in the road of our marriage, Jeff admitted to himself, *but I'm glad Rhonda and I didn't seek counseling like some other couples we know. The next time I see Orley, I'll let him know that things are going better between me and Rhonda.*

Thinking about Orley caused Jeff to remember the anniversary gift the Amish man had given him this morning. When he'd arrived home from work this afternoon, Jeff had set the box on the kitchen table after going through the mail. He still couldn't figure out why Orley would give them anything for their anniversary, since the Amish couple didn't know Jeff and Rhonda that well. Even so, the gift was a nice gesture, and Jeff was eager to find out what was inside that small box. He'd forgotten about it until now and hadn't mentioned it to Rhonda yet.

Guess I'll wait till we get home, and then I'll show her the gift and we can open it together.

"Jeff, look out!"

His wife's shout along with the two eyes shining in the road made him jump. Jeff gripped the steering wheel and hit the brakes, but it was too late. The sickening thump when Rhonda's sporty car hit the deer was deafening to Jeff's ears.

Chapter 23

"I don't know why you're so upset with me. It's not my fault a deer ran in front of our car." Jeff's shoulders slumped. "I feel terrible about hitting the poor thing. I've never run into an animal before, and I hope I never have to live through something like that again."

"It was *my* car, Jeff, and it's probably totaled." Tears sprang to Rhonda's eyes and ran down her hot cheeks as they stood on the shoulder of the road waiting for help to arrive.

"It will be okay. We have insurance, and I'll get them called right away." Jeff reached for her hand. "It could have been worse. At least neither of us is hurt like that poor animal." He pointed to the small doe lying dead by the side of the road. "I'm sorry our lovely evening had to end with me hitting the deer."

"I read in a magazine someone left at the hotel a few weeks ago that over one million deer are killed each year from getting hit by a car." Rhonda shivered even though the evening air was quite warm. "I shudder to think of how many people have been killed when their vehicle has hit a deer."

"Any loss of human life is a tragedy." Jeff let go of Rhonda's hand and slipped his arm around her. "You're trembling. Are you cold?"

"No, just shook up over what happened to the deer and my car."

"I get it. My legs are kinda shaky too."

Rhonda looked at him and grimaced. "How am I going to get to work in the morning?"

"I'll drive you there and pick you up when you're ready to leave for the day. We may have to rely on my rig alone until we can get a new one. It is doubtful that yours can be fixed."

Rhonda brought a shaky hand to her forehead. "This is one more thing that we didn't need to happen."

"I agree, but since you have full coverage on your car, we'll either be reimbursed for the repairs or given the money to buy a new vehicle."

Rhonda moved closer to her car, noticing some fur left by the animal where the dents showed. She groaned. "I wish this part of our evening had never happened. I feel so bad for that poor animal." Rhonda tried to stave off more tears as she continued to stare at her damaged vehicle. "I really liked my car, and I hope it can be repaired, but if it's not fixable, and we have to wait to buy a new one, you'll be stuck taking me to and from the hotel five days a week."

"I don't mind driving you, but it might be best if we see about renting a car. Since you have good coverage, I think our insurance company will pay for that too."

"No, they won't. With our finances being tight, I called a few weeks ago and lowered our premium by cutting back on a few things we had on our policy, including reimbursement for renting a car in the case mine was ever out of commission."

Jeff folded his arms and groaned. "You should have consulted me before you did that, Rhonda. Doesn't my input count for anything?"

"Of course, it does, but. . ."

Rhonda's words trailed off when two vehicles pulled up almost simultaneously. One was a sheriff's car and the other a tow truck. For now, their discussion was over, but no doubt it would be dealt with again when they got home.

Walnut Creek

Lois looked away from the to-do list she'd been working on and glanced at the grandfather clock across the room. It was getting close to ten o'clock—definitely time for bed.

She nibbled on one of the homemade snickerdoodles she'd made after work. It went well with the warm cup of chamomile tea she had brewed for herself. A little snack before bed wouldn't hurt anything, and it sure was tasty.

Lois's day had been busy. She'd had time to do a few chores before she and Orley went to work at the antique shop this morning. Soon after they'd opened their business, a few elderly English people, possibly tourists, had come in. Lois had introduced herself, saying that if they needed anything to let her know. She figured the ladies must be from out of town because she'd never seen them around before.

Even now, Lois had to chuckle when she thought about how those three ladies browsed as they chatted about the different things the antique shop offered. The tallest woman had pointed to an old train set and commented that it looked like the one her dad used to have.

Not wanting to wake Orley while he rested, Lois suppressed a snicker. *When a certain piece stirs up memories for a person, I guess they can't help but want to talk about it.*

Her gaze went to her husband, slouched in his favorite chair. His eyes were closed, and soft snores vibrated from his nose.

Lois couldn't figure out how Orley could doze for a few hours in his chair and go right to sleep when they went to bed. She would have to be sick or overly tired to sleep in her chair.

She finished the last cookie and drank the remainder of her tea. Then she rose from her chair and went to the kitchen to rinse the dishes and pull down the window shades. *I should put the cookie tin away first and then do up these dishes.* Lois ran the water and added some detergent in the sink while pondering a few things: *I wonder how Jeff and Rhonda are doing? I hope they are able to work things out.* While the warm water ran, she began washing the few dishes. *That young couple needs prayer, and I'll be sure to do that before I go to sleep tonight.*

Lois finished her task and went back to where Orley slept. She looked out the front-room window and saw the lights of a buggy going by. Soon it slowed to make the turn into the neighbor's driveway. *I thought so. It's the Millers. They must have been out visiting this evening. They're good people, such a nice young family, and their three little ones are so sweet.*

A lump formed in her throat. *If Orley and I could have had children, I would have tried to be the very best mother. I'm sure Orley would have been a good father too.*

Shaking her thoughts aside, Lois waited until the clock chimed ten times. When her husband didn't budge, she left her chair, walked over to him, and gave his arm a nudge. "Wake up, sleepyhead. It's time for bed."

Orley's nose twitched slightly, but his eyes remained closed.

"Ich geh noch em bett." She shook his arm with a little firmness this time.

His eyelids opened just a crack, but he made no effort to move. "Okay, you go ahead to bed. I'll be there soon."

She shook her head. "If I leave you here in this chair and go to bed by myself, you'll wake up in the morning in the same place you are right now."

Orley yawned and sat up a little straighter. "You're right as always, my dear *fraa*."

She snickered. "Jah, sure. I'm only right when I'm agreeing with you on something."

"That's not true. You're right at least fifty percent of the time."

She gave his arm a poke. "Come now, silly *mann*. We can talk about this pointless subject another time when you're not half asleep."

He got up from his chair and turned to face her. "I'll have you know that I'm wide awake."

"I'll bet you won't be once your *kopp* hits the pillow on our comfortable bed."

Orley bent his head and kissed her cheek. "Right again, Fraa."

She rolled her eyes then began to move away from his chair, but he caught hold of her hand.

"Wait a minute, Lois. There's something I've been meaning to tell you."

"Oh? What's that?"

"This morning, while you were busy doing paperwork in the back room, Jeff Davis came into our store, wanting to buy a piece of vintage jewelry for his wife because it was their anniversary."

She clutched the sides of her apron. "Oh dear. What did you tell him?"

"I said all the antique jewelry had sold, which was the truth."

"Was he satisfied with your answer?"

Orley shrugged. "I think so, but I could tell from the way his shoulders sagged that he wasn't happy about it."

"As I recall, you mentioned the day we met the Davises at one of the yard sales we'd stopped at that Jeff had bought an old but pretty pin to give his wife."

"True, but he couldn't remember where he put it, so he was looking to find something to replace the daisy pin."

"Did he look at anything else in the store or mention wanting to buy something?"

Orley shook his head. "Nope. When I suggested that he might be able to find something suitable for Rhonda in one of the gift shops here in town or perhaps Berlin, Jeff was ready to head out the door." Orley gave his beard a quick tug. "Before he left, I gave him an anniversary gift from us."

She tilted her head to one side. "Oh, what did you give him?"

"Remember that old plaque with Psalm 46:10 written on it: 'Be still, and know that I am God'? You know, the one that had been lying on one of the center display tables."

"Jah. We've had it in the store for a long time. I kept thinking someone would buy it, but the plaque's pretty much been ignored." Lois tapped her chin with her index finger. "Maybe we should put it in a more prominent place so it's more visible."

"There's no need for that now, because I put the plaque in a box and handed it to Jeff before he went out the door."

Lois's lips parted slightly before they formed a full-fledged smile. "That was a good gift to give the young couple whose marriage seems to be struggling. If they'd come to know God personally, He would be there to help them deal with any problems that might come their way."

Orley nodded. "My thoughts exactly, and for that, I'll continue to pray."

Jeff entered the house behind Rhonda and paused in the hallway. "Does it seem warmer than normal in here, or am I just overheated from dealing with the ordeal of hitting that deer?"

Rhonda stood beside him a moment and nodded. "It is quite warm. It hasn't been this uncomfortable in the house before, and it seems a little odd to me. What did you set the thermostat on before we left to go out to dinner?"

"Like usual, seventy-two."

"And did you make sure that it was set for the air-conditioning to run and not the furnace for heat?"

She must think I'm an idiot or something. Jeff's body temperature came up a notch as his jaw tightened. "It's only the first week of September, and we haven't had any cold weather yet, so why would you think I'd be stupid enough to turn on the heat?"

"I didn't say you were stupid."

"Sounded like it to me. I feel like you are treating me like a child."

"Don't be so defensive, Jeff. I was only asking if—oh, never mind. I'll go look at the thermostat myself."

"If you don't believe me, go ahead and look all you want." Jeff put both hands on his hips.

"I didn't say that."

"Don't bother checking. I'll take a look at it myself." He moved past her and hurried down the hall, although the sound of her footsteps told him she was close behind.

When Jeff viewed the thermostat, his eyes widened. "What in the world?"

"What's wrong?" Jeff felt his wife's warm breath as she peered over his shoulder.

"It's set to seventy-two, like I said, and it's in AC mode. Even so, the temperature here in the house is up to eighty. It's no wonder we feel hot."

Rhonda sagged against the wall. "This is not good, Jeff. Now we're going to have to call someone to check it out, and we'll probably end up with an expensive repair bill—or worse yet, discover that we need a whole new air-conditioning unit." She sighed. "I dread trying to sleep in this overly warm house tonight. We're going to be miserable."

"Maybe it won't be so bad. For starters, we should open some windows, which oughta help, since the outside air felt cooler than it does in here. And there's a box fan in the garage I can bring in."

"All right, but before we get started with that, I really need something cold to drink."

"Same here. Let's go to the kitchen and open those windows first, and then we can take the pitcher of lemonade out of the refrigerator."

"Okay." Rhonda turned and trudged down the hall as if in slow motion.

Jeff felt bummed about the way this evening had turned out. He'd wanted their anniversary celebration to go well. It had been so pleasant during their meal at the restaurant, but hitting the deer had put a damper on things. To make matters worse, Jeff felt sure

Rhonda blamed him for the accident. Despite the lateness of the evening, Jeff had already notified their insurance company about the accident and was told that someone would be by the house tomorrow around noon to pick up Rhonda's vehicle.

The ride home with the tow truck driver as they'd brought her pathetic-looking car back to their yard hadn't helped either. While the driver talked nonstop to Jeff the whole way, Rhonda sat silent, staring straight ahead with her arms crossed.

When they entered the kitchen, Jeff opened both kitchen windows, while Rhonda got out two glasses and filled them with ice cubes. The air coming through the open windows was a little cooler than the stuffy kitchen, but there wasn't much of a breeze. No doubt, it would be a miserable night trying to sleep, even if they opened every window in the house.

Once Rhonda poured lemonade into their glasses, they both took a seat.

"What's this?" she asked, gesturing to the cardboard box on the table.

"Oh, yeah; I almost forgot about that. Orley gave it to me when I stopped at Memory Keepers this morning."

Rhonda's forehead wrinkled. "You bought something from the antique store?"

"No. He put some item in a box before I left and said it was an anniversary gift for us from him and Lois."

She took a drink from her glass and placed it back on the table. "That's odd. Orley doesn't know you or me very well. Why would he give us anything?"

Jeff shrugged. "I don't know, but even though his wife wasn't in the room at the time, he said he was sure she would also want us to have the gift."

"Have you opened it to see what's inside?"

Jeff shook his head. "I was waiting so we could open the gift together."

Rhonda glanced at the clock on the far wall. "We may as well do it now, because in another twenty minutes, it'll be past midnight and it will no longer be our anniversary."

"Yeah, right." He pushed the box in her direction. "Why don't you do the honors?"

Rhonda pulled the flaps open and reached into the box. When she withdrew the gift, she wasn't smiling. "Why would Orley give us this?" She turned the antiquated plaque to face Jeff.

His pulse quickened and his chest tightened. "Be still, and know that I am God." He leaned back in his chair and groaned. "I thought I'd made it clear to that determined Amish man that you and I are not religious."

"Apparently, you didn't make it clear enough." She placed the unwanted gift on the table. "So now what are we supposed to do with this?"

"Beats me." Jeff turned his hands palms up. "Guess we could pitch it in the garbage."

Her mouth twisted as though she'd eaten something distasteful. "We probably shouldn't do that, in case Orley asks you about it, but I'm certainly not going to hang it on any wall in our house."

"Agreed. I'm going out to the garage and get that box-fan to use in our bedroom tonight." Jeff picked up his glass and drank the sweet liquid in just a few gulps. He had half a notion to return the old plaque but didn't want to hurt Orley's feelings. *Guess for now at least, I'll stick it out in the garage someplace where I won't have to see it.*

Chapter 24

A loud thump followed by a yelp caused Lois to sit straight up in bed. A quick glance at her husband's side of the bed told her exactly what had happened. Orley had a habit of sleeping close to the edge of the bed and had fallen out on more than one occasion. This morning was a repeat performance.

She sprang out of bed and went around to where he lay on the floor. "Are you all right?"

"I'm fine." He turned over, got up slowly, and took a seat on the bed.

"You always say you're fine even when you're not." Lois followed the comment with a click of her tongue.

"Well, it's true. All I feel is a little *glumpe* on my kopp." Orley touched his forehead.

Lois placed her fingers on the spot he had touched. "Feels more like a goose egg has formed than just a little lump."

"No matter. It's nothing for you to worry about. Now that we're awake, we'd better get dressed, do our chores, and eat breakfast so I can get out our bikes. Since we're having another sale, we don't want to be late opening the store today."

Lois glanced at the clock on Orley's bedside table to check the time. "You're right. The alarm will be going off soon anyway." She placed her hand on his arm. "I think we should call one of our drivers to take us to the store today, though."

He tipped his head back and looked up at her. "How come?"

"You always peddle fast and furious when we're biking, and with that lump you earned when you hit the floor, you might feel light-headed, or you could even faint. Then you'd be making a trip to see the doctor."

Orley stood up, planting his feet in a wide stance. "I am fine, I tell you. We do not need a driver or a doctor. When the weather turns cold and we want to stay warm, then I'll call on someone to take us to the store in their motorized vehicle."

Lois lifted her shoulders in a halfhearted shrug. "Okay, Husband, whatever you say."

~

Canton

When Jeff pulled into the hotel parking lot, Rhonda told him good-bye and got out of his vehicle. It seemed so odd not to be driving her own car today, and she couldn't help but feel sorry for herself.

"I hope your day goes well," Jeff called through the open window on the passenger's side.

With a backward wave, Rhonda nodded and hurried inside.

A few seconds after entering the hotel, she was approached by Gayle, the night desk clerk. "Lori's husband called a while ago. She went to the hospital with heavy contractions during the night, and her baby girl was born early this morning."

Rhonda's eyes widened. "Is everything all right? Lori's due date wasn't supposed to be for another two weeks."

"Both mother and daughter are doing fine," Gayle responded. "But she obviously will not be working today, so someone will need to take the next shift."

"That someone will have to be me." Rhonda took in a few deep breaths. She was exhausted, having gotten to bed so late last night, and wished now that she had hired someone to take Lori's place earlier, since she wouldn't be coming back to work at the hotel anytime soon if at all.

"Can you stay a little longer while I go to my office and make some phone calls?"

Gayle bit down on her bottom lip. "I could stay another hour, but then I'll need to go because I have a dental appointment."

"Okay, that's fine." Rhonda hurried to her office and took a seat at the desk, where she pulled out a list of people who had recently applied for a job at the hotel. She was about to call one of them to set up an interview, when her cell phone rang. Seeing who the caller was, she felt compelled to answer. "Sorry, Gwen, but I'm at the hotel, and I really don't have time to talk."

"This will only take a few minutes," her sister said. "It's about our mother."

Rhonda sat up straight. "Is something wrong with Mom? Is she sick or has she been in an accident?"

"No, she's fine physically." There was a pause. "Remember on the Fourth of July when I was about to tell you something concerning our mother?"

"Oh, yeah. . .you never finished your sentence because Megan fell into the pond."

"Right. And I've been meaning to call you ever since but haven't gotten around to it until now."

"I meant to call you as well." Rhonda was on the verge of telling her sister about Jeff hitting a deer and how their AC had gone out, but Gwen spoke first.

"Mom has been doing something out of character for her lately."

"In what way?"

"She's entered the dating game."

Rhonda's mouth nearly fell open. "Say what?"

"Yeah, she's gone out with two different men so far."

"You're kidding, right?"

"No, I'm telling the truth."

Rhonda set the phone on her desk and placed both hands against her ever-warming cheeks. *Where did Mom meet these guys?*

This is so unlike her to be dating. It's hard to picture this happening.

After a long pause, her sister spoke again. "Are you still there, Rhonda?"

She picked up the phone and held it close to her ear. "Yes, I'm here. Just in shock is all."

"It was a surprise for me too, but I've come to accept the idea because Mom deserves to be happy."

Rhonda figured with Mom going all religious these days that she must have lost her good sense. The acceptance she heard from Gwen about their mother's actions only deepened the betrayal she felt, which lit her fuse.

"Our mother deserved to be happy with Dad too, but he made sure her life and ours were miserable." Rhonda felt a tightness around her eyes, and it was all she could do to keep her voice down. "Did you forget the vow our badly shaken mother made after he walked out on her for another woman?"

"No, I haven't forgotten. Mom said she would never get involved with another man because after Dad had cheated on her not once but three times that we know of, she lost faith in men."

"And with good reason." Rhonda's head began to pound. "What brought on this sudden need for a man in her life? Mom lives close to you and gets to see her granddaughters nearly every day, so she shouldn't be lonely."

"Spending time with a man who has similar interests and is kind enough to take her on dates isn't the same as being with the girls."

"But which man? We all had to deal with the mistakes our mother made in choosing our father," Rhonda was quick to say. "And has she really learned her lesson? What if the next guy she chooses isn't any better than Dad?"

"Remember, she's just getting started in this dating phase."

"Yes, but if either of the two men she's seen are merely pretending with her, and Mom doesn't see through their lies, then things may move faster than you think."

"I don't believe she's considering marriage. Not at this time, at least. I mean, I haven't picked up on anything. She's only gone out with the one man twice and the other fellow just once."

Many questions rolled around in Rhonda's head. "Who are these men? I hope she's not involved in internet dating, like Jeff's father has recently started doing."

"No, not at this point anyhow. The two men both go to our church, and they seem very nice. I must add there seems to be a good-sized group of single, middle-aged men who belong to our congregation."

Oh great. This just gets better. My sister should be keeping a close eye on our mother. "Anyone can attend church or proclaim to be a Christian, but that doesn't mean they are. Take our father, for example. He went to church at Christmas and Easter and came to our Bible school programs. And what did that prove?" Rhonda's voice had risen a little higher, and if she didn't get off the phone with her sister soon, she might end up yelling.

"Listen, Gwen, I really do need to go. Things are hectic for me right now."

"Oh, I'm sorry. Is there anything I can do?"

"Not unless you have a magic wand to wave and make everything better in my life."

"What's wrong?"

"It's nothing you can help with, and I have to hang up now so I can take care of hotel business."

"Okay, but I want you to know that I'll be praying for you."

"Don't bother. God's never answered any of my prayers. But if you want to ask God for something, pray that Mom gets out of the dating game and concentrates on something that won't leave her with low esteem and a broken heart." Rhonda didn't give her sister a chance to respond. "Bye, Gwen," she said and clicked off the phone.

Rhonda sat several minutes, trying to digest the conversation she'd just had with Gwen. It couldn't have happened at a worse time than now, with everything else falling from the sky. *How can my sister be so casual about this?* She brought a shaky hand up to her throbbing brows and began to massage them. The pain in Rhonda's head had increased, but she forced herself to pick up the phone and call the first name on her list of employee prospects.

Jeff hoped things would go well for himself and Rhonda today. Since he was the one who'd wrecked Rhonda's car, he wanted to figure out a way to make things better.

He parked his SUV in the parking lot and headed for his restaurant. Shortly after Jeff entered the building and had talked to Russ, he went to his office to check for any messages he may have gotten on his cell phone that morning. He saw there was a missed call from his dad, but he hadn't left a message. He decided to return the call before things got busy. Hopefully, since Dad ran his own computer repair business and might not be open yet, he would have a few minutes to talk.

Jeff punched in his dad's number and wasn't surprised when he answered right away. "Hey, Dad. I saw that you called me last night, but there was no message."

"Another call came in I needed to answer, so I didn't bother to leave a message. Figured I'd call again this morning, but you beat me to it."

"So, what's up?"

"Nothing much. We haven't talked since the Fourth of July, so I wanted to see how things are going with you and Rhonda and wish you a happy anniversary."

"I should've called you too, but things got busy here at the restaurant, and now everything's kind of crazy for me and Rhonda. Our anniversary was pretty much ruined."

"What happened?"

Jeff explained about hitting the deer and mentioned that the air conditioner at their house had quit working. "Someone is coming out to look at it later today."

"I'm sorry to hear about your problems. Is there anything I can do to help? I'd be happy to pay for the AC repairs or—"

"No thanks, Dad. I can manage this on my own."

"Are you sure?"

"Yeah."

"Well, let me know if you change your mind. In the meantime, I'll be praying that things work out and you don't end up having to get a new air-conditioning unit. Those can be pretty expensive, you know."

Jeff grimaced. "I'm well aware."

"If you'd like to borrow my truck until you get a new car, let me know. I will see if one of your brothers would be free to follow me down to your place in their vehicle sometime this weekend."

Jeff lifted his gaze to the ceiling. *Rhonda would never drive that old truck.* "Umm. . .I appreciate the offer, but if we can't get another car right away, we'll probably rent one for Rhonda."

"Why throw your money away on a rental?" Dad questioned.

"I don't want to put you out. I'm sure I'll come up with something."

"It's no big deal, and it's a parent's right to help out their children."

Jeff's tone softened. "Okay, thanks for the offer. I'll let you know if I change my mind. Talk to you later, Dad."

When Jeff ended the call, he put both hands behind his head and leaned back in his chair with a groan. It was nice of his father to offer money or the loan of his truck, but Jeff wished Dad hadn't mentioned the word *prayer*.

~

Walnut Creek

Feeling winded and hot, Lois had a hard time keeping up with her husband as they rode their bikes along the shoulder of the road. Apparently, the bump on his head hadn't affected his ability to ride a bike at rapid speed. And she wasn't that surprised about it either. But in this extreme heat, she wished he would slow down. They'd been going so quickly, she couldn't enjoy the passing scenery, as she normally would. The only good thing about traveling this fast was that they'd probably get to the store with time to spare before they needed to put the OPEN sign in the front window. That would give Lois a little time to sit at her desk in the back room and write a few letters. She didn't like getting behind on things, but it seemed to be happening more often than not these days.

I need to figure out some way to get more organized and schedule the things I need to accomplish in a better way, she told herself. *There are just not enough hours in a day to get everything done.*

By the time they'd reached the store and had their bicycles brought into one of the back rooms where they kept them during business hours, Lois felt quite winded and more than ready to sit and rest awhile. Orley too appeared to be out of breath, so they took seats in their little office area. Lois found both of them a cold bottle of water, which had been in the small cooler in Orley's bicycle basket.

"How are you feeling?" She wiped some perspiration from above her brows and looked over at her husband.

"Hot and tired, but otherwise I'm fine and dandy." He touched his forehead. "The lump from this morning's mishap has gone down some, and it doesn't hurt at all."

"I'm glad to hear it." She leaned closer to him. "I've said this before and I'll say it once again—you really shouldn't sleep so close to the edge of the bed."

"I can't help it. I don't start out that way, but sometime during the night, my body shifts to the right. I guess I like to travel, especially in my sleep." Orley chuckled.

"Maybe we should get a bigger bed. You know—a king size."

"I'll give it some thought." He chugged on his water and wiped the sweat from his forehead with a tissue he'd pulled from the little box on Lois's desk. "So, I've been thinking. . ."

"About what?"

"Jeff Davis. I'm worried that I did the wrong thing by giving him that religious plaque."

"Is it ever wrong to share the Good News with others? And by the way, those doubts after doing something good aren't from Him." She pointed upward.

Orley tapped a finger against the bridge of his nose. "I suppose not, but that young man is struggling, and I don't want to do anything that might push him further from finding a personal relationship with God."

"I can relate with what you've said, and I'm trying to remember to pray regularly for Jeff and Rhonda. I understand certain things, especially when I. . ." Lois stopped talking and drank some more water. It was not the right time for this discussion. She had a letter to finish writing, and Orley should be in the front part of their store, ready to greet customers when it was time to open. They could continue their discussion about the correct way to tell others about Jesus some other time.

Chapter 25

Canton

"How'd your day go?" Jeff asked when Rhonda got into his SUV at six o'clock that evening.

"Not well."

"How come? I hope you didn't get locked in the storeroom again."

After fastening her seatbelt, Rhonda shook her head. "That door's been fixed."

"What kind of problems did you encounter?"

"To begin with, Lori's baby came early, so she couldn't work today, which meant I had to fill in for her at the desk."

"It's great that she had her baby, but I'm sorry you had a rough day." Jeff turned down the music playing on the radio. "Couldn't you have called one of your other employees to take Lori's place?"

"I tried, but everyone had either made other plans for the day or didn't answer their phone."

Jeff pulled out of the parking lot. "Guess you'll need to hire someone to replace Lori now, huh?"

The traffic was busy at that time of the evening, and instead of responding to her husband's comment, Rhonda cried out, "Jeff, watch out for that van!"

"I see him." Jeff braked and tooted his horn. "What an impatient driver. He shouldn't be allowed to drive. I wonder how he got his license."

"You need to be more careful. Remember the deer? We don't need to wreck another vehicle."

Why did she have to bring that up? "I don't need the reminder, and please stop critiquing my driving. I'm doing fine. It was the other guy who messed up. We'll be home soon and out of this dumb traffic, so try to relax."

Rhonda didn't respond.

Jeff repeated his question about hiring a new employee.

"Yes, I will need to find a replacement for Lori. I made several calls from my list of recent applicants, so tomorrow I'll be conducting a few interviews." Rhonda sighed. "Hopefully, I will find someone suitable soon, because there are many things I need to do that won't get done if I'm at the reception desk too many hours."

"I hate to tell you this, but I have some news that won't make your day any brighter."

"Is it about my car or the air-conditioning?"

"Both. I went home around noon and met with the cooling-and-heating technician."

"What did he say?"

"The compressor went out, and since it's an older one, they can't get new parts to repair it. So, our only alternative is to get a new air-conditioning unit, which of course will be expensive."

"And impossible at this time."

"Are you willing to sleep in a sweatbox like we did last night with only a few open windows and a box fan that didn't cool our bedroom enough?"

"The Amish do it, and they survive."

"We're not Amish, Rhonda, and we aren't used to sleeping in an overly hot room."

"We'll have to get used to it because we have no extra money to put out for a new AC."

Jeff couldn't miss the determination in his wife's voice. *Should I say something about my dad's offer to help?* Although he didn't want to accept money from his father, for the sake of keeping the house cool until winter set in, he might do it. Since the furnace hadn't been affected, only the air conditioning unit, they should be fine for heat all winter.

"We could put a new AC unit on one of our credit cards," Jeff suggested.

"No way!"

His wife's shrill tone caused Jeff to have second thoughts about telling her the second piece of news he had to report. But she needed to know what they were faced with, so Jeff plunged ahead.

"We can discuss the AC situation later, but on another note, while I was at the house, our insurance company sent someone out to pick up your car, and they hauled it away to wherever they do their estimates. They'd called first and said when they'd be coming, which was good since our gate is kept closed when we aren't there." Jeff grimaced. "Now it's the waiting game until we find out if the car's totaled or by some chance can be fixed."

"I doubt it can be repaired, Jeff. You know how terrible it looked. Either way, this is really putting a hardship on us." Rhonda's voice broke, and Jeff figured she was close to tears.

He glanced her way. Sure enough, tears rolled down her flushed cheeks.

"Ah, honey, don't cry." Jeff let go of the steering wheel with one hand and reached over to touch her arm. "We'll figure something out, but let's wait till we get home to talk more about it. Okay?"

She swiped her hand across her face and gave a brief nod.

With a determined set of his jaw, Jeff focused on the road ahead.

Walnut Creek

As Rhonda and Jeff sat out back on their patio, eating sandwiches and chips for supper, neither of them said much at first. They'd agreed earlier that they didn't feel like cooking anything and did not want to heat up the kitchen any more than it already was from the house being closed all day. Jeff had offered to put some meat on the grill, but Rhonda said she'd rather eat something cold, so she'd made ham and cheese sandwiches.

Rhonda was nearly finished with her sandwich, when she pushed her plate aside and told Jeff about the phone call she'd had from Gwen. "I can't even express how surprised I was to learn that my mother has begun dating. If she's not careful, she could end up going from the frying pan into the fire with one of those men, who I doubt she knows very much about." Rhonda paused to put a few chips on her paper plate. "Just because they go to her church doesn't mean they can be trusted."

"My dad goes to church, and he's trustworthy," Jeff said.

Rhonda pointed a finger at him. "We're not talking about your dad. We're talking about two strangers we've never met."

"Okay, but there's nothing you can do about it. Your mother's a grown woman and can make her own decisions."

She glared at him but chose to say nothing. *I wouldn't expect you to understand.*

Jeff ate quietly for a while, and Rhonda picked at her food.

"My dad called me today, and after I told him about hitting a deer and our AC going out, he offered us some money and also the loan of his truck."

With determination, Rhonda shook her head. "I am not interested in driving your father's truck, but if you don't mind using it, then I'm willing to drive your SUV."

Jeff tugged on his lower lip. "Why don't you talk to your mom and see if she would loan you her car? Since she lives close to your sister, she probably has transportation available to her whenever she needs to go someplace. You should at least call and tell her what's happened."

"I don't see the point. She'd probably do like your dad did and offer to loan us some money. Besides, Mom needs her car to go to and from the dentist's office where she works as a receptionist."

"I'm not sure Dad's offer was a loan," Jeff said, giving no response to Rhonda's last comment.

"We're not charity cases, Jeff, and as responsible adults, we need to figure something out on our own."

"That's what I thought at first too, but now that I've had more time to think about it, maybe we shouldn't let our pride get in the way. I think we oughta go ahead and at least accept his offer to loan us the truck. Like you said, I can drive it and let you have my rig."

Rhonda mulled over what Jeff had suggested. Her facial muscles relaxed a bit as she finished her iced tea and set the glass down. "That will help, and with access to two vehicles again, we will be freed up to go about our normal routines." She looked toward their house and frowned. "But it doesn't take care of the situation with our air conditioner. I dread going back into the house, where it's so uncomfortably warm."

"You said it yourself—we can't afford to buy a new one, and I'm sure you don't want to max out our credit cards."

"No, I don't, but you could part with some of your antiques."

Jeff looked at her with raised brows. "You've gotta be kidding, Rhonda. Even if I could find a buyer for any of my old things, a new central air unit, plus installation, would cost anywhere from five to ten thousand dollars. I don't have any antiques valued at that amount."

"Then we'll just have to get by without AC until sometime next year and hope that our townhouse has sold by then."

Jeff thumped the tabletop with his knuckles. "It should've sold by now. I think we should get a new Realtor."

"How's that going to help? If homes like ours aren't selling, another Realtor wouldn't have any better luck than the one we have now." She pursed her lips. "We made a mistake buying this place—let's face it."

He shook his head vigorously. "No, we didn't, Rhonda. We're just dealing with a rough spot right now, and we need to work our way through it."

Her eyes narrowed as she swatted at the air. "I'm working. . . you're working. . .but nothing's working out for us. One problem crops up, and another one's right on its heels."

Jeff heaved a heavy sigh and got up from his chair. This discussion was getting them nowhere, and he needed to be by himself for a while. His first thought was to go watch TV in the man cave, but it was too hot in there to enjoy watching anything. So, Jeff headed for the pond and took a seat on one of the creek benches to watch the fish swim around. He needed to feed them but didn't feel like going to the shed to get the food right now. It would have to be done before he went back to the house, however. Although having a pond with fish was nice, it also meant more work.

Maybe after I've sat here awhile, I'll feel better. Jeff leaned forward with his elbows on his knees and closed his eyes. *How can I make things better? Is there anything I can do to solve our financial problems? Maybe Rhonda's right—we probably should have been satisfied to stay at our townhouse in Canton. The question is, where do we go from here?*

New Philadelphia, Ohio

June had taken a seat at her kitchen table to eat the shrimp salad she'd made for her supper, when someone rapped on the back door. A few seconds later, Gwen stepped into the room.

"How many times have I told you to keep your doors locked, Mom?" She stood in front of June with both hands on her hips. "Some stranger could walk right in, uninvited."

"You just did." June cracked a smile.

Gwen scrunched up her face. "I am not a stranger, Mom. And I only turned the doorknob to see if it was locked. Of course, when I found out it wasn't, I came in." She pulled out a chair at the table and took a seat. "You really should be more careful."

Ignoring her daughter's pointed expression, June said, "I'm surprised to see you here at this time of the day. Shouldn't you be fixing supper for your family?"

"We've already eaten. My considerate hubby brought pizza on his way home from work." Gwen gestured to June's salad. "Looks like you're eating light tonight."

"Yes. I didn't feel like cooking."

"Sorry, Mom. I should have invited you to join us for pizza."

"That's okay. This nice cold salad is fine for me." June drank some water. "So, what's the reason for your visit? I'm sure it has to be more than checking to see if my door was locked."

Gwen nodded. "I wanted to talk to you about Rhonda."

"What about your sister?"

"I spoke to her today, and she sounded pretty stressed."

"Did she explain why?"

"No, but she mentioned that things were hectic at the hotel."

June poked a shrimp with her fork. "That's nothing new. Ever since your sister began working there, things have been crazy."

"True, and she's probably used to all the challenges of being a hotel manager by now, but I think something else may be stressing her."

"Such as?"

Gwen shrugged. "I don't know, but maybe if you give her a call, she'll tell you what's bothering her."

June placed her fork on the plate without eating the shrimp. "It has been awhile since I talked to Rhonda. I'll give her a call as soon as I finish my salad." She looked at Gwen. "Would you like to be here when I call, so you can hear what she says? I can put it on Speaker mode, and then you could ask her a few questions too."

"No, I'd better not stay for that. Rhonda might not appreciate me asking questions or putting in my two cents."

"Okay. I'll make the call after you're gone, or if you'd like to stay, I just won't put it on Speaker."

"I really should go." Gwen pushed back her chair and stood. "I promised the girls that we could roast marshmallows this evening, and they're probably waiting for me in front of the firepit, along with their dad."

June got up and gave her daughter a hug. "Thanks for dropping by. If what Rhonda has to say is anything important, I'll let you know."

"Okay, Mom. I'll talk to you again soon."

After Gwen went out the back door, June finished her salad and put the dishes in the sink. Then she picked up her cell phone and punched in Rhonda's number.

Walnut Creek

Rhonda was about to enter the master bedroom when her cell phone rang. She didn't feel like answering, but if it was hotel business, she probably should.

She looked at the caller ID, and seeing that it was her mother, she answered. "Hi, Mom. How are you?"

"I'm fine. In fact, I'm more than fine."

Rhonda couldn't miss the bubbly tone of her mother's voice. "That's good. Sure wish I could say the same."

"What's wrong?"

"Pretty much everything right now."

"I'm sorry to hear that. Do you want to explain?"

Rhonda began by telling her mother about the need to find a new front-desk clerk at the hotel, then she brought up the subject of their air-conditioning going out. "And if that's not bad enough, Jeff hit a deer last night when we were leaving a restaurant near Charm, where we'd gone to celebrate our anniversary."

"Oh my, I forgot it was your anniversary. I hope neither of you were hurt."

"We're both fine, but my car is probably totaled. The front end doesn't look good at all."

"I'm sorry to hear it. Is there anything I can do?"

"Not unless you have a lot of money lying around."

"I could help a little, but I don't have enough to buy you a new car or. . ."

"I am not expecting your help, Mom. Our insurance will pay to either fix the car or replace it, and we're not going to worry about the AC until next year when the hot weather hits."

"But it's warm right now. And from what I saw on the weather channel the other day, it sounds like the heat wave might continue for a few weeks. I may have a fan or two around here I could lend you. Do you have any fans you can use there now?"

Rhonda entered her bedroom and took a seat on the edge of the bed. "Yes. We have a box fan in our room, and I'll tell Jeff about your offer of the extra fans. We plan to open all the windows once the sun goes down each evening. So, we'll pretend we're Amish for the rest of September." She gave a forced laugh. "Can you picture that—me dressed in plain Amish clothes, sitting in a rocking chair and reading a book by a gas lantern?"

"No, I certainly cannot. You're used to having a cell phone, computer, and many other modern things."

"Yeah, and up until now—air-conditioning."

"Are you sure I can't help by chipping in on that?"

"Yes, Mom, I'm sure, but thank you for offering." *If Jeff wouldn't accept money from his dad, I certainly can't take my mother up on her offer. We'll just have to deal with this on our own.*

"Gwen mentioned that she'd talked to you earlier today."

Her mother's comment pushed Rhonda's thoughts aside. "Uh, yeah, that's right. She called while I was at the hotel, so we didn't talk long."

"Did she tell you that I've gone out a couple of times with two men who go to our church?"

"Yes, she mentioned it."

"She thinks it's good that I'm dating again. What are your thoughts, Rhonda?"

"If that's what you have chosen to do, then my opinion really doesn't matter."

"Yes, it does. I'm open to your input, just as I was to Gwen's."

"Okay, then, here goes. . . After what my father pulled on you, I think it's a mistake to get involved with another man." There, it was out, and Rhonda felt better for having said it.

"These men aren't like your dad. They are kind, Christian men."

"People who call themselves Christians are not perfect, Mom."

"I didn't mean to imply that they were. It's just that—"

"Look, I don't want to throw cold water on your excitement over dating, but you need to be careful. Either one of the men you've been seeing might appear to be nice, but they could be wolves in sheep's clothing."

There was a long pause before Rhonda's mother spoke again. Rhonda figured she was either mulling over her statement and giving it some consideration or had become irritated because Rhonda hadn't shared in her excitement over entering the dating game again.

"I appreciate your concern, dear, but I am being cautious. Now, I have to go, but I'll talk to you again soon."

I can't be excited for her, Rhonda told herself after she'd said good-bye and clicked off the phone. *And I won't put my stamp of approval on Mom dating anyone—Christian or not.*

Chapter 26

Jeff stretched out on his patio lounge chair, placing both hands behind his head. "I'm glad our weather's finally cooled down. Looks like fall is here to stay."

Rhonda took a deep breath and released it slowly. "At least it solves one of our problems. We just need to pinch our pennies and try to save up for a new AC before the hot weather takes over next year."

Jeff's cell phone rang from where he'd laid it on the table beside his chair. He picked it up and looked at the caller ID. "It's our Realtor. Maybe she has some good news."

Rhonda sat quietly as he conversed with the woman they'd hired to sell their townhouse. They needed an offer, and soon. She folded her arms. *I hope our townhouse sells for the price we're asking. It's hard not to be impatient over this since we've been waiting for several months without even a nibble.*

When Jeff got off the phone a few minutes later, he looked over at Rhonda and smiled. "We have an offer."

She sat up straight. "Really? Is it a good one?"

"Well, yes and no. The couple interested in purchasing the townhouse wants to be in there within thirty days, which is a good thing. The downside is that they want us to lower the price by ten thousand dollars."

"You're kidding."

"I wish I were, but that's the buyer's offer."

Rhonda's stomach clenched as her eyes widened. "That's a lot less money than our asking price, Jeff. What are those people thinking?"

"They probably can't pay the full price and are hoping we'll come down so they can buy the place."

How disappointing. I wish they would've accepted our offer. Instead, all this will do for us is add more frustration and stress as we decide what to do. Rhonda shook her head. "We can't lower the price that much. We need to make enough money so we can pay off the loan on this place."

"If we accept their offer, it'll give us enough to knock the balance down here, which would mean we could pay off the rest of this mortgage sooner."

Rubbing her arms briskly, she leaned forward. "I think we should make a counteroffer and agree to sell the townhouse for five thousand dollars less."

Jeff thumbed his ear. "I don't know, Rhonda. They could decline our offer and walk away. As you keep reminding me, we need to get our old place sold."

"Of course, we do, but we can't give it away. Don't forget, in addition to wanting to pay off this house, we'll need money for a new air-conditioning unit next year."

"I'm well aware, but we'll have even less money if we don't sell the townhouse." Jeff looked directly at her. "And don't forget, we've been saving quite a bit of money because I'm borrowing my dad's truck, and we didn't have to rent a car for you to drive while we're waiting for insurance money to come through."

"Yes, I know." Using her fingertips, Rhonda closed her eyes and made little circles all over her tight forehead. She remembered how two days after their accident, Don and Eric had driven down to deliver Don's truck. She'd been grateful and had fixed them a nice meal before they headed home in Eric's vehicle.

Jeff nudged her arm. "You okay? You're not dealing with another headache, I hope."

"Not yet, but it may be forthcoming."

"Want me to massage the back of your neck?"

"No, that's okay. I'll feel better once we resolve this problem." She tilted her head from side to side, weighing their choices. "What if we give a counteroffer of eight thousand dollars less than our asking price? Does that sound reasonable to you?"

Jeff bobbed his head. "The couple who want our townhouse may not think so though." He picked up his cell phone. "Should I call our Realtor back and let her know of our decision?"

"Yes, please do."

While Jeff made the call, Rhonda leaned her head against the back of the chaise lounge and closed her eyes. If she believed in the power of prayer, Rhonda would say one right now, asking that the prospective buyers would accept their counteroffer.

~

Canton

The following morning, Rhonda sat in her office at the hotel, looking at a list of supplies the head of housekeeping had turned in. The number of items looked larger than the previous month and had thrown her off guard.

I'm sure that's because of the renovation work and that for a while we were shy ten to fifteen rooms to put up our guests for the night.

Rhonda had always worked hard, and she carried the weight of her job. The stress of it meant a headache most of the time, however.

I'm so tired of dealing with all this. I'd much rather be at home making out my grocery list right now. Rhonda pursed her lips. *There are too many responsibilities here, and I'm tired of it.*

One of those responsibilities was hiring new employees when needed. After going through ten potential desk clerks, Rhonda had finally hired one last week. It was a relief not to have the extra responsibility of working behind the front desk.

A knock sounded on the office door, and Rhonda called,

"Come in." She was surprised when Lori entered the room with a baby in her arms.

"I came by to show you my little sweet pea." Lori smiled as she moved closer to Rhonda's desk. "I hope you're not too busy to take a peek at her."

"No, of course not." Rhonda's throat swelled as she gazed at the wee infant in the young mother's arms. "She's beautiful, Lori. Congratulations."

"Thank you. Derek and I are so happy we've become parents."

"What did you name her?"

"Natalie—after my great-aunt. She's the sweetest lady."

When the baby stirred and emitted a sweet cooing sound, Rhonda's throat tightened to the point she could barely swallow. Although she was happy for Lori, she couldn't help feeling envious. After all these years of being unable to have children, she did not understand why it still hurt so much when she saw other people's babies.

"Would you like to hold her?" Lori asked.

"Umm. . .I feel like a cold might be coming on, and I don't want to expose your little girl, so I'd better not."

"Oh, okay. Maybe some other time."

Rhonda nodded. Then, realizing she hadn't thought to buy the baby a gift, she retrieved her checkbook and wrote a check for fifty dollars. "Please use this to buy the baby something." She handed the check to Lori.

Lori's soft brown eyes filled with an inner glow. "Thank you so much. That's very kind of you."

"You're welcome." Rhonda glanced at the paperwork on her desk. She needed to get busy working but didn't want to be rude. Besides, the longer Lori stood here, the more Rhonda's heart filled with regrets.

"I'm not sure when or if I'll be returning to work for you." Lori looked at her and then at the baby. "As busy as this place is, you'll no doubt need to hire another person, and I certainly understand."

"Yes, and someone has been hired to take your place. However, if at a later date you choose to come back to work here, there will hopefully be a spot for you. Or at the very least, I'll be happy to give a good reference if you should ever decide to apply for another job."

"Thank you, Rhonda," Lori responded. "I'd better go and let you get back to work."

Rhonda smiled, despite the tears she struggled to hold back. "Feel free to come by some other time."

"I will, but next time I'll call before I drop by." Lori said goodbye and turned toward the door.

She is so blessed with her sweet newborn. If only I could be a mother. It was difficult for Rhonda to shake away the desire of having her own child. She could hardly hold back the idea as it resonated within her.

After Lori left, Rhonda booted up her computer. Although she still had paperwork to do, not to mention answering review comments, she went to the internet and typed in "What are the reasons a couple can't get pregnant?"

Several sites came up, and she clicked on the first one that caught her interest, listing several reasons for an inability to conceive. "Number one," she said quietly. "A woman's cycle and ovulation might be irregular. Number two: the younger a woman is, the easier it is for her to get pregnant."

Rhonda continued to read more reasons. Being either overweight or underweight. The man might be sterile. Endometriosis could contribute to fertility problems. A woman's Fallopian tubes could be blocked due to scar tissue or adhesions. An endocrine disorder or some underlying medical condition. Uterine fibroids. Too much stress.

Rhonda paused to drink some of her lukewarm coffee and groaned. She and Jeff had been tested, and the doctor hadn't found anything physically wrong with either of them. He had mentioned stress, though, and said that they should both eat a balanced diet, exercise regularly, and look for ways to lower their stress.

"Yeah, right." She tapped her left foot and frowned. *How's a person supposed to ease their stress when it keeps on coming? Even waiting to hear something back from our Relator is causing me stress. If the people who are interested in our townhouse don't accept our counteroffer, I don't know what we're going to do.*

Rhonda clicked out of the page she'd been looking at and found another one that pertained to eating a healthy diet. The doctor who'd written the article recommended eating plenty of vegetables, fruits, whole grains, lean protein, and healthy fats. He also stated that there were several specific nutrients a woman should focus on to support her fertility. The main ones he'd listed were folate, CoQ10, iron, vitamin D, zinc, and omega-3 fatty acids.

Maybe I should make an effort to eat healthier and take the supplements listed here, Rhonda told herself. *Although I don't know why. After thirteen years of not conceiving, I doubt that eating healthier and taking certain supplements would make any difference.* She shifted on her chair. *If I do decide to make some changes regarding my health, I won't say anything to Jeff. He'd probably say what I read was a bunch of hooey and give me a lecture on learning to be content without children.*

Walnut Creek

When Rhonda arrived home that evening, she found Jeff in the kitchen, talking on his cell phone. She put her things away and took a seat at the table to wait until he was done. *I'm guessing it isn't his father. It sounds more like he's speaking to our Realtor about the townhouse.*

Rhonda looked down at her nails and picked at a hangnail. *If only we could be free from our old place and focus all our attentions on this new home.*

She let her mind go blank while her husband continued to talk.

"That was our Realtor," Jeff said when he'd clicked off his phone. "The people who want our townhouse have agreed to our terms."

Rhonda heaved an audible sigh. "What a relief. That's one less thing we'll have to worry about now. Did she say anything else?"

"Just that the deal should close within the next thirty days, and once it does, we'll have our share of the money."

Her face scrunched a bit. "If we could have sold it ourselves, we wouldn't have been obliged to pay a commission."

"True, but we're both too busy to be bothered with trying to sell a home on our own. We did the right thing by hiring her."

"I suppose." Rhonda heaved another sigh. "Whew! I'm exhausted."

"Rough day at the hotel?"

"Just the usual, but the biggest stress of my day was when Lori came by to show me her baby."

He raised his brows. "Why would that be stressful?"

"You know how much I want children. Seeing Lori's beautiful little girl was just another reminder that we will never become parents or have the privilege of raising a child."

Jeff looked at her pointedly. "It's wrong for you to be jealous of everyone who has a child. You should find something to get your mind off it and quit harping on the topic so you can focus on other things."

Hurt by his comment, Rhonda stood up and moved over to the refrigerator to take out something for supper. *How can Jeff be so unfeeling? Is he really content not to have children?* She took out a bag of premade salad ingredients. *I wonder if Jeff would change his mind if I ever did get pregnant.*

Rhonda woke up the next morning with a pounding headache. She'd been dreaming when the alarm went off, nearly jolting her out of bed. In the dream, Rhonda and Jeff were parents. She held a fair-skinned, curly-headed girl on her lap, while watching Jeff play on the floor with their dark-haired son. Even now, fully awake, Rhonda remembered the joy she'd felt when the little girl had called her "Ma-ma." *If only it were true and not a dream.*

She figured that the events of yesterday had made an impact on her. Rhonda had tried not to be jealous or harbor any regrets about her life without a child, but it seemed impossible to shake those feelings. She rubbed her forehead and sat up in bed, but when the room began to spin, she laid back down. *What's going on? Why do I feel like this? Did the cold I felt coming on yesterday become a reality? Could my sinuses and ears be so plugged that it's affected my equilibrium?*

Rhonda turned her head slowly to the left and realized that her husband was not on his side of the bed. She lay there a few moments, wondering if he might be in the kitchen fixing breakfast. Her stomach roiled at the thought of food. Although she'd been hungry enough last night when they ate supper, Rhonda had no appetite for food right now. Between the nausea and headache, she felt certain that she'd never be able to get dressed and go to work this morning. In fact, Rhonda didn't think she could even get out of bed. *Could this be a migraine, or have I come down with the flu?*

She called out to Jeff several times, but he didn't answer. *Maybe when I don't show up in the kitchen, he'll come back to our room to check on me.* Rhonda closed her eyes, which did nothing for the headache, but at least it helped the dizziness subside.

I need to call my assistant manager and let her know that I won't be coming in to work today. She rolled onto her side and reached for her cell phone, but before she could punch in the number, Jeff entered the room.

"How come you're still in bed? I figured you'd be up and dressed by now."

Rhonda moaned, and through half-closed eyelids, she looked at him standing by her side of the bed. "I'm sick, Jeff. There's no way I'll be going to work today." She held the phone out to him. "Would you call my assistant manager and let her know that I won't be in today?"

"Sure, honey." He placed his hand on her forehead. "Your head feels hot. You must have a fever."

"I wouldn't be surprised. My head is also pounding, and I'm real woozy and nauseous."

"I'll make the call and then fix you a cup of ginger tea. That should help your stomach settle." He took a seat on the edge of the bed and clasped her hand. "It sounds like you must have the flu. Would you like me to take the day off and stay home with you? I don't feel right about leaving you here alone when you're not feeling well."

"No, don't do that; I'll be okay. Just bring me the tea and a few bottles of water. I'll spend the day in bed, and hopefully by the time you get home this evening, I'll feel better."

"Are you sure you don't want me to stay?"

"Yes, and there's no need for you to worry."

"Okay, but if you take a turn for the worse, please give me a call and I'll come right home."

"I will." Rhonda closed her eyes again. Her head hurt less when she didn't have to see any light in the room. *At least I know Jeff cares about me. Guess that's something to be grateful for. I just wish. . .* Her thoughts gave way to slumber.

Chapter 27

Berlin, Ohio

On the way home from work that afternoon, Jeff decided to stop at the pharmacy to pick up a few things he hoped would make Rhonda feel better. He had called her several times during the day and always felt bad if he awakened her. The last time Jeff called to let her know he would be leaving the restaurant soon, she had mentioned having a sore throat. He'd mentally added throat spray and lozenges to the list of things to buy.

Pulling into the pharmacy parking lot, Jeff noticed several horses and buggies at the hitching rail. It was nice that the shopping complex, which the pharmacy was a part of, had provided a place for the Plain people to park while they shopped.

Jeff parked his dad's truck and got out of the vehicle. He would be glad when he got the SUV back. Their insurance company had pronounced Rhonda's car totaled, but it could be a few more weeks before they received a settlement check. They would wait till then to begin looking at new cars, and Jeff hoped his wife would find one to her liking. She'd enjoyed her sporty vehicle, so it might be a difficult decision to choose another car unless it was comparable to her previous one.

Jeff pushed those thoughts out of his mind and entered the building. He'd gone down the first aisle when someone tapped his shoulder. Jeff turned and was surprised to see Orley behind him.

"It's good to see you." The Amish man smiled. "Lois and I were talking about you and your wife the other day and wondered if you had a nice anniversary."

"It wasn't the best." Jeff dropped his gaze to the floor.

"Mind if I ask why it wasn't the best?"

"On the way home from dinner at the Chalet in the Valley restaurant, I hit a deer." Jeff raised his head and looked at Orley, hoping his negative outlook wasn't too obvious.

"Sorry to hear that. Were either of you hurt?"

"No, but the front end of Rhonda's car sure was, and the impact killed the young doe."

Orley gave a slow shake of his head. "That's a shame, but praise God neither of you was hurt."

Ignoring Orley's comment, Jeff said, "To top it off, when we finally got home that night, it didn't take us long to realize that our air-conditioning unit had a problem. The house was so hot, we weren't sure we could sleep inside."

"We did have some warmer than normal evenings a few weeks ago."

"How do you and your wife cope with hot weather?"

"We open several windows for a cross-breeze and set a battery-operated fan near our bed."

"We used an electric box fan, but it didn't do much good. We're used to sleeping with a cooler temperature, so we were both pretty miserable." Jeff reached around to rub the back of his neck.

"Our weather has cooled considerably now," Orley stated. "I'm sure you must be more comfortable."

"Weather-wise, yes, but this morning Rhonda woke up sick. I think it's some type of flu." Jeff gestured to a bottle of aspirin and other medicines. "That's why I'm here. I came for something to take away Rhonda's headache and to help her throat."

"You might also consider stopping by the health food store in town. There's a homeopathic remedy specifically used to help alleviate symptoms of the flu."

Jeff's interest was piqued. "What's the name of it?"

Orley scratched behind his left ear. "Sorry, but I can't remember what it's called. I'm sure someone who works at the health food store could help you with that though."

"Okay, I'll stop by there after I leave here." Jeff was about ready to say goodbye and move on down the aisle, when Orley spoke again.

"Did you and your wife like the anniversary gift I gave you from me and Lois?"

Jeff shuffled his feet nervously. He felt trapped and uncertain about how best to answer. He didn't want to admit that they were none too thrilled with the religious plaque, but at the same time, it would be a lie to say that they liked it. Some quick thinking kicked in and Jeff replied, "It was kind of you to think of us."

Orley produced a wide smile in response. "Just remember, Jeff, that a personal relationship with God is the only way to find peace and true happiness."

Jeff held his arms tightly at his sides, feeling as though he'd been backed into a corner. *Why does this Amish man have to be so persistent? Doesn't he realize I have no need of his religious beliefs? Why can't he leave well enough alone?*

"I'd better get the things I came in for now and head for home. Rhonda's probably wondering what's taking me so long." Jeff took a few steps away from Orley.

"Please tell your wife that Lois and I will be praying for her to get better soon. Oh, and don't forget about stopping by the health food store."

"Yeah, thanks. See you around, Orley." Jeff grabbed a bottle of aspirin and hurried to the next aisle, where remedies for coughs and sore throats were sold. The last thing he'd needed today was a push from Orley Troyer in the direction of God.

—✦—

Walnut Creek

After Jeff entered the house that evening, he put some of the things away that he'd purchased in Berlin, picked up the rest of the items he thought might help Rhonda feel better, and went to check on her. He found his pale wife propped up in bed, drinking from a bottle of water.

"How are you feeling?" Jeff took a seat on the edge of the bed, holding the bag of remedies.

She held up her hand. "Better not get too close to me. I'm pretty sure what I have is the flu, and it's no doubt contagious. We don't need you getting sick too and missing work."

"I'm not worried about it, and even if I do get sick, Russ will cover for me at the restaurant until I'm better."

Rhonda peered at the bag Jeff held. "What did you bring me?"

"I got some cold-and-flu remedies that I hope will help you feel better."

Setting the bag aside, he placed his hand on her forehead. "I think you have a fever. Have you taken your temperature today?"

She shook her head.

"I'll get the thermometer." Jeff went to the bathroom and took the digital thermometer from the medicine cabinet. When he returned, he handed it to her. "Please put this under your tongue."

"I know what to do with it." Rhonda quirked a smile and did as he'd asked. When it beeped, she removed the item and handed it to Jeff.

"Not too bad. Just a little over one hundred."

"I think it was higher than that earlier today because I did a lot of sweating, and then I got the chills." She moaned. "I hate being sick and missing time off work."

"As frustrated as you've become with work, I wouldn't think you'd miss it."

"I can't argue the point that my job is usually frustrating." She squinted at him. "If we were on a relaxing vacation, it would be one thing, but taking sick days off is no fun."

He smoothed back Rhonda's damp hair from her face. "Most of the items I picked up after work are from the pharmacy in Berlin, and at Orley's suggestion, I dropped by the health food store and bought a homeopathic remedy that is supposed to help curtail flu symptoms."

"Where did you see Orley?"

"At the pharmacy. It was there that he told me about the all-natural remedy." Jeff grimaced. "He also asked if we liked the anniversary gift they'd given us."

Rhonda covered her cough with the palm of her hand. "What'd you tell him?"

"I didn't provide a direct answer. Just skirted around it by saying we appreciated their gesture." He glanced at the thermometer still in his hand then back at Rhonda. "Can you imagine what he would have thought if I'd told him that I put the old plaque inside a cupboard in our garage?"

"He'd probably be offended."

"I'm sure. Now enough about the gift. I'm going to the kitchen to open a can of chicken noodle soup. I got you some saltines to nibble on too. It's the one food that seems to be more tolerated when a person feels nauseated. Oh, and I bought a box of real fruit ice pops and organic chocolate-covered ice-cream bars from the health food store. Those should help your sore throat feel better." Jeff stood. "I'm going back to the kitchen now and heat the soup."

"I'm not hungry, Jeff, but thanks for offering."

"You need the nourishment, Rhonda. Now please rest, and I'll be back soon to check on you."

"I saw Jeff Davis at the pharmacy today," Orley said when Lois took a seat next to him at the dining-room table, where they'd chosen to have their dessert after supper.

"How are he and Rhonda doing?" Lois cut into her piece of apple pie and took a bite.

"They're going through a rough time right now."

"In what way?"

"First of all, he mentioned their anniversary."

Lois drank her tea. "Did they like the plaque you gave them?"

"I'm not sure. When I asked him that question, Jeff just said he appreciated our thoughtfulness. He also mentioned that he'd hit a deer on the way home from their anniversary dinner."

"Oh, no! Were either of them hurt?"

Orley shook his head. "Only the deer and Rhonda's car. Actually, the doe died." He paused to eat a bite of his pie then continued. "To make matters worse, when they returned home that evening, they discovered that their air-conditioning had quit working. So, of course, they spent a miserable night trying to sleep in an overly warm house."

Lois wiped her mouth with a napkin before speaking again. "We are not used to having air-conditioning, so we've come up with ways to deal with the heat, but most English people—especially those who rely on air-conditioning—have a hard time staying cool when the weather is hot and muggy."

"Jah, that's right." Orley used his napkin to wipe up a bit of coffee that had spilled on the table. "It's good that the weather has cooled now, though, because Jeff mentioned that Rhonda has the flu. She'd no doubt be even more miserable in a hot, stuffy house."

Leaning both wrists against the table, Lois sat with her hands lightly folded. "We need to continue praying for that couple. They seem to be having more than their share of trials."

"I agree. We do need to keep praying for them." Orley's lips pressed together. "Wish I'd thought to ask for Jeff's phone number so I could call and check up on them."

"That would be a good idea. Maybe Jeff will drop by Memory Keepers again, and you can ask for it then."

"I hope so. I don't know all the reasons, but I'm sure the Lord directed that young man to our store for a purpose beyond looking at antiques."

"I believe you're right, Husband." Lois pushed her chair back and stood. "I'm going to do up these dishes and join you in the living room, where we can relax for a while before it's time for bed."

"Sounds good to me. Think I'll take a look at the newspaper while you're doing that." Orley rose too.

"All right, I'll be in there soon."

When Lois entered the living room a short time later, she found Orley in his favorite chair, wearing his reading glasses, and holding the newspaper near his face.

"Let me get a light going in here so you're not straining to see." Lois grabbed a lighter and lit the kerosene lamp. "How's that?"

"Much better. Danki."

Lois took a seat in the chair beside him, where she often sat when she wanted to chat. But she wasn't sure how much talking they would get done this evening since her husband seemed engrossed in whatever he was reading.

She reached into the wicker basket on the other side of her chair and withdrew her knitting needles and a ball of yarn. Maybe when Orley finished reading the paper, they could talk. If not, then Lois would be content to begin a new knitting project, as she'd wanted to make a winter stocking cap for her husband.

Lois had barely begun to knit when Orley gave a deep chuckle. "You've gotta be kidding."

She turned her head in his direction. "What was that?"

He rapped the paper with his knuckles and rolled his eyes. "I've been reading that Dear Caroline column, and I can't believe some of the dumb things people can come up with to write her about."

She leaned closer to him. "Such as?"

"Well, here's one that I'm sure you'll get a kick out of. Listen to what it says: 'Dear Caroline: My husband leaves his clothes lying around on the floor and never puts them in the hamper, like I've asked him to do many times. On a few occasions, I have tripped over them. What should I do about this? Fed Up.'" He looked over at Lois and lifted a single eyebrow while closing his opposite eye. "How *lecherich*! Can you believe anyone would waste the time to write a letter to someone they didn't even know about something so trivial?"

Lois poked her tongue against the inside of her cheek and inhaled a long breath. "I don't think it's ridiculous at all. The woman who wrote that letter is obviously upset about her husband's carelessness and most likely hoped that Caroline could offer some suggestions."

"Well, listen to what the columnist said in response. 'Dear Fed Up, Nagging probably won't help, so my suggestion is don't continue to pick up your husband's clothes. Don't launder them even if they are dirty. Eventually, he will run out of clean clothes to wear, so he will have no choice but to pick them up himself.'"

Orley grunted. "That's just common sense. Doesn't take a genius or someone like Caroline, who thinks she is a counselor, to come up with something so sensible. I've spoken to people with bigger problems than that and—"

"You are not the only person who can give out advice, you know." Lois followed her statement with a noisy huff. "I am sure that Caroline is trying to do her best and give sensible answers to those who have asked her advice."

Orley's chin jutted out. "Why are you defending that woman? It's not like you know her personally."

Lois took a deep breath and blurted, "Actually, I am well acquainted with Caroline."

"Oh?" He tipped his head, looking at her with a curious expression.

Lois pointed to herself. "Caroline is me."

Orley snickered. "Jah, right. Are you pullin' my leg?"

She gave a slow shake of her head. "I've been writing that column for nearly a year."

His eyes widened, making them appear bulged. "B. . .but how can that be? Until now, you've never said a word about this to me."

Lois slid her finger around the rim of her teacup as she searched for the right response to her husband's question. "I didn't want you to know that the paper had hired me to write the column."

"So, they know who the author is, but no one else—not even me?" Orley's gaze flicked upward, and then he looked at Lois with a glassy stare. "I feel betrayed."

Her chin quivered as she reached over and touched his arm.

"I'm sorry, Orley, but I wasn't sure you would approve. I wanted to do something meaningful that could hopefully help people who are hurting and need guidance."

"Oh, and you can't accomplish that in our store like I do when I recognize that someone needs a bit of mentoring?"

Lois sucked in her cheeks as she pulled her hand back. "I have done that many times, but my newspaper column reaches a lot more people than the few that come into our store and open up about their problems."

Orley sat quietly, staring into his coffee cup. Then he looked back at Lois and frowned. "It hurts that you made an agreement with our local newspaper to pose as Caroline and chose not to tell me."

"I was going to tell you but wanted to give it a try first and see how things worked out." She swallowed hard. "After the first issue came out and you made some joke about the column, I couldn't muster up the courage to tell you. You've done that several times since, so I felt certain that you would ask me to quit writing as Caroline."

"You're right, I probably would have discouraged you, but if that's what you really want to do, then you have my blessing."

"Really?"

"Jah."

"Danki." She smiled and clasped Orley's hand. "Again, I am sorry for not telling you, and I hope you'll forgive me."

Orley gave her fingers a gentle squeeze. "I do, and I'm glad we've had this discussion. Keeping things from one another is not healthy for a marriage." He paused a moment and then spoke to her in a calm, gentle tone. "All those times when you had errands to do, and I didn't know where you were headed off to, it was because of Dear Caroline, right?"

"Jah."

Orley gave a brief nod and went back to reading the paper.

Lois sighed with relief. Although there were a few things from her past that she hadn't told him about, since the day she and Orley had gotten married, this was the first time she'd deliberately deceived him. How thankful she was that he'd forgiven her and given his blessing to continue writing as Dear Caroline.

Chapter 28

Cleveland

Rhonda kept her eyes on the road as she followed Jeff in his dad's truck. Driving her new silver compact car with its soft leather interior was nice, and she'd been getting more familiar with its options. While she missed her old vehicle, this one would be a good replacement. They'd bought her new car yesterday, and Jeff said he felt it was best not to keep his dad's truck any longer. Rhonda appreciated Don loaning them the rig, and she was aware that Jeff was eager to get his SUV back from her. She was equally eager to drive something more to her liking. The car she'd chosen wasn't as sporty as her previous one, but it was cute and got good gas mileage. That was a plus since she commuted to and from the hotel five days a week.

Rhonda was glad that she felt like her old self again. The flu bug she'd contracted had lasted for over a week. Fortunately, Jeff had not gotten sick. Either his immune system had been stronger than hers, or it was because, at her request, he'd slept in the room set up for their overnight guests. Things were pretty much back to normal now and would be even better once the deal closed on their townhouse. It was set to happen in two weeks. What a relief it would be to hand over the keys for their old place to the new owners. Even better would be receiving the check.

Jeff changed lanes, and Rhonda followed, easing in behind the truck. Traffic wasn't too bad for a Saturday, which was nice. Hopefully, not many cars would be on the road when they returned home later today.

Maybe they could stop for a bite to eat at one of their favorite restaurants.

Rhonda had already decided that she would let Jeff drive back to Walnut Creek. It would give him a chance to get a feel for her new car, and she could relax in the passenger's seat. Since they'd be leaving Don's place before it got dark, they'd be able to see anything that might be on the road, including deer.

Rhonda thought about the information she'd read online about the importance of looking for ways to de-stress. Suggestions included doing deep breathing exercises, drinking calming herbal teas, and soaking in a bathtub filled with warm water. Another idea was to take a cold shower to relieve anxiety. Rhonda hoped she'd be able to implement a few things that might help her relax.

She gripped the steering wheel a little tighter and frowned. *With a job like mine, I'll probably never be free of stress. And dealing with traffic when I have to commute to work all the time sure doesn't help.*

Jeff's blinker came on again, only this time he took an exit. Rhonda followed him off the ramp and through some streets leading to his dad's place. Although the trip to Cleveland didn't take long, she was ready to get out of the car and stretch her legs.

For some reason, her mother came to mind. *I wonder how things are going with her these days?* It had been several weeks since she'd found out from Gwen about her mom dating. *I don't like the idea of Mom going out with strange men, and I can't believe she's entered the dating scene and is willing to try again.* She gripped the steering wheel tighter. *Knowing Mom, she'll probably end up liking the wrong guy and have her heart broken.*

Rhonda dreaded the time when she'd have to talk to Mom about her dating again. It seemed Jeff's relationship issues with his father paled in comparison to her problem with Mom. Rhonda hoped things would go well during their brief visit with Don. It always upset her whenever Jeff became defensive around his dad.

Of course, Rhonda reminded herself, *more often than not, I'm the same way with my mother.* Her jaw clenched. *I would never put up with a cheating man the way Mom did when she kept giving my dad second chances and more.*

At times Rhonda's mother got on her nerves—especially if she tried to cram religion down Rhonda's throat. *She ought to know that I'm not about to start going to church or attend some Bible study. I mean, why should I? That God she talks about has done nothing for me.*

Jeff looked in his rearview mirror and was glad to see that Rhonda's new car was behind him. He'd been keeping an eye on her vehicle ever since they'd merged onto the main highway. Although the silver-tone car she had chosen to buy wasn't her first choice, it was the best they could do with the amount of money they'd received from their insurance company.

At least it's nice looking and seems to handle well on the road. Hopefully, Rhonda has enjoyed driving it today.

Jeff turned left at the next intersection, drove a few more blocks, and pulled the truck into his father's driveway. He made sure to park close to the garage, leaving enough room for Rhonda's car to pull in behind him.

Jeff and Rhonda had no sooner gotten out of their vehicles than Jeff's dad came out of the house. He came right over and gave Rhonda a hug then stepped up to Jeff and did the same.

"How was your trip?" Dad questioned. "Were you slowed by traffic?"

Jeff shook his head. "There were fewer vehicles on the road than I thought there'd be." He gestured to Rhonda's car. "What do you think of my wife's new set of wheels?"

"Looks good." Dad went over and gave the car a quick once-over. "Does it drive well?" he asked, directing his question to Rhonda.

"Yes, it handles quite nicely." She smiled. "It's not as sporty as my other car, but I think it's going to work out okay for me."

"That's good." Dad looked back at Jeff. "How'd my truck work out for you? Did you have any problems with it?"

"Nope, none at all. It got me to and from my restaurant with no problems as well as to all the other places I needed to go."

"Glad to hear it." Dad clasped Jeff's shoulder. "Come inside and I'll fix you both something cold to drink. It'll be nice to sit and visit awhile."

Jeff looked at Rhonda, and when she gave him an approving nod, he said, "Sure, Dad. But we can't stay too long."

"Do you have someplace else you need to go?"

Jeff couldn't miss his dad's look of disappointment. "No, just home, but we'd like to get back before dark," he replied.

"That's several hours from now." Dad motioned them to follow him onto the front porch. When he opened the door, a yappy little terrier darted out and pawed at Jeff's leg.

He bent down and gave the hyper animal a few pats. "When did you get a dog, Dad?"

"He showed up at my place a few weeks ago with no collar or identification tags. I ran an ad and asked around, trying to find his rightful owner, but had no luck." Dad looked down at the dog and shook his head. "The little fellow worked his way right into my heart."

"What'd you name him?" Jeff asked.

"Dancer." Dad grinned. "He's a smart little guy and dances on his back feet whenever he wants a doggie treat."

Jeff resisted the urge to roll his eyes. He figured Rhonda was probably amused by the statement too.

They entered the house, and Dad invited them to take a seat in the living room, saying they should make themselves comfortable while he went to the kitchen to get some cold apple cider. "Unless you'd rather have it warm?" he added.

Jeff looked at Rhonda, and when she shook her head, he replied for both of them. "Cold is fine, Dad."

"Okay, I'll be right back."

After his father left the room, Jeff seated himself on the couch. Rhonda had no more than taken a seat beside him when Dancer leaped into her lap and began licking her hand. She wasted no time in picking up the dog and setting him on the floor. A few seconds later, Dancer jumped up again. This time the mutt put his paws on her chest and slurped her chin.

"Eww. . ." Rhonda's nose wrinkled as she looked over at Jeff. "If this keeps up, we'll be leaving a lot sooner than your father expects."

"Sorry, hon." Jeff took the dog from her and placed him back on the floor. "Go lay down, Dancer." He pointed to the doggie bed that had been positioned near his dad's recliner.

The stubborn animal made no effort to move. He sat looking up at Jeff with his head cocked to one side. *"Yip! Yip! Yip!"*

Jeff looked at Rhonda to see her reaction, but she sat silently with her arms crossed. He figured she might be trying to protect herself in case the dog tried to jump up on her again.

"What do you think of my pooch?" Dad asked when he entered the living room with a jug of apple cider and three paper cups.

Jeff glanced at the dog. "Well, um. . ."

"Would you like to see him dance?"

"Sure."

Dad set the cider and cups on the small table near the couch, reached into his shirt pocket, and pulled out a small doggie biscuit. As soon as Don held the biscuit, Dancer scurried over, stood up on his hind legs, and danced around. The crazy animal yipped and yapped until Dad let the treat fall. With one quick snap, Dad's furry companion snatched the biscuit then dashed out of the room.

"Where's he going?" Jeff asked.

"He'll either eat the treat or hide it someplace to consume later." Dad chuckled as he poured them each a glass of cider. "I've found biscuits in some mighty strange places."

"It seems as though you've taken an eccentric dog under your wing," Rhonda spoke up. "Where do you put Dancer when you're at your business or out making calls?"

"I put plenty of old newspapers on the floor and barricade him on the utility porch, with enough food and water so he can get by till I get home. I'm not about to let him have free rein of the house while I'm gone." Dad took a seat in his recliner. "Eventually, I'll build Dancer a dog run outside, but with the weather turning colder, I wouldn't feel right about leaving him outside for too long. A bigger dog could take it but not a little terrier like mine." He took a drink of cider and smacked his lips. "Boy, this sure is good."

Jeff's brows drew together. He didn't know what to think. He'd never seen his dad this hyper before. Was it acquiring a new dog or something else? He was about to ask when Dad posed a question.

"How are things going with the sale of the townhouse? It's been a few weeks since you called and said you had a buyer."

"We do, and we're supposed to close in two weeks," Rhonda said before Jeff could respond.

"That's great!" Dad's smile stretched wide. "It just goes to show what the power of prayer can do."

Yeah, right. What good did prayers do on Mom's behalf to keep her from dying? Jeff wanted to say the words out loud, but what good would that do? His dad would probably say something lame like, "It must have been your mother's time to die." Jeff had heard that line before, and it only made him angrier. He wasn't sure he could forgive God for taking a sweet woman like his mother away from her family.

In order to temper the fury boiling inside him, Jeff lifted his glass of cider and took a drink. The tangy, cold liquid helped cool Jeff's parched throat. Too bad it couldn't do the same for the hot anger churning in his soul. Whenever Jeff was at the restaurant, overseeing things and visiting with customers, his anger at God would dissipate, or at least he didn't think about it so much. The same held true when he was at home with Rhonda, enjoying their private retreat. But a few minutes spent in his father's presence or even talking with him on the phone often opened Jeff's old wounds. If only he could find some way to let them go permanently.

"So, you have a new car now, and you'll soon receive the money from the sale of your old place, but what about your air-conditioning? Have you been able to get that replaced?" Dad directed his question to Jeff.

"No, and we're not going to do anything about it until spring, when we have a better feel for our finances," Jeff replied.

Dad bobbed his head like a woodpecker attacking the bark on a tree. "That's smart thinking." He looked at Rhonda and grinned. "Aren't you glad I raised my boy to think things through?"

"Well, actually—"

"So, Dad, other than acquiring a dog, what else is new with you these days?" Jeff set his paper cup down and leaned slightly forward. It was definitely time for a topic change.

Dad moved to the edge of his recliner, with his shoulders straight and pulled back. "Well, Son, I'm glad you asked. As I've mentioned to you previously, I'm back in the dating scene."

Jeff slowly nodded his head.

"After going on a few dates and looking at many women's profiles on the dating site I've been using, I have finally found one that I feel could be my soulmate. Of course, I haven't met her on a date yet."

This sounds utterly ridiculous! I don't know how my dad could get a good feeling about a person without even meeting her. "Better not get your hopes up, Dad," Jeff was quick to say. "If none of the other women worked out for you, this one you're so excited about might not be the one for you either."

"Don't be so negative, Son. I've been praying about this, and if it's the Lord's will for me to find another helpmate, He will lead me to the right one, and I'll have an assurance about it."

Jeff's gaze flicked upward. *Right, Dad. Of course, you will.*

New Philadelphia

June picked up her purse and was almost to the door, when it swung open and Gwen stepped in.

Gwen shook her finger like June was a child. "For goodness' sakes, Mom, when are you going to remember to lock your doors?"

"And when are you going to remember to knock?"

Ignoring June's question, Gwen said, "The girls and I are heading out to do some shopping, and I was wondering if you'd like to join us."

June shook her head. "I can't today because I'm going to get my hair done. After that, I have a manicure appointment."

"Let me guess—you have another date tonight with Walt. Or is it Robert this time?"

June's face heated up. "Neither. This man's name is Andy. I met him on a Christian dating site a few weeks ago, but tonight will be the first time we've met in person."

Gwen frowned. "Do you think that's a good idea?"

"I don't see why not."

"I don't trust those dating sites, Mom. This fellow could be some kook, pretending to be something he's not."

"That's why I'm meeting the man tonight, so I can get to know him better and find out more about his relationship with the Lord. And if it doesn't work out, I'll try someone else whose profile is a closer match to what I'm looking for."

"And what would that be?"

"He has to have the same standards and similar interests as me."

Gwen pulled in her bottom lip then released it. "Does Rhonda know you've visited a dating site?"

"No, but then I haven't talked to her in a few weeks."

"What do you think she'd have to say about it?"

June shrugged.

"She wouldn't approve, Mom, and you know it."

"You're right, but not because I'm connecting with a man on a Christian dating site. Your sister doesn't want me to date anyone, and it has nothing to do with whether he's religious or not. She's worried that if I got married again, my husband might cheat on me the way your father did."

"She may be wrong about that, but I think you ought to be cautious and not—"

June opened her purse and withdrew her car keys. "I don't have time to debate this with you, Gwen. If I don't leave now, I'll be late getting to the styling salon."

"Okay, I'll let you go. We can talk about this some other time."

June smiled and gave her daughter a hug. "Try not to worry about me. I'm a grown woman, and whether you and your sister realize it or not, I am perfectly capable of taking care of myself. I'm also relying on God to help me make good decisions."

Chapter 29

Walnut Creek

Rhonda glanced over at Jeff and noticed how tightly he gripped the steering wheel. She reached over and placed her hand gently on his arm. "Are you stressed from all the traffic we encountered after leaving your dad's place or is it something else?"

"The traffic didn't bother me so much. It's Dad's foolish behavior."

"Him having a dog or the idea that he's seeking women to date?"

"Both. Dad hasn't been the same since he bought that flashy-looking convertible." Jeff groaned. "I'm convinced that he's dealing with some sort of midlife crisis."

"My mother must be going through one too because she's definitely not thinking straight these days."

"At least she hasn't bought a convertible or taken in some hyper mutt." Jeff let go of the steering wheel with his right hand and reached up to rub the back of his neck—one more hint that he felt stressed out.

"Please use both hands on the wheel. You don't have good control with just one hand."

His brows furrowed. "I do too. A lot of people drive with one hand on the wheel."

"But they're not driving my car."

"Should I pull over so you can drive?"

Rhonda couldn't miss her husband's sarcastic tone. "Don't be silly; we're almost home."

Jeff put his hand back on the steering wheel. "There, are you happy now?"

She combed her fingers through her hair and flipped it back behind her ears. "Are you angry about what I said, Jeff, or just taking your frustrations over your dad's actions out on me?"

"Guess it's mostly my feelings about Dad. Sorry for snapping at you, honey. I think we'll both feel better once we're in our own home where we can fully relax."

"You're right," Rhonda agreed. "I'll fix us a snack, and then maybe we can watch a movie together in your man cave."

He glanced her way and grinned before looking back at the road. "That sounds great. Since we stopped for an early dinner on the way home, I'm not all that hungry, but in an hour or so, a snack might be nice. I'll make some popcorn to go with whatever you fix."

"That would be nice."

As they approached their home, he reached for the remote to open the gate. "And the best part is that the two of us will be spending some quality time together."

⁓

"It was nice we had a chance to spend some time fellowshipping with your brother, Samuel, and his wife, Esther, after the rest of the people went home today," Lois commented as she and Orley headed for home in their buggy. "I still have some of my snack mix left over. It's setting behind my seat in the red container."

"There were plenty of snacks to nibble on earlier today, but I can always make room for a little more." He chuckled.

"It was good to visit with some familiar faces while we ate and even afterward during the cleanup time in the kitchen."

He bobbed his head. "Jah, since today is our off-Sunday, I'm glad we could attend church services with my brother's church district this morning. It was also nice that it was held at Samuel and Esther's home."

"Speaking of homes. . .that one there is certainly beautiful." Lois pointed up ahead.

Orley squinted. "And you know what? I believe that is Jeff and Rhonda Davis in the car going into that yard through the open gate."

"How do you know it's them?"

"The woman in the passenger's side turned her head to the right, and I recognized her face."

As Orley's horse, Biscuit, approached the gate, he pulled back on the reins to make the gelding stop. "Jah, it's them all right. Jeff parked the car by that big garage, and now he's getting out. If I had a horn, I would give it a few toots."

"Since you don't, we should keep going."

"Nope." Orley handed the reins to Lois and climbed down from the buggy.

"What are you doing?" she called to him.

Ignoring his wife's question, he stood outside the closed gate, cupped his hands around his mouth, and hollered, "Hello, Jeff Davis!"

A few seconds passed before Jeff looked his way and waved.

"He sees us." Orley glanced over his shoulder at Lois before turning to look back at Jeff, who was now headed his way.

When the young man stepped up to the gate, Orley smiled and reached his hand over the top of the barrier. Jeff followed suit and gave Orley's hand a firm shake.

"It's nice to see you again," Orley said. "I have driven by here many times but didn't realize this was your place." He gestured to the house. "It certainly looks grand from the outside."

"Yeah, the inside's pretty awesome too. If you have the time, you're welcome to come in for a tour."

"We have plenty of time. Lois and I are on our way home from my brother's place, where church was held this morning, but we're in no hurry to get home."

"Okay then. I'll open the gate and let you in." Jeff pulled a remote from his shirt pocket, and when his thumb came down on it, both sides of the gate swung open. "You can pull your rig in and secure the horse to a section of our fence."

"Sounds good." Orley climbed back in the buggy and turned to face Lois with a grin. "We're goin' in."

She tipped her head. "Into the Davises' yard?"

"Jah, and then into their house. Jeff is gonna give us a tour."

"But they just got home from somewhere," she responded. "They might not appreciate us barging in."

"Jeff extended the invitation, so I'm sure it's okay." He took the reins from Lois and guided his horse into the yard. When Jeff pointed to the place along the fence where he wanted him to go, Orley directed Biscuit to that spot, gave Lois the reins again, and got out. After the horse was secured, he waited for Lois to climb down from the carriage. Then they both walked with Jeff up to the house, where Rhonda stood on the front porch.

"Hello." She offered them a smile, but it appeared as though it may have been forced. Or perhaps the pretty young woman was just tired. "Jeff said you would like to see our house."

"That would be lovely," Lois was quick to say, "but if this isn't a good time, we can come by some other day."

"No, it's okay." Jeff unlocked and opened the front door. "We just got back from Cleveland, where we went to return my dad's truck that he loaned us after I hit the deer I told Orley about."

"I was sorry to hear the sad story," Lois said as she and Orley stepped into the spacious entryway behind Rhonda and Jeff.

"Is the vehicle you were driving to replace the car you wrecked when you hit the deer?" Orley questioned.

"Yes, it is," Rhonda spoke up. "But I don't like it as much as the one I used to have."

Orley could not miss the disappointment in her tone, and he didn't understand why she would be dissatisfied with such a nice car. Then again, many things confused him about the way some English people thought, not to mention all the modern, fancy gadgets they owned.

"Okay now, if you're ready for the tour, we'll start on the left side of the house." Jeff's comment pushed Orley's thoughts aside.

"Yes, we are ready to see what your home looks like." Orley glanced at Lois and was pleased when she gave a nod.

~

As the Davises showed them through each room in their beautiful home, Lois was astounded. She'd never been in a house so fancy before and wondered why this young couple had bought such a large place for just the two of them.

Each to his or her own, she thought. *Unless Orley and I had a big family, I sure wouldn't want a house that large.*

When Jeff showed them a room at the end of the long hall he'd said was his "man cave," Lois held both hands against her cheeks. "I've never seen such a large television screen." She pointed to the place where it hung on the wall.

"I didn't realize you Amish had TV's in your homes," Jeff commented.

"We don't," Orley spoke up. "But we've seen the television sets in some of our English neighbors' homes. But none were as large as yours."

Jeff shrugged his shoulders. "What can I say—I like to see what I'm seein' in a big way."

"He's not kidding about that," Rhonda interjected. "If there was a bed in here, I think my husband might sleep in this room."

Jeff nudged his wife's arm. "Very funny, Rhonda."

His eyes narrowed into tiny slits, and Lois couldn't mistake the look of irritation on the young man's face.

"Now that you've had the full tour of the inside of our home, let's go out back and I'll show you around the yard." Jeff looked at his wife. "Would you mind fixing us that little snack you had talked about before we pulled into our yard a while ago? We can eat it on the back patio."

"That's okay. Don't go to any trouble on our account." With a shake of her head, Lois held up her hand.

"It's fine," Rhonda said. "There's a container of creamy cucumber dip that I made yesterday in the refrigerator. We can have it with some cut-up veggies and crackers if that sounds good to everyone."

"It's fine with me." Orley was the first to respond and then looked at Lois. "We have your snack mix out in the buggy that we could contribute. Let me go grab it." He turned and went out the front door.

While he was gone, Lois looked around some more. She noticed that while they'd toured the home, there were only a few antiques on display. Most of their furnishings were modern pieces that fit nicely with the house's upscale designs. Lois asked Jeff when the house was built.

"When our Realtor showed us the place, she said it was five years old," Jeff responded.

Soon Orley came back inside with the container and handed it to Lois. "Here you go."

Lois thanked him and turned to look at Rhonda. "It's filled with a few different types of crackers with nuts mixed in."

"That sounds good." Rhonda smiled.

"Is there anything I can help you with in the kitchen?" Lois asked.

Rhonda shook her head. "I can manage. Why don't you go out with the men and look at our yard? There's a table on the patio you can set your snack mix on so you can be hands-free while you take a look around."

Lois hesitated a few seconds but finally nodded. As she stepped out the back door behind the men, her breath caught in her throat. "This yard is beautiful. The grass is so green, the flowers are lovely, and there's even a pond with waterfalls." She placed her container on the patio table and pointed in that direction.

"Let's take a walk out there so you can see our fancy fish." Jeff led the way.

Lois stood between Orley and Jeff, barely able to take it all in. The fish swam near the edge of the pond as though begging to be fed, and the cascading waterfalls, which Jeff had turned on, made Lois feel as if she were near a mountain stream.

"If I had a place like this, I'd never need to go anywhere for a vacation," Orley commented. "Think I could set up a hammock and lie out here all day, listening to the gurgling water as it cascades into the pond."

Lois had to agree. This yard was so relaxing. *If Orley and I had a yard like this, during warmer weather, I'd sit outside and answer the letters that are forwarded to me from the newspaper for my Dear Caroline column. I bet I could think more clearly and give better answers if I had a place this serene to do my writing. Of course,* she reminded herself, *I'd probably never get any work done in the house or at our store. So, I will not allow myself to long for something that really isn't necessary.*

"Shall we go back up to the patio now and wait for Rhonda to bring the snacks out?" Jeff's question broke into Lois's thoughts.

"You two go ahead and relax," she said. "I'd like to help Rhonda bring the refreshments out." She hurried up to the house.

When she entered the kitchen, Lois said to Rhonda, "Your yard is beautiful and such a relaxing place to spend time outdoors."

Rhonda set a tray of veggies on the table and turned to face Lois. "Yes, the yard and pond were one of the reasons we bought this home, but there's a lot of upkeep that goes with taking care of it. Since both Jeff and I work five days a week, it's hard for us to do all the things that need to be done in the yard or here in the house."

"Have you considered hiring someone to help with the chores?"

"Oh, we've considered it all right, but it would be one more expense we don't need at this time."

"I understand." Lois gestured to the paper plates and napkins on the counter. "Should I take those out to the patio?"

"Yes, please. You can set them on the table."

"What else can I bring out?"

"Plastic cups are in that cupboard." Rhonda pointed. "And there's a jug of apple cider in the refrigerator. I'll get a tray and bring out the crackers, dip, and cut-up vegetables."

"Okay." Lois gathered the items and took them outside to the picnic table, where the men sat talking. They glanced her way, smiled, and continued their conversation on the topic of antique clocks. Rather than interrupt them, she went back inside.

"Our husbands are talking about vintage clocks," she told Rhonda.

The young woman lifted her gaze to the ceiling. "That figures. I've never been able to understand Jeff's fascination with old things."

"You don't care for antiques?"

Rhonda shrugged her slender shoulders. "They're okay, but a lot of them—at least the ones Jeff's interested in—are quite expensive." She moved closer to Lois. "Jeff hasn't been back in your store looking to buy anything else, I hope."

"Just that time when Orley mentioned that Jeff had come in, looking for an old piece of jewelry to give you for your anniversary, but Orley informed him that all the vintage jewelry had sold."

Rhonda pressed her lips together a few seconds before speaking. "I believe my husband is addicted to old things, and it hasn't done anything to help our marriage. Quite the opposite. His obsession has made things between us more stressful because he refuses to part with any of his collectibles."

Lois was on the verge of saying something, when Jeff stepped into the kitchen, looking directly at Rhonda. "Are you about ready with the snacks?"

"They're right there on the table. I was just getting ready to bring them out."

"Great!" He grabbed the tray filled with crackers, dip, and veggies. "I'll take them out for you."

"Thanks." Rhonda grabbed a few bananas and apples from the fruit bowl. "I'm trying to eat a healthier diet, which includes plenty of fruits and vegetables," she told Lois as they followed Jeff out the back door.

Lois smiled. "Orley and I enjoy healthy snacks too."

⁓

As they ate and drank their refreshments, Jeff noticed that Rhonda directed most of her conversation to Lois and barely looked at him, even when he asked her a question. *Is she upset with me because I invited the Troyers in for a tour of our home? Or maybe she's put out with me for suggesting that she fix us some snacks.* Jeff chomped on an apple. *But that makes no sense, since we'd already agreed that we would enjoy having snacks while we watched TV. Of course, it was supposed to be just the two of us. Maybe Rhonda resents the intrusion of two people neither of us knows very well.*

"Say Jeff, I was wondering about that plaque I gave you for your anniversary. I didn't see it hanging on the wall in any of the rooms we walked through on the tour of your house. Did you not like the gift?"

Orley's question jolted Jeff out of his contemplations. "Um. . . no, it was a nice gift. I just haven't had the time to hang it yet."

"I can understand why," Lois interjected. "Between working full time at your restaurant and taking care of this big home and yard, I doubt you have much free time at all."

"You're right about that," Jeff agreed. "Sometimes I wish I could sell my business and find a job closer to home." He glanced at Rhonda, who sat with her arms folded. "You wish that too, right?"

She gave a noncommittal shrug and reached for her glass of cider.

"We should probably get going and let these two have what's left of the day to themselves." Lois gave her husband's arm a nudge.

"Yeah, sure." Orley pushed his chair back and stood. "Before we go though, I was wondering if I could get your phone number, Jeff. That way we can keep in touch."

"Sure thing." Jeff reached into his pocket and pulled out a pen and small tablet. After he'd written his cell number down, he tore off the paper and handed it to Orley.

"Thanks. If I don't call before, I'll definitely let you know when winter sets in and there's enough snow on our hill for sledding." Orley grinned. "It'll be fun to watch you try out that old sled you bought the first day you visited our store."

Jeff smiled. "That'd be great. I'll look forward to that call."

Chapter 30

Autumn's chilly fingers had blown away the colorful leaves on the trees in Jeff and Rhonda's yard. Now the smell of an early winter drifted on the brisk breeze that had whooshed in last night and covered their yard with a blanket of fluffy white snow.

"Oh, boy." Jeff rubbed his hands together in the anticipation of finally getting to try out his old sled on the Troyers' hill. Of course, he wouldn't go there without checking with Orley first.

This would be a good day for sledding, Jeff thought, looking up at the heavy snow coming down. *Since I'm not working today, maybe I could drop by their house and see if Orley might be home.*

"How come you've been standing in front of the kitchen window so long?" Rhonda asked, stepping up to him.

"Just watching the snow come down and wishing I could try out my sled." He turned his head in her direction. "Since neither of us has to work today, why don't we bundle up in warm clothes and take a ride over to the Troyers' place?"

Her thick lashes fluttered like a bird in flight. "You're kidding, right?"

Jeff gave a quick shake of his head. "Orley said when it snowed, I could try out my sled on that hill at the back of his property." He rubbed his hands together again. "I'm just itching to give my old sled a try."

"This is only the third week of November, Jeff. It won't officially be winter until December twenty-first."

"It looks and feels like winter, and by next month there might not be any snow, so I'd like to take advantage of it now." He clasped her arm. "Come on, Rhonda, please say you'll take a ride with me to the Troyer's Place."

"I don't feel right just going over there unannounced. Shouldn't you try and call Orley first? What if they're not home?"

"It will be okay, and come to think of it, that day he asked me for my number, I should have gotten his as well. Don't know why I didn't."

Rhonda muttered something under her breath.

"What was that?"

"Oh nothing."

"I'm gonna get my sled and go over there. Please come along and keep me company. Besides, the scenery will be pretty as we take a drive out to their place." Jeff gave a quick pout and followed it with a grin. "Then we'll come back here, turn on the gas fireplace, and veg out the rest of the day."

"If Orley and Lois are at home, what am I supposed to do while you're sledding? We have so few days when we're both not working, and I'd hoped we could do something fun today."

"And so we shall. We can take turns sledding down the Troyers' hill." Jeff's excitement mounted as he continued to gaze out the window at the freshly fallen snow.

"I'm not interested in sledding, Jeff." Rhonda bumped his arm with her elbow. "The last time I got on a sled, I lost control and ended up in a snowbank with icy-cold snow up my nose."

"If you don't want to sled, you can stand on the sidelines and cheer me on." Jeff slipped his arm around Rhonda's waist and pulled her close.

"The last thing I want to do is stand around in the snow and shiver while I watch you act like a big kid on that antiquated sled of yours. Which, by the way, might not even be safe."

"It's not in that bad a shape. I mean, I've dusted the sled off and looked it over. I'd like to do some minimal work on it so that it doesn't take away from its original look, but it's all cosmetic, and I'm sure I can still make it work." Jeff turned to face Rhonda and gave her a kiss. "There's no need to worry. I'll be fine, honey. You'll see."

⌒

"It sure is nice having a day at home together," Orley said when he entered the small room he and Lois used as their home office.

She looked up from where she sat at the desk and nodded. "I always appreciate the days off we take from the store. It gives me a chance to catch up with things around here." Lois gestured to the stack of letters lying before her. "Not to mention being able to get some of these letters answered that were sent to my newspaper column. There doesn't seem to be enough hours in a day for me."

Orley frowned. "I'd kinda hoped we could go play in the *schnee* together."

She swatted the air. "Go on with you now. I have work to do here, and we're too old to be playing in the snow."

Orley shook his head vigorously. "One is never too old to play in the snow, and if you're too busy answering letters, then allow me to help, and you can get it done quicker."

Her brows lifted. "Let me get this straight. You want to help me come up with answers to the people who have written to Caroline?"

"Jah, that's right."

"Okay then, how would you respond to this one?" Lois picked up the letter on top and read it to him. " 'Dear Caroline: I have a finicky cat that won't eat unless I'm holding her in my lap. It's probably my fault because I began feeding her like this when she was a kitten. I've tried everything to get her to eat from her dish while it's on the floor. Is there anything I can do to break my cat's habit? Powerless Pet Owner.' "

Orley's eyes widened. "Is that the kind of letter you normally get?"

"Sometimes. Of course, there are other letters involving more serious issues like this one: 'Dear Caroline: My father left my mother for another woman when I was a teenager. Now she's in her fifties and has begun dating. I'm afraid she'll make a mistake and end up getting involved with the wrong man. How can I make her listen to reason? Desperate Daughter.'"

She looked at him with squinted eyes. "Any ideas how I should respond to either of those letters?"

Orley gave his beard a couple of pulls. "Well, for the first one, I'd tell that person to put food in the *katz's* dish, set it on the floor, and walk out of the room. I bet in no time the furry critter would be gobbling up that food."

Lois pursed her lips and gave her chin a few taps. "Hmm. . .I will definitely consider that. Now what about the second letter?"

Orley gave his beard a couple more tugs. "That one's a little more difficult since it involves a daughter and her mother. I might need to think about that awhile. I'll ponder it while I step outside and check the weather."

"Okay, but I may have come up with a reply to the letter by the time you return." Lois gave him a sly little grin.

"I wouldn't be one bit surprised." He winked and left the room to get his jacket and stocking cap.

When Orley went out the door and stepped onto the porch, he breathed in the chilly air as a few birds chattered at a nearby feeder. It was always nice to enjoy the serenity of a quiet day.

Orley soon saw a familiar vehicle drive into the yard. After it stopped near the house, he went out to greet Jeff and his wife, who had both gotten out of the SUV.

"Hello." He extended his hand to Rhonda and then to Jeff. "This is a nice surprise."

Grinning widely, Jeff shook Orley's hand. "I couldn't remember what days the antique store was closed, so I wasn't sure if you'd be home."

"Yep, today is one of our day's off," Orley responded. "I assume both of you must not be working today either."

"That's right, and since we have all this unexpected beautiful snow, I was hoping I might be able to try out my sled on your hill." Jeff pointed in that direction.

"Sounds like a good idea, and I'd like to join you." Orley gestured to the house. "Let's go inside, and I'll let Lois know you're here. Maybe the four of us can take turns sledding."

Rhonda shook her head. "I only came along to watch."

"Okay, well maybe you'll change your mind once you see how much fun Jeff and I have." Orley opened the door and invited them in. "I'll get Lois and see if she'd like to do any sledding or would rather stand on the sidelines and watch."

When Orley entered the room where he'd left his wife a short time ago, he found her still hard at work on her letters. "The Davises are here," he said. "Jeff and I are going to do a little sledding, but Rhonda said she'll watch. How about you, Lois? Would you like to join us men on the hill or wait down below with Rhonda?"

Lois splayed her hands out wide and flexed her fingers. "I'm not finished here yet, but I probably do need a break." She rose from her chair. "I'll bundle up and come outside to watch and visit with Rhonda while you and Jeff play in the snow."

He wrinkled his nose at her. "We won't be playing, Fraa. We'll be sledding."

She snickered. "Same difference."

⁓

"Those two sure seem to be having fun, don't they?" Lois commented as she and Rhonda stood off to one side at the bottom of the hill, watching Orley and Jeff carrying on like a couple of kids.

"I'll say." Rhonda slipped her gloved hands inside her jacket pocket. "It would be a lot more fun if Jeff and I had a child and I was witnessing him or her sliding down that hill."

"So, you're unable to have children?"

"Apparently, although we've never been given a logical reason, not even after all the tests we'd had run."

"And you're sad about that?"

Rhonda nodded. "Don't you feel the same because you and Orley have no children?"

Lois moved closer to her. "I learned some time ago that I could have a happy life even if I couldn't have children. I had to be willing to accept life with its conditions and on its terms not my own. And I decided that my life was a gift from God, and my happiness was not dependent upon children, a husband, or any of the other things I had once thought were the source of happiness. It's about being able to accept the bitter and sweet parts of life."

Rhonda bit her lower lip. "I've had plenty of bitter."

"Do you associate not having children with feelings of failure?" Lois asked.

Rhonda nodded.

Lois gently patted her arm. "I understand, and it's normal to feel that way, but it's not true. The first step is to find other things that bring you happiness without having children."

"I've tried, but nothing, not even my busy managerial position at the hotel, makes me feel fulfilled."

"Perhaps you might consider taking up a hobby you enjoy or doing some charitable work."

"Maybe, if I had the time. My job is quite demanding."

"I understand. Mine can be as well."

Rhonda couldn't imagine that owning an antique store could be demanding, but she chose not to voice her thoughts.

"Another thing you can do," Lois continued, "is to talk about your feelings of pain and loss. Have you done that, Rhonda?"

"I have, but only to Jeff." Rhonda looked down as her eyes filled with tears. "He gets upset when I bring up the topic, so I try not to mention it to him anymore."

"Perhaps it's a touchy subject because he too is hurting."

"I thought he was at first, but now I'm not so sure. Jeff seems to find his fulfillment in other things—like collecting antiques that we can't afford and watching favorite programs on his large-screen TV."

Lois's forehead wrinkled. "Oh, I see." She leaned closer to Rhonda. "May I ask you another question?"

"Sure."

"Do you have a personal relationship with God?"

Rhonda bristled. *Now why is she asking me that? And what business is it of hers anyway?* "Jeff and I aren't the religious types," she mumbled. "We don't go to church either."

"I'm sorry to hear that. A permanent feeling of peace and acceptance is what we all need, and it can only come from a relationship with God. The Bible tells us that. . ."

Rhonda was glad when Orley yelled down to Lois, asking her to fix them something warm to drink. It had felt good to discuss the way she felt about not having children until Lois brought up the topic of God.

Rhonda shivered, pulling the scarf around her neck a little closer. *If I'm going to discuss anything of a serious nature again, I'll write another letter to the Dear Caroline column. At least she doesn't try to cram religion down my throat.*

"One last trip down the hill, and we'll be ready for hot chocolate," Orley hollered.

"Let's watch his final run with the sled, and then we'll go inside," Lois said. "By the time the men come in, I'll have something hot ready for us all to drink."

"Okay." Rhonda was sure Jeff would want a hot beverage, so she really couldn't say no to Lois's invitation. She stood silently watching as both Jeff and Orley pushed off on their sleds and sailed down the hill. Jeff's sled did fine, but Orley's must have gotten hung up on a clump of snow or something else. In a split second, he was off the sled and lying face-down, unmoving in a pile of snow.

"Oh dear! I believe he might be hurt." Lois tromped through the snow and dropped to her knees next to her husband.

With her heart pounding, Rhonda followed. By the time she reached them, Orley had rolled over and was laughing so hard, tears rolled down his rosy cheeks. "What a ride that was! Reminds me of when I was a boy and lost control of the sled one time. I ended up hitting a tree and breakin' my naas."

Frowning, Lois shook her finger at him. "That's not funny, Orley. When you were lying there, unmoving, I thought you had been seriously hurt."

He shook his head. "Nope. Just couldn't catch my breath for a few seconds. And with the snow being so cold and seeping into my boots and up my sleeves, I didn't think I could move."

"I'm glad you're okay." Rhonda looked over at Jeff. "The way you two were carrying on, either one of you could have been hurt."

Jeff shrugged his shoulders. "We were just having fun. Right, Orley?"

The men said they'd be in after a few more runs down the hill, so the ladies went into the house. Jeff couldn't believe how much fun it was to be out playing like a kid again on his old sled, and he had a nice friend to keep him company. He was glad he'd discovered the relic in Orley's shop. And what were the odds of finding one just like his grandfather's?

"If we continue to have snowy days all winter, I'd like to come back and do this again sometime," Jeff said as he and Orley pulled their sleds back up the hill.

Orley grinned. "Same here. Maybe next time we can talk our wives into joining us."

Jeff shook his head. "I doubt Rhonda would be willing."

"Speaking of your wife, did you ever find that daisy pin you'd wanted to give her?"

"No, but hopefully one of these days it'll turn up."

Orley nodded and brushed some snow off his leg. "When we go inside and have the chance, I'd like to show you some of the treasures I've found."

"That'd be great." Jeff positioned his sled, sat down on it, but didn't push off.

"I found a few of the better ones at an auction. The one my wife likes, we got a few years ago at an auction in Florida. Have you been to any of the auctions locally?"

"No. I'm sure that would be interesting though."

Orley took a seat on his sled and looked over at Jeff. "It is a good way to find some nice pieces. And there's usually food to eat, so you can recharge your energy."

"Sounds like fun."

"It is. Lois and I like to go from time to time. We often see familiar faces and enjoy visiting with new people too. My wife and I like being together, and when we go to auctions, we sometimes make a whole day out of it."

"Think I'd like that too." Jeff looked off toward the horizon. *I wish my wife were as interested in antiques and collectibles as I am. Also wish I knew what we need in our lives to have a better marriage. I can't help wondering how Orley and Lois seem so content with each other.*

Orley cleared his throat. "Are you ready to go?"

"Yes, let's do it." Jeff pushed off the hill.

His companion did the same, and they slid quickly downward. At the bottom, they came to a stop, both wearing smiles. Orley looked toward the neighbors' place and waved. An Amish man with a couple of little boys waved back, and the neighbor called out some words in Pennsylvania Dutch. Orley answered him back. Jeff was curious about what was being said, but he felt no need to inquire on the topic.

They headed back up the hill again and came down at the same time. Jeff was happy with his sled. It rode well, and he decided it was worth every penny he'd spent. He glanced over at Orley, with his pink cheeks and big smile. It was obvious that this man liked to have fun. He also conveyed a sense of peace that came from within.

Jeff heard his wife call his name. "We're ready for you guys to come in now."

He cupped his hands around his mouth and hollered in response, "Be right there!"

"And now," Orley said, "let's put our sleds away and head to the house for hot chocolate. I bet my wife has some of her tasty banana bread set out for us too."

As Jeff pulled his sled toward the house, he listened as Orley whistled a pleasant tune. *Sure wish I knew where that man's joyful attitude and peaceful expression comes from. I'd like a taste of it myself.*

Chapter 31

"Here's the newspaper." Jeff handed it to Rhonda. "It's a very nice Thanksgiving edition, and after a quick glance through it, I saw ads from plenty of stores that will be having big sales tomorrow morning."

"I won't be one of those frenzied shoppers." Rhonda shook her head. "Dealing with all the crowds is too stressful, and I've been looking for ways to lower my stress levels."

"Is that why your yoga mat is on the floor in the spare guest room?"

She nodded. "I decided to put that room to good use as a place where I can unwind."

"Good idea. And speaking of unwinding. . .since we don't have to be at your mom's place for dinner till two o'clock, I'm going out front to build a snowman." He rested his hand on the kitchen table. "It'll be fun. You wanna join me?"

"No thanks. I had enough exposure to the snow the day I stood beside Lois, watching you and Orley sledding down that snowy hill behind their house."

Jeff chuckled. "That was a fun day. Made me feel like a kid again, when my cousins and I used to slide down the hill at my grandpa's place."

With a small laugh, she rolled her eyes. "I never would have guessed."

He bent his head and kissed her. "If you change your mind, I'll be outside creating Mr. Snowman."

When Jeff left the room, Rhonda fixed herself a cup of peppermint tea and took a seat at the table to read the paper. She heard the front door open and close, and a short time later, she saw Jeff through the window, beginning his task of rolling a small snowball across the yard.

She watched him for a couple more minutes. *I'm satisfied staying inside and keeping cozy warm. Knowing Jeff, he'll want some hot cocoa when he's finished playing out there.*

Looking back at the newspaper, Rhonda scanned through the ads and went straight to the Dear Caroline column, hoping a reply to her recent letter might be there. Sure enough, there it was.

"Dear Caroline," she silently read. *"My father left my mother for another woman when I was a teenager. Now she's in her fifties and has begun dating. I'm afraid she'll make a mistake and end up getting involved with the wrong man. How can I make her listen to reason? Desperate Daughter."*

Rhonda's gaze went to Caroline's response. *"Dear Desperate Daughter, Although it's often difficult for a grown child to see their single parent begin dating, it's important to remember that your mother is an adult. She needs to feel that she has your support and is given the opportunity to make her own decisions. Your mother may be lonely or feel the need for male companionship. In all fairness, you need to give her the freedom to make her own decisions. It's also important that you be there to support her if those decisions don't turn out well."*

Rhonda sat quietly, sipping her tea and pondering Caroline's response. She reflected on how it would be if she were in her mother's place and had a grown daughter who opposed her desire to start dating.

If Jeff ever left me for another woman, she thought, *I don't think I could ever trust another man. Of course, Mom and I are different, and what feels wrong to me obviously doesn't to her. Guess I need to stop worrying about it and just be there for Mom if and when she needs me.*

"What would you like me to do next, Mom?" Gwen asked after she'd finished cutting dill pickle slices.

June gestured to the stack of her good plates on the kitchen table. "Why don't you take those to the dining room and ask your girls to set the table in there? They'll need to include silverware, napkins, and glasses."

"No problem. I'll oversee them to be sure the chore is done correctly." Gwen picked up the plates and left the room.

June opened the oven door to check on the turkey. When she pulled back the foil covering the big bird, a tantalizing aroma drifted up to her nose. Soon, the whole kitchen smelled delicious. The thermometer she'd placed in the turkey's breast showed that the meat was done, so she turned down the heat and covered it again, before closing the oven door. She would leave the bird there until everyone she'd invited arrived.

June rubbed a sweaty palm against the fabric of her apron. *Perhaps I should have told Gwen and Rhonda about the other guest I invited today rather than keeping it a surprise.*

Although it was unlike June to be so impulsive, she'd invited a man she had met on the internet dating site to join them for dinner today and couldn't help feeling a bit apprehensive. Would both of her daughters approve of him? Would they mind that she'd included him in their Thanksgiving plans? *Maybe I have made a mistake.* June closed her eyes and sent up a little prayer.

Hearing the sound of a vehicle pull into the yard, June opened her eyes and looked out the kitchen window. *Guess I'll know soon enough, because he's here, so there's no turning back now.* She removed her apron and headed for the front door. *Now if Rhonda and Jeff would just get here, we can eat our Thanksgiving meal.*

When Jeff pulled into June's yard, his eyebrows squished together as he peered out the front window of his SUV.

"What's wrong?" Rhonda questioned.

"That looks like my dad's truck parked over there. In fact, I know it is because I recognize the license plate." He pointed. "What would he be doing here? Last I heard, he'd made plans to be at Eric's place today."

"Did he know we were invited to my mom's for Thanksgiving?"

Jeff shrugged. "I'm not sure. I may have mentioned it when we talked on the phone the other day, but he never said anything about coming down."

"Maybe he wanted to surprise you."

"Oh, I'm surprised all right. And I hope he got your mom's permission and didn't just barge in unannounced." Jeff tapped his knuckles on the steering wheel. "My father's been quite impulsive lately and acting kind of weird ever since he bought that convertible."

Rhonda nodded. "He and my mom would make a good pair. They've both been acting out of character for the last several months."

Jeff rolled his eyes. "Yeah, right. Now wouldn't that be something to talk about—your mother and my father. They barely know each other, and as far as I can tell, they have nothing in common."

Rhonda laughed. "Well, we can't sit here any longer, talking about such a ridiculous scenario. We need to get the food I brought and go inside."

"You're right." Jeff opened his door and Rhonda did the same. When they got out, he reached into the back and took out the box of food Rhonda had prepared.

Walking up to the house, she looked over at him and smiled. "Try to relax, Jeff. If your dad is here, I'm sure he has a good explanation."

They stepped onto the porch, but before either of them could lift a hand to knock, the door swung open. Rhonda's mother greeted them with a pleasant smile. "Happy Thanksgiving!"

"Same to you, Mom," Rhonda said.

"How were the roads between Walnut Creek and here?"

"Not too bad," Jeff responded. "Since we haven't had any heavy snowfall for a couple of days, the roads were mostly clear."

"That's good to hear." Mom glanced at the box Jeff held. "If that's the food you brought, I can take it to the kitchen." She held out her hands.

"No, that's all right," Jeff said. "I'll do the honors."

"Okay."

Jeff started for the kitchen but stopped and turned to face Rhonda's mother again. "Is that my dad's truck parked in your yard?"

Circles of pink erupted on her cheeks. "Umm. . .yes, as a matter of fact it is. Don's in the kitchen, carving the turkey for me."

Rhonda expected Jeff to ask why his dad was here, but instead he headed down the hall, straight for the kitchen. Rhonda's mother followed, and Rhonda was right behind her. She wasn't about to miss out on Jeff greeting his dad.

⁓

Jeff entered the kitchen, set the box on the table, and stepped up to the counter, where his father stood carving the turkey. "What are you doing, Dad?"

"I'm carving a turkey, Son." Grinning, he bumped Jeff's arm with his elbow. "And it's a tender one too. See how it falls right off the bone?"

Reaching up to rub the back of his hot neck, Jeff said, "I can see that. What I'd like to know is, what are you doing here?"

"Rhonda's mother invited me." Dad turned and motioned for her to join him at the counter.

Smiling, June did as he'd asked. "Today is our first official date."

"What?" Jeff and Rhonda said simultaneously. He looked at his wife and noticed that her eyes had widened and her mouth hung slightly open. No doubt, she was as shocked as he was.

"We met on that Christian dating site I told you about," Dad explained.

June bobbed her head. "It was a surprise to both of us when our profile pictures came up and we realized that we already knew each other."

"Yeah, and we were equally surprised to discover that we have several things in common. So, rather than meet somewhere for our first date, June invited me to join her family for Thanksgiving dinner today." Dad turned back to his job of cutting the turkey.

Meanwhile, Rhonda pulled out a chair at the table and sat down. She either didn't have anything to say or had decided it was best not to voice her thoughts. Jeff felt certain, though, that his wife could not be happy about this unexpected development. Rhonda had stated many times that she didn't think her mother ought to be dating. He was sure she hadn't changed her mind about that, even if it was his dad her mother had suddenly taken an interest in. This whole thing of their parents entering the dating world again had become more surprising.

Although there was plenty he wanted to say, Jeff decided to keep quiet—at least until he had a chance to speak to his dad alone. *There's no point in me getting upset and ruining everyone's holiday*, Jeff told himself. *But at some point, I will express my feelings to Dad. Even though I've known June since Rhonda and I got married, and she's a nice enough person, no woman can ever replace my mom.*

~

A short time later, everyone gathered in the dining room, and Don led the family in prayer. Rhonda chanced a peek at Jeff, who sat beside her, looking down but with his eyes open. She couldn't miss the way a vein on the side of his neck protruded. *He's unhappy about my mother and his father dating. Although it does seem a bit odd, at least Mom didn't invite some stranger to join us today. Guess that's something to be grateful for.* Rhonda reached over and clasped Jeff's hand, and he gave her fingers a little squeeze. *I wonder if his thoughts are the same as mine.*

When Don's prayer ended, the platters and bowls of food were quickly passed around, and everyone began eating. Rhonda was careful about what she ate, choosing only healthy items, like the fruit salad, cut-up veggies, and cucumber dip she'd made to bring along. She also chose a piece of turkey, but no gravy or stuffing, and just a dab of potatoes.

"For goodness' sakes, Rhonda, you're certainly not eating much," Mom commented. "Are you on a diet to lose weight, because if that's the case, you're already thin enough."

Rhonda grimaced. "No, Mom, I am not on a diet. I'm just trying to eat healthier these days."

"I heard from Mom that your townhouse has sold," Gwen interjected. She glanced at Jeff and then settled her gaze on Rhonda. "I bet you're relieved."

Rhonda nodded. "We had to lower the price some, but we were glad when the deal finally closed, and we received our check. Now we'll be able to buy a new air conditioner in the spring and hopefully pay off the mortgage on our new place in Walnut Creek."

"I still don't understand why you need a house and yard that big. It would make more sense if you had children, but for just the two of you, it seems like a waste of space to me."

Gwen's comment hurt, and Rhonda struggled not to make a caustic response. *It's none of my sister's business how big our place is. She's probably jealous because her home isn't as spacious.* Rhonda's fingers curled into the palms of her hands as she held them firmly in her lap. *And did Gwen have to remind me that we have no children? Doesn't she care how much it hurts me to be unable to have babies?*

As though sensing her irritation, Rhonda's mother reached over and gave her arm a gentle pat. Then she looked across the table at Gwen and stated firmly, "That comment was unnecessary. Jeff and Rhonda have both worked hard ever since they got married, and they deserve to have a large home if that's what they want. They also didn't need the reminder that they are unable to have children."

"Sorry." Gwen dropped her gaze. "I didn't mean to put a damper on the otherwise nice day. Will you forgive me?"

Rhonda nodded. What else could she do with everyone staring at her?

On the way home that evening, Rhonda brought up the subject of Jeff's dad and her mother dating. "It was a surprise to find out that our parents met on a dating site and that today was their first date."

Jeff kept his gaze straight ahead and said nothing.

"I don't particularly like the idea, but at least they're dating someone we both know, so we don't have to worry what kind of person they are seeing socially."

Still no response from Jeff.

Sensing his reservations, Rhonda decided not to push. She thought about the letter she'd sent to Caroline and reflected on the columnist's reply. *Perhaps I do need to follow Caroline's advice and accept my mother's decision to try dating again. If it doesn't work out, Mom will learn from her mistakes. She doesn't need me telling her what to do.*

Walnut Creek

"That was some tasty meal we had at my *bruder*'s house today." Orley yawned and patted his belly. "But now I'm ready to settle into my favorite chair and take a *leie*."

"Nap, nothing." Lois tapped his shoulder. "If you're that tired, you should go to bed."

"Jah, maybe I will." He gave another noisy yawn. "You coming too?"

"I'll be there in a little while. I need to put my pie pans away, and I may do a little reading before I turn in."

"Okay." Orley pulled Lois into his arms and gave her a warm hug. "I love you."

"I love you more." She poked his stomach teasingly. "That's why I made your favorite chocolate cream pie to take to our family gathering today."

"I appreciated your kind gesture." He tweaked Lois's nose and followed it with a kiss on her lips. "If I'm asleep when you come to our room, would ya turn out the lamp on my side of the bed?"

"Of course," she replied, "but there's no need for you to leave it on. If I use my flashlight, I'll be able to see just fine coming into the room without you having to burn more batteries on the lamp."

"All right." Orley kissed her again and ambled out of the room.

Lois went to the kitchen, and after putting the pie pans away, she got out her Bible and took it over to the table. Their house was silent, with her husband already in bed.

She read a few passages from the book of Psalms and bowed her head for prayer. *"Heavenly Father,"* Lois silently prayed. *"Thank You for the many blessings You have given to me and Orley, which include our extended family. It was a joy to spend time with the adults who attended the function, but talking to our nieces and nephews was also most pleasant."*

Lois paused from her prayer and opened her eyes. *I wonder what it would be like if Orley and I had children of our own.*

With her elbows on the table, she placed both hands against her cheeks and reminded herself of the things she'd told Rhonda that snowy day when Orley and Jeff went sledding on their hill. Lois had to admit that she'd always wanted to raise a child or maybe several, but she had never let on to Orley. She didn't want to hurt his feelings or cause him to think that she blamed him because they couldn't have children.

Maybe it's best that we have no children, she thought. *While I don't think we would have been too strict, Orley and I might have been too permissive and ended up spoiling our kinner.* A few tears seeped from her eyes and rolled onto the table. *But oh, what a joy it would have been to be able to hold a boppli—a baby we could call our own.*

Chapter 32

The resonance of a rooster crowing pulled Jeff out of a fitful sleep. But that made no sense; they didn't have any chickens, and neither did any of their closest neighbors. Could one have somehow wandered into their yard?

Then, as Jeff came more fully awake, he remembered fooling with his ringtone last night and setting it to the sound of a rooster crowing to see if he would like it. Well, he didn't. It was annoying!

Groggily, Jeff reached over to his nightstand, and when he picked up the phone, he saw the time and recognized Russ's number. *What's he doing calling me in the middle of the night?*

Jeff pulled himself up and padded into the bathroom to take the call. "What's up, Russ? Have you no idea what time it is?"

"Yeah, Boss. It's two o'clock in the morning, and I'm calling with bad news."

"What's wrong? Are you sick? Have you been hurt?" Jeff's mind raced with all sorts of negative possibilities.

"I'm fine, but your restaurant caught fire. It burned fast, and there isn't much left."

"What?" Jeff blinked rapidly as he tried to process what he'd heard. "How'd you find out, and why wasn't I notified by the authorities?"

"It happened a short time ago. The sirens woke me up. Since my apartment is near the restaurant and the sirens sounded close,

I got dressed and headed over there." Russ's voice cracked with the emotion he obviously felt. "There are emergency vehicles up and down the block, and they're sure it was arson because three other businesses in the area also burned down."

Jeff's heart pounded, and his legs felt like sticks of rubber. He had to lean against the counter for support and couldn't help seeing his shocked expression in the mirror. *Who would do such a thing, and why'd they target my business?* Jeff frowned. *And why would God allow this to happen?*

"Are you still there, Boss?"

"Yeah, just trying to come to grips with what you've told me and wondering why this happened."

"Who can say? There are a lot of crazy people in our world who don't care about others and just want to wreak havoc."

Jeff leaned forward and massaged his forehead. He sure never expected anything like this to occur. Just when things seemed to be going better in his life, and now he had this to deal with!

"I'll get dressed and head your way. I need to see for myself how bad it is, and I'm sure the authorities will want to ask me some questions."

"Okay. I'll be here waiting for you. I'll also let the fireman in charge and the police know that you've been told and will be on your way."

"Thank you. I'll see you as soon as I can get there." Jeff clicked off his phone and went to the walk-in closet to get dressed. He'd picked out a pair of jeans to put on when Rhonda came in.

"What's going on?" Her sleepy eyes squinted against the well-lit bathroom light. "Who was on the phone, and why are you getting dressed at this time of the morning?"

Speaking rapidly, Jeff told her what Russ had said.

Rhonda's eyes widened, and she covered her mouth with the palm of her hand. "That's terrible, Jeff. What are you going to do?"

"Russ's waiting for me, and I'm going to Canton to see for myself how bad it is. Then my next step will be to contact my insurance company and file a claim for the loss of my restaurant."

Tears rolled down Rhonda's cheeks as she moved closer and gave him a hug. "I'll get dressed and go with you."

Jeff inhaled through his nose and exhaled through his mouth. "There's nothing you can do there, and there's no point in both of us losing sleep." He gave her arm a pat. "Please go back to bed. I'll wake you when I get home."

Rhonda shook her head. "I'm fully awake now, and after hearing this devastating news, there's no way I can go back to bed and sleep."

"Well, whatever you do, try not to worry. I'll call you when I get there." Jeff finished getting dressed, gave Rhonda a kiss, and hurried out of the room.

～

After Jeff left, Rhonda sat on the edge of their bed, filled with disbelief. How could something like this have happened? Without the income from Jeff's restaurant, how were they going to make it financially? In addition to her concern over losing the restaurant, Rhonda felt hurt that Jeff didn't want her to go with him. Did he not need her support? Or had her distraught husband been in such a hurry to get to Canton that he didn't want to wait for Rhonda to get dressed?

There was no way Rhonda could go back to bed now, so she slipped her robe on and plodded out to the kitchen to brew a cup of calming herbal tea. Fortunately, she didn't have to go to work until Monday, as she'd taken Thanksgiving, plus three more days off to get a few things done and rest when needed.

As she sat at the kitchen table, staring into her cup of tea, tears sprang to her eyes. She'd thought that, with determination, she and Jeff could get through anything in their own strength, but now she realized they couldn't. Certain things, like Jeff's restaurant burning down, were out of their control. The insurance policy Jeff had taken out on his business would no doubt pay enough so he could build a new restaurant, but that would take time. And since they'd have to pay their deductible first, what money they did receive might not be enough to build a new restaurant.

Rhonda sipped her tea. *I never imagined this kind of trouble would happen to Jeff and me.* She wished she could talk to someone about this right now, but she didn't want to wake her mother or sister during the middle of the night. She couldn't call Lois, either, because the good-natured Amish woman would surely be in bed. In addition to that, the Troyers didn't have a phone in their house. Even if she called and left a message on the answering machine in their phone shed, they probably wouldn't listen to it until later today.

At this moment, Rhonda desperately needed to talk to someone, so she did the only thing she could think of—she prayed. It was the first prayer Rhonda had uttered since she'd begged God to keep her dad from leaving home. That prayer had gone unanswered, because Dad had walked away from Mom and his daughters without looking back. Although he had paid child support, he'd rarely come around. He cared more about his new wife and the stepdaughter he'd inherited than he did his own girls.

As more tears fell, Rhonda prayed out loud, "Lord, if You're listening, and if You care about me, would You please provide answers and let Jeff and me know what direction to take now? We can't make it on my income alone, and it could be several months before Jeff is able to rebuild and get his restaurant open for business again."

Rhonda paused and pulled a tissue from the pocket of her robe to dry her eyes and blow her nose. Although she still felt concern, a small sense of peace pervaded her soul.

I wonder where that Bible is that I received for perfect attendance when I went to Bible school as a girl. Maybe I should look for it and do some reading while I'm waiting for Jeff to return.

An hour later, Rhonda sat on the living-room sofa with a Bible in her lap. After searching through several boxes in her closet, she had located the book.

Unsure of where to begin reading, Rhonda opened the New International Version of the Bible to a section where a purple ribbon had been placed by one of the Bible school teachers. It was the book of Romans, chapter 10. As an adult, she had never read from the Bible, but she remembered reading it and even memorizing some verses when she was a girl.

Maybe it's time for me to read it now, she told herself.

Rhonda began reading out loud with the first verse. When she came to verse 9, her throat clogged, and she had to swallow several times before going on. "If you declare with your mouth, 'Jesus is Lord,' and believe in your heart that God raised him from the dead, you will be saved."

Rhonda thought about the question Lois had asked her when they'd stood out in the snow, watching Orley and Jeff on their sleds. *"Do you have a personal relationship with God?"*

Rhonda had admitted that she and Jeff weren't the religious type and didn't go to church. She could still picture the look of concern on the Amish woman's face as she'd expressed her sorrow over hearing Rhonda's admission. She had tried to block out Lois's next statement about everyone needing a permanent feeling of peace and acceptance, which could only come from a relationship with God. But now, after reading the verse found in Romans, she realized that to have a relationship with God, one must first accept His Son as their Lord and Savior.

Rhonda bowed her head and closed her eyes as she prayed a heartfelt prayer: "Jesus, I believe that You are Lord, and I believe in my heart that God raised You from the dead. Please fill my life with Your peace and strengthen my faith no matter what trials I might face." Rhonda ended her prayer by asking God to keep Jeff safe and to provide for their needs.

As she sat holding the Bible in her lap, Rhonda felt such a sense of peace that she wanted to share it with someone right now. She wished it could be Jeff, but knowing how adamant he was about having nothing to do with religion, she had second thoughts. In fact, the more Rhonda thought about it, the more she realized the best thing she could do was say nothing—at least for now. It would not be good to get him any more riled up than he was already, and she didn't want anything to come between them. Perhaps if Jeff saw a change in her, she would feel free to share her conversion with him.

Canton

Jeff had given Rhonda a call once he'd arrived, and now he stood in his restaurant's parking lot next to Russ, staring at the remains of his restaurant while slowly shaking his head. "I can't believe this happened not only to me but to three other businesses as well."

"I know. It makes my blood boil to think that anyone could do such a horrible thing."

"There's absolutely nothing salvageable. That fire had to be really hot to do this kind of damage." Jeff continued to eye the smoking rubble while slowly shaking his head. "It feels like my whole world's crashed in on me."

"I can say this with certainty—I believe we are put through trials for a reason." Russ spoke with a softened tone.

Jeff's brows furrowed, but he didn't verbalize his thoughts. *Trials? But I'm a good person. Why does God allow bad things to happen to people like me?*

Russ placed his hand on Jeff's shoulder. "What are you gonna do, Boss? Do you plan to rebuild?"

Jeff's shoulders slumped, and he leaned slightly forward as he massaged his pulsating forehead. "I honestly don't know. There's so much to think about, and I'm feeling pretty overwhelmed right now."

"Of course, you are. Anyone would be if they'd just lost their business."

Jeff sucked in a deep breath and let it out slowly. "There are so many things to consider—how much my insurance will pay—how long it will take until the claim is settled—how much money it would take to rebuild—and what to do about my employees who are now out of a job."

Russ gave a nod. "You do have a lot to think about."

"What about you?" Jeff asked. "Will you take unemployment and hold out, hoping you'll get your job as manager back? Or would you rather move on and find something else?"

"Well, I. . .uh. . ." Russ put his hands in his jacket pockets as he rocked back and forth. "Guess I could get by on unemployment if I knew for sure you were going to reopen within a reasonable timeframe. Otherwise. . ."

"I wish I could offer you, as well as my other employees, a guarantee that you'd be returning to work soon, but I can't." Jeff's voice wavered. "Right now, all I can think about is the need to contact my insurance company with the bad news that my restaurant is gone, and I'll proceed from there." He looked once again at the pile of rubble before him and swallowed against the lump that had formed in his throat. When he'd arrived on the scene nearly two hours ago, he'd talked to the police and firemen and answered all their questions, but now it was time to go home. Jeff had hoped that after he'd left, Rhonda could go back to bed and fall asleep. But when he'd called earlier to let her know he'd arrived, she had answered right away. During their brief chat, she'd told him that she was too upset to go back to bed. Jeff asked her to try and get some sleep and told her not to worry. If he found her asleep when he arrived home, he'd go to bed too rather than try to think things through with a foggy brain.

Walnut Creek

When Jeff arrived home, he found Rhonda asleep on the couch in the living room. She looked so peaceful, he didn't want to wake her. He made his way quietly down the hall but didn't stop at the master bedroom. He was no longer tired, so instead of going to bed, Jeff headed for the garage to take care of some business.

Skirting around Rhonda's car, Jeff made his way over to the spot where his SUV should have been parked, had it not been for all the boxes of antiques and collectibles yet to be unpacked. He'd planned to put up more shelves in order to display his old bottles and jars but hadn't gotten around to it yet. Now, it no longer seemed important. Instead of sleeping, Jeff would go through each box and pick out the items he thought would bring in the most money.

Rhonda woke up and glanced at the antique clock on the mantel above the fireplace. It was 6:00 a.m., which meant she'd been sleeping at least three hours.

She pulled herself off the couch and went to the front window, relieved to see that Jeff's rig was parked outside. *I bet he went to bed after he got home from Canton, but I wonder why he didn't wake me.*

Rhonda looked in their room, but there was no sign of her husband. *He must be in his man cave.* She hurried down the hall and opened the door, but Jeff wasn't there either. *Could he be in the garage?*

When Rhonda entered the garage a few minutes later, she was surprised to see Jeff squatted next to several opened cardboard boxes. "What on earth are you doing?" she questioned.

He looked up at her and grimaced. "I'm doing what I should have done a long time ago. I'm going to sell most of my antiques if I can find the right buyers."

Rhonda blinked rapidly as she stared at him. "How come?"

"I won't be getting a settlement from the insurance company for at least thirty days, and we need money more than I need a bunch of old things sitting around collecting dust. So, my plan is to take most of these old things over to the Troyers' antique store and see if they will buy them. I may also run an ad in the paper."

Rhonda stood with her mouth slightly open.

"With Christmas just a month away, some people might be interested in buying some of my collectibles to give as gifts or even to keep for themselves." Jeff stood up and walked over to where she stood. "So, I'm gonna head over to Memory Keepers after breakfast. They should be open by then. Would you like to go with me?"

She shook her head. "But I would like you to tell me how bad the fire was and what happened while you were in Canton earlier this morning."

"I'll go over all that with you while we're eating breakfast."

"Okay." Rhonda gave Jeff a hug. "We've been through rough times before, and we'll get through this too. We just need to. . ." She stopped talking and gave his shoulder a pat. "I'll go get breakfast started while you finish what you're doing."

"Okay. Let me know when you're ready to eat."

She gave a brief nod. *Oh, how I wish I could share Jesus with Jeff right now. But I'm sure he would not be receptive.*

Jeff scratched the back of his head. He couldn't put his finger on it, but there was something different about Rhonda today. Despite the uncertainty of their future, there was a sense of calmness about her. In fact, her expression, which often revealed stress, was one of peace.

How odd, Jeff thought as he knelt again and pulled another box over to him. *It's not like my wife to appear so calm when we're in the middle of a crisis. Maybe it's all that relaxing herbal tea she's been drinking lately. Yep, that must be it.*

Chapter 33

"You look different this morning," Jeff said when he took a seat at the breakfast table. "Are you wearing different makeup?"

She shook her head. "I'm not wearing any makeup."

"Maybe it's the way you're wearing your hair."

"It's a ponytail, Jeff. There's nothing special about my hair." She took a bite of her scrambled eggs. *My husband appears to be avoiding the topic of what happened to his business. I'm sure he's holding in his thoughts and feelings.* "Are you going to talk about the fire now?"

"Yeah, sure." Jeff drank some of his coffee then set the mug down. "There's not much left of my restaurant. Nothing salvageable at least. It's hard to come to grips with what's happened to my livelihood, not to mention my employees, who will now be out of work." His eyes misted. "I had the awful job of calling the cooks and waitresses to let them know they'll need to go on unemployment or begin looking for new work elsewhere. Russ and I even drove around and looked at the other buildings that had burned, and they were all destroyed too." He pounded his fist on the table, causing some of his coffee to spill over. "It's not fair! I'm out of business and my employees have no jobs."

"But you'll rebuild and start over, right?"

"I—I don't know." Jeff's forehead wrinkled as he pushed his hair off his forehead. He needed a haircut, but that was not a priority—at least not today. The first order of business was to see Orley Troyer.

"Have you called your dad and told him what happened?"

"Not yet. How about your mom? Does she know?"

"No, but I plan to call her sometime today."

"I may have to ask Dad for a loan."

"Are you sure? In the past you haven't wanted to ask him for money."

"True, but I've never needed it this bad before." Jeff ate the last of his toast and pushed back his chair. "I'm gonna load all the boxes I've filled and head over to Memory Keepers now. Hopefully, I'll be able to sell some of the things today, and I won't have to ask my dad for as much money to borrow." He gave Rhonda a kiss before hurrying out of the room.

After Jeff's SUV pulled out of the yard, Rhonda put their breakfast dishes in the dishwasher and went to her home office to boot up the computer. Using her browser, she searched for a women's Bible study in her area. She found one listed and bookmarked it. As nice as it would be to fellowship with other Christian women, it would mean being gone from home, which would also mean she'd have to come up with an explanation to Jeff if he asked where she was going. *I'd like to tell him everything, but he'd be shocked at my change of heart—especially since we've agreed for a long time that neither of us wanted anything to do with religion.*

Rhonda was pleased when she discovered an online Bible study she could take, which might work better since it wouldn't compete with her work schedule or take her away from home. The topic Rhonda was most interested in was prayer, and they certainly needed a lot of that right now.

Rhonda turned away from the computer, picked up the phone, and called her mother. "Hi, Mom, there's something I need to tell you."

"What is it, Rhonda? You sound excited about something."

"I'm a Christian now, Mom. In the early hours this morning, I prayed and accepted the Lord as my Savior."

"Oh, Rhonda, that's wonderful. It's such an answer to prayer."

"Please don't say anything about it to Jeff, because he'd be upset if he knew."

"I won't mention it to him, but I don't think you should keep such an important occurence from your husband."

"I'll tell him when I feel the time is right." Rhonda paused and drank some of her sparkling mineral water. "There's something else I need to tell you."

"What is it, Rhonda? Is it more good news?"

"No, just the opposite. In the wee hours of this morning, Jeff's restaurant was destroyed by fire."

Rhonda heard the intake of her mother's breath. "Oh no! How did it happen?"

Rhonda told her what little she knew and ended by saying that three other businesses had also been burned. "The officials told Jeff that they're sure it was arson, so of course there will be an investigation."

"I hope they find out who did it. A crime like that should not go unpunished."

"If there were no witnesses, we might never know who was responsible."

"I would assume that Jeff has good insurance on the building."

"Yes, but it could be a month or even longer before the claim is settled."

"Will you be able to manage financially until then?" Mom asked.

"I—I think so. Jeff's going to sell some of his antiques, and he may talk to his dad about borrowing some money."

"I'm sure Don would loan it to him too." Mom spoke in an uplifted tone. "He's such a nice man. I still can't get over the way we found each other on that Christian dating site."

"Any plans to see him again?" Rhonda questioned.

"Yes. Before Jeff's dad left after our Thanksgiving gathering, he asked if he could take me out to dinner at a restaurant here in New Philly next Friday evening. I guess he doesn't mind the commute."

Hearing the excitement in her mother's voice, Rhonda smiled. "I'm sure you'll have a pleasant evening, Mom."

"Yes, I'm certain of it."

"Will you be seeing Don exclusively now or continue to see other men as well?"

"Our relationship is too new for me to speak for him, but as far as I'm concerned, I have no desire to date anyone else right now. Even during our family gathering on the Fourth of July, I enjoyed visiting with Jeff's father. It may be too soon to say this, but I have a good feeling about the possibility of a permanent relationship with Don."

Rhonda drank some more water and tried to picture Jeff's father and her mother as a married couple. *I wonder if it will ever come to that.*

"I hate to end this conversation, Mom, but I need to get some laundry done, so I'd better hang up."

"Okay. Thanks for calling, and remember, I'll be praying for both you and Jeff. I don't have a lot of money saved up, but if there's anything I can do to help, please let me know."

"Thanks, Mom. Have a good day."

When Rhonda hung up, she rose from her desk and walked over to the window to look out. The clouds had parted, and the sun shone brightly, making the snow that was left in their yard look like tiny diamonds that had been scattered about. Although their future was uncertain, she felt an inner peace that hadn't been there until she'd found a personal relationship with the Lord. Now if only Jeff would do the same.

~

Carrying one cardboard box in his hands, Jeff entered Memory Keepers and placed it on the front counter, which Orley stood behind.

"What have ya got in there?" the Amish man asked.

"Old milk bottles I'd like to sell. I have more in my vehicle, along with some canning jars, a few gas lamps, and some insulators."

Orley tipped his head and looked at Jeff through squinted eyes. "You want to put all those items on consignment here?"

Jeff opened the flap on the box so that the items inside could be seen. "I need some money right now and was hoping you might be able to buy some or all of them outright."

Orley slipped both thumbs under his suspenders and gave them a light snap. "With it being this close to Christmas, some of these items could sell right away, but I'm not in a position to buy everything from you today."

"Oh, I see." Jeff dropped his gaze.

"Whatever I'm not able to pay you for can be left here on consignment, though. Could be those might sell between now and the holiday as well."

"Okay. I'll go get the other boxes, and after you've looked through them, you can let me know which items you're able to buy from me today." Jeff started to move away from the counter but stopped when Orley posed another question.

"Mind if I ask why you're in need of money? Are you looking to buy something special for your wife's Christmas present?"

Jeff shook his head. "Somebody set fire to my restaurant last night, so I'm out of business, which means, except for what Rhonda makes, there's no other income for us right now."

Orley's eyes widened. "I am sorry to hear this. Do you know what started the fire?"

"Three other businesses in the area were also burned down, so it was obviously arson."

"That's a shame. It's hard to understand why a person would do something so hateful."

"Tell me about it." Jeff's fingernails bit into his palms as he curled his fingers into them.

"I'll tell you what... I'll pay you a fair price for the items in this box, and when you bring the rest in, I will write them up to be sold on consignment." Orley leaned closer to Jeff. "My wife and I will be praying for you and Rhonda during this difficult time."

Prayers, prayers, prayers. Jeff gritted his teeth. *Why do Christians believe that prayer is the answer for everything?*

~

After Jeff left the Troyers' antique store with a few hundred dollars, he decided it was time to give his dad a call. Still sitting in the parking lot, he picked up his cell phone and clicked Dad's number.

"Hey, Son, I was about to call your number, but you beat me to it." A short pause ensued. "I heard what happened to your restaurant, and I wanted you to know how sorry I am."

"Who told? Did my wife call and let you know?"

"No, I heard it from Rhonda's mother. She called me a while ago."

"I see. Guess Rhonda must have called her after I left the house."

"You're not at home?"

"No, I just left the antique store here in Walnut Creek."

"You went out shopping for antiques?"

Jeff's facial muscles tightened. "No, Dad, I was not shopping. I need money right now, so I went there to sell off some of my collectibles."

"You don't need to do that, Son. I'm more than happy to provide whatever money you'll need to get by on until your insurance pays and you're able to rebuild the restaurant."

"I appreciate the offer, Dad, and I'll pay you back just as soon as I can. The only thing is, I may not build a new restaurant."

"How come?"

"For one thing, I'm getting tired of the commute. I'd like to find some other kind of work closer to home."

"What type of job?"

"I don't know. There are quite a few restaurants in our area. Maybe one of them is hiring."

"Doing what, Jeff?"

"Beats me. I'll wait tables or cook if I have to. I started out that way, remember?"

"Of course I do, but I can't imagine you going from owning your own business to working for someone else in any position."

"One does what one has to when the going gets rough." Jeff gripped his cell phone a little tighter.

"Don't let bitterness take control and keep you from making wise decisions."

"I don't need any lectures, Dad. The only help I need right now is..."

"Just give me a number, and I'll put a check in the mail for you. Or would you rather that I come down there and give it to you in person?"

"No, that's okay. You can mail the check." Jeff stated the amount he needed and was about to say goodbye when his dad spoke again.

"Ever since June called and told me what happened, I've been praying for you—that God will provide for your needs and bring you back to Him."

Great! More prayer and more preaching. What's my dad trying to do—make me feel guilty for turning my back on God?

Jeff gritted his teeth. "Okay, Dad, thanks in advance for your willingness to help out. I need to go now, but I'll let you know when the check arrives."

"All right then. I'll talk to you again soon. Oh, and please tell Rhonda I said hello and that my prayers are with her too."

"I'll give her the message. Bye, Dad."

Jeff clicked off his phone and put his key in the ignition. It was time to go home and give Rhonda the news that, thanks to his father, they'd be okay financially until the insurance check came in.

As Jeff drove out of the parking lot, his stomach knotted. *First Orley and now my dad trying to cram their religious views down my throat. I don't know why they won't let up, but I wish they'd keep their opinions to themselves. Makes me want to avoid them both, but it wouldn't be right to ignore my own father.* He rapped his knuckles on the steering wheel. *And in spite of Orley's religious inclinations, he's a nice guy and we have our enjoyment of antiques in common.* Jeff hated to admit it, but the truth was he liked hanging around the Amish man.

A few miles down the road, Jeff spotted a sign nailed to a fence post bordering someone's land. As he drew closer, the words came fully into his view: You Matter to God.

He groaned. "Sure don't remember seeing that sign before."

A little farther on, he saw another sign. This one read: Are You Having Problems? Give Them to God.

Disgusted, Jeff looked away and kept his focus on the road. *What kind of a religious fanatic would tack signs like that along this country road?*

He could hardly believe it, but one more sign came into view: Trust in God at All Times.

"This is getting ridiculous! Is someone trying to tell me something?" Jeff shook his head. Maybe he was seeing things because of fatigue. After all, he'd only had a few hours of sleep last night before that crazy rooster crow tone woke him. *I need to go home and take a nap*, Jeff told himself. *I'm bound to feel better after a few hours of sleep.*

⁓

Rhonda's stomach growled. *Could it be lunchtime already?* She glanced at the clock near the bottom of her computer screen and was surprised to see that it was half past noon. She'd been so engrossed in the Bible study for new Christians that she'd found online, time had gotten away from her. She'd learned a lot so far—from the scriptures listed as well as the study leader's comments. One of those statements was that when a person receives Jesus, they become a child of God.

I don't have to dwell on the failures of my earthly father anymore, Rhonda thought. *From now on, my focus should be on my heavenly Father, who loved me so much that He sent His Son to earth to die for me.* A lump formed in her throat. *I only wish Jeff would accept God's gift of salvation too. I need to keep praying for him until he does.*

Hearing their front gate open, Rhonda looked out the window and saw Jeff's SUV pull into the yard. *Oh, good, he's home. I hope everything went okay.*

She left her office and headed down the hall. A short time later,

Jeff entered the house and took off his boots, leaving them in the hall near the coat tree. "How'd it go at the antique store?" Rhonda asked. "Did Orley buy any of the items you'd brought?"

"Just one box. The rest he took on consignment." He released a heavy sigh. "I called my dad, and he's agreed to loan us some money. Said he'd put a check in the mail."

"That was good of him, but we could have driven up to his place to get it."

"I thought of that, and he even mentioned coming here with the money, but I asked him to mail it instead."

"How come?"

Jeff scrunched up his face. "Because I didn't want to hear more of his religious babble. I've had enough religion crammed down my throat for one day."

Rhonda cringed inwardly. Now was definitely not the time to tell her husband about the prayer she'd uttered early this morning. If Jeff knew she'd given her heart to Jesus, he'd pull away from her emotionally and maybe even physically.

"Are you hungry?" she asked. "Shortly before you arrived, I was thinking about fixing some lunch."

Jeff shook his head. "I don't want anything to eat, but I am exhausted, and I need to take a nap."

"Of course you do. It's been too many hours since you've slept." Rhonda put her arms around Jeff and rubbed the small of his back. "Sleep well, and if you're hungry when you wake up, I'll fix you something to eat."

"Thanks." He kissed her forehead then pulled away and shuffled down the hall.

Rhonda remained in the entrance. Taking a seat on the bench near the door, she bowed her head. *Heavenly Father, Please soften my husband's heart and open his eyes to the truth. Show Jeff how much You love him, and please bring him to a saving knowledge of Christ. In Jesus' name, Amen.*

Chapter 34

"What's all this?" Lois asked when she came out of the back room and found Orley kneeling beside several cardboard boxes in the middle of their store.

He looked up at her with eyebrows drawn together. "Jeff Davis came by a while ago and asked if I could buy all this from him." Orley pointed to each of the boxes.

Lois tapped a finger against her lips. "That seems odd. As much as he likes antiques, I'm surprised he'd be willing to part with any of his collectibles."

"Under normal circumstances, I don't think he would, but his restaurant in Canton burned down, and he's in need of money right now."

"I'm so sorry to hear that." Lois knelt on the floor beside her husband. "Were you able to buy everything from him?"

He shook his head. "We don't have that much cash on hand, and I would never have done that anyway without consulting you. So, I bought one box, but the rest of the items he left on consignment, and I'm hoping for his sake they will all sell."

Lois put both hands against her cheeks. "I feel bad for Jeff and Rhonda. They've been through a lot the past few months, and I'm sure it's been hard on their marriage as well as their finances."

Orley nodded and rose to his feet. Then he reached out his hand and helped Lois up. "When Jeff was here, he seemed so despondent, wearing an almost hopeless expression. I told him we'd be praying for them, but I don't believe my words meant that much to Jeff."

"I think he's trying to bear the burden of all this on his own shoulders." Lois pinched the skin just above the neckline of her dress. "What that young couple needs the most is a personal relationship with the Lord. If only one of them could make a commitment to the Lord, maybe the other one would in time."

"I agree, but it's not something we can force them to do. They must both come to a place where they realize their need for Jesus."

"Very true. So, we'll keep praying for them like we have been— that something will happen to open their eyes—and in the meantime, we'll ask God to show us if there's anything more we can do to help out."

He bent his head and rubbed noses with her. "Sure am glad the Good Lord brought such a *schmaert* woman into my life."

She smiled and gave his belly a little poke. "I had to be smart to choose a wonderful Christian man like you."

~

Jeff stood in front of the bathroom mirror, a pained expression staring back at him. The skin around his eyes bunched, and he felt a deep ache at the back of his throat, making it difficult to swallow. *I'm glad Dad was willing to loan us some money, but if I don't rebuild the restaurant, I'll need to find a job so we have two incomes to make it through. My wife doesn't need the extra stress of thinking she'll have to work longer hours to compensate for my lack of income either.*

Jeff massaged his temples while he lingered in front of the mirror. He figured he and Rhonda could get caught up with their debts, but now losing the restaurant had set them back. He'd worked hard to make his restaurant a success, and for what—to see it lying in a heap of rubble and ashes?

Maybe this is God's way of punishing me for turning my back on Him and denying that He even exists. Jeff clenched his jaw until it throbbed. *I have every right to be angry at God. He took my mother when I needed her the most.*

How many times had he told himself this? One hundred— maybe more? Sometimes the anger Jeff tried so hard to hold in caused him to explode over little things, which of course had not been good for his and Rhonda's marriage.

There had been times when his wife had compared the situation with her dad walking out on her family to him losing his mother to cancer. As far as Jeff was concerned, there was no comparison. Although Rhonda's father had abandoned his family, he was still alive. Jeff's mother's body had died, and maybe her spirit had too. He wasn't sure that the people who'd professed Christianity while they were alive went to heaven when they died. Jeff didn't know if there really was a heaven. Some people believed that when a person passed away, their consciousness died along with their body, and they just evaporated into nothingness like vapor.

To stifle his disconcerting thoughts and give himself a boost, Jeff grabbed a washcloth and wet it with cool water then rubbed it all over his face. Normally, this would have revived him but not today—he was too exhausted.

I need to sleep and quit thinking about things, Jeff told himself. *All the speculation in the world won't change the fact that my mother is gone and so is my restaurant. I can rebuild my place of business, but I'll never see Mom again.*

Jeff's shoulders curled forward as he shuffled wearily out of the bathroom. He grabbed the folded blanket at the foot of the bed, flopped down, and covered himself with it. It wasn't long before Jeff drifted off to sleep.

~

"Jeff.. .Jeff.. .Jeff.. . Come to me, Son. Follow the light."

Jeff recognized his mother's voice, but he couldn't see her face. It was as though he had fallen into a black hole or had gotten trapped in some dark cave.

He turned his head to the right and then the left, searching for some sign of light, but there was none. Jeff groped around with both hands, hoping to find something familiar he could grasp, but it was useless. No matter how hard Jeff tried, he couldn't get his bearings and saw no sign of light.

"Let go of your fear and take a step forward."

Jeff did as the voice asked.

"That's right. Now take another step and then two more. Soon you will see the light."

Once more, Jeff did as he was told. To his relief, he saw a tiny ray of light in the distance. In desperation, he kept moving forward. "Mom, is that you?"

"Yes, Son, keep moving toward the light."

Jeff continued, until he was bathed in a glorious radiance like he had never seen before. He blinked against the brightness and stood in awe at the sight before him. There stood his mother, dressed in white and holding a gold-plated sign etched with elegant lettering in one hand. It read: BE STILL, AND KNOW THAT I AM GOD.

But Mom's not God. Why is she holding that sign? It resembled the one Orley had given him, only this was more elaborate and beautiful.

Jeff's mother turned to her left, making a sweeping gesture with her other hand.

He inhaled a deep breath as his gaze became fixed on a magnificent city—every building and all the streets were made of gold. Could this be heaven? Jeff gulped in another breath. Am I dead?

He shook his head. No, I can't be. I don't remember dying. But if I am dead, then I don't deserve to be in heaven because I turned my back on God and rejected His Son.

"Please, Jeff, don't be mad at God for taking me away. I'm in a much better place." His mom spoke in a pleading tone.

Hot tears rolled down Jeff's cheeks and spilled onto his shirt as his mother's image began to fade. "Don't go, Mom," he shouted. "Please don't leave me like you did before."

"If you accept Christ as your Savior, I promise, we will see each other *again. Goodbye, Son. I love you very much." As quickly as she'd appeared, Jeff's mother vanished.*

"I love you too." Jeff dropped to his knees and sobbed. Is it true, Mom? If I accept Christ, will we be reunited when I die?

⟶

Jeff's eyes snapped open, and he blinked multiple times. He sat up straight, his body drenched in sweat. *Was it a dream? A figment of my imagination? Or did I actually speak to my mom?* It had seemed so real. Whatever it was, Jeff felt certain that God's hand had been in it. For the first time since his mother died, Jeff knew without reservation that God was real, and when his mom's soul left her body, she had gone to heaven.

"I want to go there someday too." With assurance, he spoke out loud.

Jeff got up and knelt on the floor along his side of the bed. As he prayed and gave his heart to the Lord, tears flowed down his face. "Forgive me, Father," he murmured. "I know that Your Son died on the cross for my sins, and I'm sorry that I have been breaking Your commandments while living in this world." Jeff paused a few seconds and swallowed hard. "Please fill my life with Your love and peace."

Jeff remained on the floor in prayer for several more minutes before standing up. He remembered how he'd been so desperate at the Troyers' shop and hoped Orley could come through for him. Calling on his dad to rescue him from his financial situation had also shown how worried Jeff was. Yet all the while, God had waited for Jeff to call upon Him and pray for his needs. *I'm glad my heavenly Father is so patient and forgiving.*

He combed a hand through his tousled hair. As much as Jeff wanted to share the wonderful experience he'd just had with Rhonda, he couldn't do it today. If he told her that he had given his heart to the Lord, she would be upset and think Jeff was trying to pull her into Christianity. So for now, at least, he would keep his conversion a secret.

This experience felt right, and he remembered how, back in his youth, he'd enjoyed going to Sunday school and learning about Jesus. Jeff remembered praying before going to sleep and at the beginning of their meals with his family. It was good reuniting himself with that, and this time he would make sure not to turn his back on Jesus ever again. It would be hard not to share his return to Jesus with Rhonda, but for now he'd try. Someday, however, when he felt the time was right, Jeff would witness to his wife. He hoped when that time came, she would be open to the idea of accepting Christ as her Savior too.

Rhonda had opened the door a crack and peeked into their bedroom a short time ago. The room was quiet except for the familiar soft rhythm of breathing that was soothing to her ears. She'd found Jeff sprawled out on the bed sound asleep. He had changed into some sweatpants and looked content while he slept there. It was good that he'd gone in to take a nap. Between lack of sleep and dealing with the stress of losing his restaurant, she felt sure he'd been on the verge of collapse. If only he could experience the sense of peace in his heart that she'd felt since accepting Christ as her Savior. Rhonda struggled with the desire to tell him about it, but if he reacted negatively, their marriage could suffer even more than it had in the past. She couldn't chance it right now.

Rhonda closed the door to insure that her husband continued to receive the rest that he needed. She turned to leave, and out of the blue, the words of the plaque the Troyers had given them popped into her mind. *I'd almost forgotten about that. It should still be out in the garage where Jeff put it. I hope one day we can agree to hang our anniversary gift from Orley and Lois in a special place here in our home.*

Rhonda tiptoed down the hall and went into her office. Since Jeff was asleep, this was a good time to read more scripture. As she entered the room, her nose wrinkled. "My office seems a little stuffy. I need to let in some fresh air." She stepped over to open the window and paused to watch some birds feeding at a nearby feeder. *They sure are fun to observe.*

Rhonda took in enough air to fill her lungs and then released it slowly. *I do feel at peace. . .thank You, Lord.*

She moved from the window, took a seat at the desk, and opened her Bible to a list of topics at the back. Perhaps there would be some verses that would help her know exactly how to pray for their situation right now. Before she got started, the strong need for a snack led her to reach into her desk drawer for the protein bar she'd put there the other day. After removing the wrapper, she indulged herself with its sweet chocolate covering and the rich peanut butter center. *I'm glad there was only one of these in my drawer,* she mused, *or I'd be tempted to eat more.*

As Rhonda enjoyed her treat, she thought about the positives in her life. *I'm married to a hard-working man; I am healthy; I have a job that pays well; and the best thing of all is I have the Lord in my life.* She reached for a tissue and wiped off her hands before grabbing the Bible again.

As Rhonda turned several pages and looked at the different topics, her gaze came to rest on the word *Forgiveness*. Underneath it was written: "Un-forgiveness is like a cancer—if you do not take care of it, the disease will eat away at your soul."

Rhonda wrote down some of the passages about forgiving that were listed, and then she turned in her Bible to Matthew 6:14–15 (NIV). A feeling of guilt crept into her soul as she read the words silently: *"For if you forgive other people when they sin against you, your heavenly Father will also forgive you. But if you do not forgive others their sins, your Father will not forgive your sins."*

Rhonda's thoughts went to her father, and she realized that she had never forgiven him for what he'd done to her mother, which in turn had affected her and Gwen's lives as well.

"So, if I don't forgive my dad, my Father in heaven will not forgive me," Rhonda whispered, nearly choking on the words.

Tears pooled in her eyes and dripped onto her hot cheeks. *I can't call myself a Christian if I'm unable to forgive.*

Rhonda closed her eyes and bowed her head. *Dear Lord: Forgive me for harboring ill feelings toward my dad all these years. Although what he did was wrong, I have been guilty of not being willing to forgive him.* She paused to swipe at her tears. *Forgive me, Jesus, for every bad thought I've had about my dad. Please give me the courage and the right words to write Dad a letter, letting him know that I have forgiven him.*

Rhonda had finished her prayer and was about to look at some other Bible passages, when she heard footsteps coming down the hall. Quickly wiping her eyes, she put the Bible in her desk drawer and left her office. As Jeff approached Rhonda in the hall, she was surprised to see his unfocused gaze. His face and neck were flushed with color. Perhaps he was still groggy from having just gotten up.

"You didn't sleep very long," she said. "Did you get enough rest?"

"I slept as long as I needed to." Jeff kept walking. "I need my cell phone. Think I left it in the kitchen."

"Are you sure? I don't recall seeing it there when I heated some soup for my lunch."

"It's okay. I'll find it." Jeff stopped walking and looked at Rhonda.

She tipped her head. *Is that a look of peace I see on my husband's face? Could a short nap have been all that he needed to calm down?*

Jeff slipped his arm around Rhonda's waist. "There's no need to worry about anything, honey. I'm confident that it's all going to work out."

Rhonda stood speechless. Could this be the same man who'd trudged down the hall nearly two hours ago with a look of defeat? She had no idea what had happened between then and now to lift Jeff's spirits, but it didn't really matter. She was pleased to see the improvement.

Chapter 35

Monday morning when Jeff went to the mailbox, there was an envelope from his father. Much to his relief, the check had made it. Jeff waited until he was back in the house to open it. Dad's check should get them by for at least a month. He had also included a note saying that if Jeff needed more to let him know.

Should I tell Dad about the dream I had a few days ago? Jeff felt the need to tell someone, and he was sure his father would be happy to hear that he'd given his heart to the Lord. He'd just have to make it clear that he didn't want Rhonda to know.

Since she had gone to work at the hotel, Jeff had the house to himself. That gave him the chance to make the call to his dad and not have to worry about her hearing what he said.

Jeff took off his jacket, hung it on the clothes tree, and headed to the kitchen to get coffee. It felt strange being home on a workday, knowing he no longer had a restaurant to run. He'd have to adjust to not seeing his employees and visiting with the customers who came in.

Jeff grabbed a mug from the cupboard and filled it with the steaming brew. Once that was done, he got his cell phone and took a seat at the table. Jeff punched in his dad's number and was disappointed when a voice message came on, saying Dad was unavailable now and to please leave a message.

"Hey, Dad. It's Jeff. I got the check today and wanted to say thanks. I'll pay you back as soon as I can." Jeff paused, trying to decide whether to say anything about his dream but decided to wait until he could speak directly to his dad. "Please give me a call when you have the time. There's something else I want to tell you."

Jeff hung up, grabbed his coffee, and headed down the hall to his man cave. This time, though, instead of watching TV, he planned to spend some time praying about the future. After that, he would make a trip to the Christian bookstore in town to buy a study Bible. Afterward, he might drop by the Troyers' house to talk with Orley. He certainly needed to tell someone about his good news. Since Memory Keepers was usually closed on Mondays, he hoped he would find the kindly Amish man at home.

Orley had just finished chopping and stacking firewood when a vehicle pulled into the yard. He smiled after the driver got out and began walking toward the house.

Orley extended his hand. "It's good to see you, Jeff."

The young man nodded. "I'm glad to see you too. I have some good news I want to share." Jeff grinned widely. "Actually, there are two pieces of good news."

"I'm always eager to hear positive news." Orley gestured to the house. "Let's go inside where it's warmer, and you can tell me about it."

"Sounds good."

Orley led the way, and when they entered the house, Lois greeted them at the entryway. She shook Jeff's hand. "It's nice to see you. Is your wife along?"

"No, Rhonda's working at the hotel today."

"Orley told me what happened to your restaurant. I was sorry to hear about it." Lois spoke in a soothing tone of voice. There was no mistaking the sympathy she felt.

"Yeah, it was a real shock," Jeff said. "But in the long run, it could turn out to be a blessing."

"Let's take a seat and you can tell me about it." Orley gestured to the living room.

"Would you two like some coffee or hot chocolate?" Lois asked.

"Hot chocolate sounds good," Jeff replied.

"I'd like some too." Orley smiled and gave his wife's arm a pat. "Danki."

"You are most welcome."

When Lois headed to the kitchen, Orley and Jeff seated themselves in two adjacent chairs with a small table between them.

"I'm eager to hear your good news," Orley said.

"For one thing, my dad loaned me enough money to get by until my insurance pays the claim I put in for the loss of my restaurant."

"Good to hear. Your father sounds like a nice man."

"He is. Unfortunately, I haven't always appreciated him the way that I should."

"Sometimes we tend to take people—especially family members included—for granted. It's important for us to focus on their good qualities instead of looking for things we don't like about them."

"True, and I've been guilty of doing that in the past—especially where my dad is concerned." Jeff shook his head. "But not anymore. From now on, I'm going to focus on his positive traits and try to show my appreciation."

"Good thinking. If I had a son or daughter, I'd hope they would feel that way too."

Jeff sat quietly for a few minutes before he spoke again. "I've been thinking about my restaurant and whether or not I should rebuild it."

"Is there a reason why you wouldn't want to?"

"For one thing, I'm getting tired of the commute." Jeff crossed his feet at the ankles. "It's also a big responsibility to provide jobs for my employees and oversee everything that needs to be done."

"What would you do if you didn't rebuild?" Orley questioned.

Jeff shrugged. "I'm not sure. Maybe see if I can find a job closer to home or even something I can do while working from our house."

"I see."

Lois came into the room, carrying a tray with cookies and two mugs of hot chocolate. She set the tray on the table between them and started to leave the room.

"Aren't you going to join us?" Orley asked.

"I have some things I need to do at my desk, but you two go ahead and enjoy the snacks while you visit." She looked over at Jeff. "Please tell your wife I said hello, and I'll look forward to seeing her sometime soon."

Jeff smiled and reached for a cookie. "Thanks, I'll give her your message."

After Lois left the room, Orley picked up his mug and took a drink. "Ah. . .there's nothing quite like hot chocolate to warm a body on a chilly day such as this."

"I agree. Now would you like to hear my other good news?"

"Of course."

Jeff leaned closer to Orley's chair and whispered, "Can you keep what I'm about to say a secret—at least from my wife?"

Taken by surprise, all Orley could do was give a brief nod. He did not like keeping secrets but didn't want to hurt Jeff's feelings. And if Orley said no, most likely Jeff would not open up and say whatever was on his mind.

"When I came back from Canton after looking at what little remained of my restaurant, I felt exhausted and went to the bedroom to take a nap."

Orley listened as Jeff went on to say that he'd had a dream—one that felt as though it was actually happening.

"I saw my mother," Jeff said. "She talked to me, and I responded. It seemed like we were standing on the outskirts of heaven." He paused and took a drink from his mug. "She held a sign with the same verse of scripture on it as the one you gave Rhonda and me for our anniversary."

" 'Be still, and know that I am God?' "

"Yeah."

Orley couldn't help wondering where this was leading, but he remained quiet and listened as Jeff went on to tell him all the things that his mother had said.

"I believe God gave me that dream or whatever it was for a reason. He wanted me to understand, without a doubt, that He is God and there is a heaven where believers go after they die." Jeff's voice cracked, and tears welled in his eyes. "When I woke up, I got on my knees and prayed. I asked God to forgive my sins and told Him that I believe His Son, Jesus, died for me." Jeff reached into his pocket, pulled out a handkerchief, and blew his nose. "I'm a believer now, Orley, and for the first time since my mother died, I feel a sense of peace."

Overcome with emotion, Orley had a hard time holding back his own tears. How thankful he was that God had answered his prayers for Jeff. It gave him the reassurance that whenever there was a need, a Christian should never quit praying. "Pray without ceasing," the Bible said.

"Thank you for sharing this wonderful news with me," Orley stated with conviction. "I'm just a bit confused as to why you don't want your wife to know about your conversion."

"Rhonda is against all things that involve religion. Well, let me back up a bit. We both used to be against religion for our own reasons. Rhonda and I felt justified in feeling that way because we felt that God had let us down in the past." He wiped away an escaped tear. "If you don't mind, I'll share my wife's story with you. It won't take long."

When Orley nodded, Jeff continued speaking. "She used to go to Bible school when she was a girl, but when her dad divorced her mother and married another woman, Rhonda became bitter and angry with God for not answering her prayers."

"I see."

"If Rhonda knew that I, who used to feel the same way she does, now have a personal relationship with Jesus, she would be very upset." Jeff took another drink and set his mug down. "We've had our share of marital problems, and I'm sure many of them were my fault." He reached up and rubbed the back of his neck. "I feel certain that if she knew I was a Christian, it would put an even bigger strain on our relationship. She might walk away from the marriage. So, I do not see any option but to keep it a secret. Don't you agree?"

Orley felt as though he was on the hot seat right now. He remembered the things their bishop had said to him and Lois before pronouncing them man and wife. The minister had stated that they needed to practice good communication in their marriage and divorce was not an option. It didn't make sense to Orley that anyone would leave their spouse because they said they'd become a Christian. Their belief in Christ had always been an important part of his and Lois's marriage. In fact, Orley looked forward to the time of devotions they had together after supper each evening. No way would their religious views put a wedge between him and his wife. *But unlike me, Jeff is English and in a different situation with his wife. It's clear that he's trusting my character enough to share what's on his heart. For that I feel honored.*

Speaking kindly but with every assurance that what he was saying was true, Orley said, "I will not repeat anything you have said to me today to your wife, but personally, I think you are wrong to not tell her."

Jeff stiffened. "You don't understand. Rhonda is as adamant about having nothing to do with God as I was before I had that dream. Which, by the way," he added. "I'm sure was ordained by God."

Orley reached over and placed one hand on Jeff's knee. "As I stated previously, I won't mention any of what you have said to Rhonda, but I will be praying that God gives you the courage to tell her when you feel the time is right."

Jeff slowly nodded. "I hope I'll eventually be able to do that, because it's not easy holding in something that was life changing for me. In the meantime, though, I want to be a good husband and try to make up for all the times I said hurtful things to Rhonda."

"That should add strength to your marriage, and perhaps after she sees the change in you, she'll be more open to hearing about your new relationship with the Lord."

"That's what I'm hoping." Jeff took another cookie and dunked it in what was left of his hot chocolate.

Orley pulled his fingers through his beard as he tried to reason things out. *Although Jeff said he didn't want me to tell Rhonda, he said nothing about Lois. I'd like her to be praying for Jeff and Rhonda too, so after he leaves, I'm going to tell her what he said.*

⁓

Jeff had just pulled into his own yard when his cell phone rang. Seeing that it was his dad, he shut off his SUV and took the call. "Hey, Dad, did you get my message?"

"Yes, I sure did. Glad to know the check got there okay."

"I'll pay you back as soon as I get my insurance check."

"No problem. I'm not worried about it." There was a slight pause on Dad's end. "You mentioned in your message that there was something else you wanted to talk to me about."

"Yep, there is." Taking a deep breath, Jeff launched into the story about his dream and what had followed when he'd awakened.

He heard his dad's quick intake of breath. "Wow, Jeff, that's amazing! I'm so happy for you. This is certainly an answer to prayer."

"I wish you could have seen her, Dad. Mom was absolutely beautiful. Her face appeared to be glowing."

"You are blessed to have had a dream like that."

"I know, and since I have plenty of time to myself these days, I'm going to check around and see if there are any men's Bible study classes near me that I could attend."

"Sounds like a good plan. Spending time in the Word will help to strengthen your faith."

"I made a trip to our local Christian bookstore earlier today and bought a study Bible."

"That's great. So, what did Rhonda say when you told her about turning your life over to Christ?"

"I–I haven't said anything to her about the dream or my prayer afterward. She has no idea I accepted the Lord as my Savior."

"Shouldn't you tell her something as important as that? Wouldn't it be great if your testimony led her to Christ?"

"Yes, it would, but to be honest, before my conversion, Rhonda and I both felt that God had let us down in big ways. We agreed it was best to stay away from anything of a religious nature. But now that's behind me, and I'm ready to pursue a new life with Jesus. My biggest concern, though, is that my wife needs the Lord too. Rhonda's always been adamant about her feelings toward God. When she was a girl, she used to pray that her father and mother would stay together, but her prayers were not answered in the way she wanted. Since that time, she's held a lot of bitterness in her heart toward God as well as her father."

"Wasn't that the way you felt before your conversion?"

"Yeah, I was angry at God for taking Mom. But now I feel different. I have a new understanding of things."

"I'm sure you do, which is why you might be the one who can reach your wife."

"But she might get angry and accuse me of trying to cram religion down her throat. That's how I used to feel when people stated that they were praying for me or said preachy things that did nothing but irritate me."

"I understand your apprehension where Rhonda is concerned, but I wish you would give it more thought."

"I will, Dad. I really do want to share Jesus with her, but now is not the right time."

"Any time's the right time to share God's love and the redemption He offers because of His Son. Pray for the right words to say, and speak them from the heart with love."

Jeff looked in his rearview mirror and saw Rhonda's car pulling in. "I'd better go, Dad. My wife just got home."

"Okay, I'll talk to you again soon. And if we don't see each other before, I'm hoping we can enjoy each other's company on Christmas Day."

"Umm. . .Rhonda and I haven't made any plans yet for Christmas."

"I figured you hadn't, so I was thinking it might be nice if you came here to my place for Christmas this year. I'm planning to invite June as well."

"I'll talk to Rhonda about it and get back to you, okay?"

"Sure, Son. Oh, and Jeff. . ."

"Yeah, Dad?"

"I love you."

"Love you too."

When Jeff hung up, he got out of his rig, waved at Rhonda before she pulled her car into the garage, and went inside to wait for her. Jeff didn't know whether he had the courage to speak to Rhonda about God today, but he looked forward to spending time with her.

Chapter 36

Jeff left the Christian bookstore whistling and with a spring in his step. Inside the bag he carried was a daily devotional, which he would keep hidden in a safe place in his man cave since Rhonda rarely came in there anymore.

Jeff still hadn't figured out what was going on with his wife. When she wasn't cooking or doing some chore around the house, she often retreated to her office. Jeff figured she was either doing hotel work from home or playing some computer game. Her favorite was a word game that claimed to help strengthen a person's brain. So, whenever Rhonda was holed up in her office, Jeff took advantage of the time to read the Bible, which helped to bolster his faith.

It had been two weeks since Jeff's restaurant burned down, and with each passing day, he became more convinced that he did not want to rebuild. It had been a difficult decision, but yesterday Jeff had called each of his employees and given them the news. Most said they understood and had already begun looking for new jobs, but Russ had been a little put out with Jeff's decision. Jeff apologized, and after explaining his reason in detail, Russ finally said he understood and wished his boss well in whatever he decided to do for employment.

Jeff unlocked his SUV and put his purchase on the passenger seat. *Even though I'm going through rough times right now, the Lord is giving me hope.* He glanced again at the bag. *I can't wait to start using my new devotional this evening.*

Since the Christian bookstore wasn't far from the antique store, Jeff decided to make that his next stop. He hadn't talked with Orley since he'd dropped by his house to share the news that he'd become a Christian, so it would be nice to connect with the kindly Amish man again and let him know what he'd decided. Hopefully, his new friend wouldn't be too busy with customers and would have some time to talk.

⁓

When Jeff entered Memory Keepers a short time later, he saw Orley talking with an elderly Amish man at the counter, while Lois visited with an Amish woman, who Jeff figured might be the older man's wife.

Since they were both busy at the moment, Jeff wandered around the store, looking at the few milk bottles on display. He didn't see any of the ones he'd brought in and left on consignment, so he hoped that meant they had sold. Although the money he'd put in the bank from his dad's check would keep them afloat as far as paying bills and buying gas for their vehicles as well as grocery items, it would be nice to have some cash to buy Christmas presents. The holiday was getting closer, and after discussing it with Rhonda, they had decided to accept the invitation they'd received to spend Christmas Day at his dad's place in Cleveland. Jeff looked forward to it, but he wasn't sure about Rhonda. She'd been acting out of character ever since his restaurant burned. Although she was much nicer to him than she had been previously, Jeff had a feeling his wife was keeping something from him. He wanted to ask but didn't want to start a discussion that could end up in an argument.

When Orley and Lois's customers left the shop, Jeff smiled and walked over to Orley. "Do you have a few minutes to talk?" he asked.

"Sure do." Orley grinned in his usual friendly manner. "Why

don't we go in the back room where it's private?"

"Are you sure? What if more customers come in?"

"It won't be a problem. I'll ask Lois to let me know."

Before Orley had a chance to speak to his wife, she spoke up. "I heard what you said, and don't worry, I'll let you know if things get busier than I can handle." She glanced around and smiled at Jeff. "Looks like you came here alone again today."

"Yeah, Rhonda's at work."

"How's she doing?"

"From what I can tell, Rhonda's okay. She's been working longer hours than normal so she can take a few extra days off the week of Christmas. The extra money is nice, but we don't get to spend as much time together as I would like."

Lois gave a sympathetic smile along with an understanding nod. Then she motioned to the door of the back room. "You two go on now and enjoy your chat. There are bottles of water in the cold bag I brought from home this morning, as well as some mighty good apples to snack on."

"Thanks," Jeff said. "I might take you up on that offer."

When they entered the small room, Orley invited Jeff to take one of the chairs, and then he placed the cooler bag on the desk and seated himself in the other chair. "I have some good news for you."

"Good news is always welcome," Jeff said.

"Nearly everything you brought in on consignment has sold. So, you have money coming."

"That's great. It'll give me some cash to buy a few Christmas presents." Jeff took the bottle of water Orley held out to him.

"Would you like an apple?" Orley asked.

"Are you going to have one?"

"You bet."

"Guess I will then too."

Orley reached into the cooler and withdrew two perfectly shaped red apples. "These are not only sweet, they're nice and crispy."

Jeff took a bite and drank some water. "I've made a decision, Orley."

"About what?"

"The business I lost. I've decided not to rebuild the restaurant."

"Mind if I ask why?"

"I'd like to find a job closer to home. Eventually, I hope Rhonda will be able to do the same." Jeff stopped talking long enough for another bite of apple and more water, and then he spoke again. "When we're gone so much from home, it's hard to keep up with everything that needs to be done in and outside the house. There's also the problem of Rhonda and me having less time to spend together."

Orley gulped down most of the water in his bottle and set it on the table. "I know a lot of people in the area. Would you like me to put my feelers out and see what jobs are available right now?"

"Sure, that'd be great." Jeff twisted the gold wedding band around his finger. "I still haven't told Rhonda about the dream I had or that I committed my life to Christ. There doesn't seem to be a right time to tell her."

"The longer you wait, the harder it will be."

"I know, but I'm afraid of her reaction."

"I assume you've prayed about it?"

"Yes, but I haven't gotten a clear answer yet."

"You will. The Lord always answers in His time." Orley pointed upward. "I remind myself daily that He knows what's best for me."

"I know that I need to trust Him."

"Right." Orley glanced at the newspaper lying on the desk. Lois had been looking at it earlier to see if her most recent column had been included. Out of curiosity, he turned to the page that gave listings for homes and places of business for sale. One jumped out at him. "Now here's something that might interest you, Jeff." He pointed to the page.

Jeff left his seat and came over to stand beside Orley's chair. "What is it?"

"Seems there is an inn for sale right here in Walnut Creek. If becoming an innkeeper is something you think you might enjoy, here's the name of the Realtor to contact." Orley pointed to the woman's name and the telephone number to call.

Jeff rolled his neck from side to side, rubbing it as he did so. "Hmm. . .that does sound like an interesting prospect. I could cook meals or at least breakfast for the guests, and Rhonda could handle the business end of things. Managing the hotel in Canton has given her plenty of experience."

Orley wrote the name of the Realtor and her phone number on a piece of paper and handed it to Jeff. "If you decide to talk to this woman, please let me know how it turns out. In the meantime, I'll be praying about the situation."

Jeff gave Orley a wide smile. "Don't know what I'd do without a friend like you. You're so positive about things, and it's been a real encouragement to me."

Orley smiled and gave Jeff a pat on the back. "I think of you as a friend too. Now, my friend, let's go up front to the cash register, and I'll pay you the money you have coming."

Canton

As Rhonda entered her office at the hotel and took a seat at the desk, her thoughts went to Jeff. Ever since his restaurant burned down, Rhonda had been concerned about him. He was gone more than usual, and when she would ask where he'd been, he usually gave little explanation. Whenever they talked, Jeff acted upbeat, but she suspected that he was trying to hide his real feelings about what had happened to his business. If that was the case, Rhonda wouldn't push, but she hoped Jeff would eventually open up to her about it. She knew from experience that it wasn't good to hold things in.

Last night, Jeff had told Rhonda that he had decided not to rebuild his restaurant. The announcement had come as a shock, and when she'd asked why, his response was even more surprising. Jeff had stated that he was tired of the commute to Canton and wanted to find a job closer to home. This seemed strange to Rhonda, because when Jeff had tried to convince her to sell their townhouse and move to Walnut Creek, he'd said he didn't mind commuting to the restaurant.

Why the sudden change? she asked herself. Rhonda had to admit that she would also prefer to work somewhere closer to home. She had even looked into the possibility. Unfortunately, none of the local hotels was in need of a manager at this time, and all the other positions had been taken.

Rhonda's biggest concern was their finances. If Jeff didn't rebuild his restaurant and wasn't able to find a decent paying job near home, they'd never be able to live off her income alone.

Refocusing, Rhonda turned on her computer. While waiting for it to boot up, she closed her eyes for a silent prayer. *Dear Lord, Please help me not to worry about the future and to trust You to provide for all of our needs. Give me the wisdom to know when I should tell Jeff that I'm a Christian, and help him to be receptive to the idea.*

Rhonda's prayer was interrupted when Marian, the new desk clerk she'd hired after Lori left, came into the room.

"Good morning, Mrs. Davis. I thought you might like a cup of coffee." Marian placed the steaming cup of strong-smelling brew on Rhonda's desk. The pungent odor wafted up to Rhonda's nose and caused her stomach to churn. *What's going on? The smell of coffee has never done this to me before. Maybe it's a new brand, or I may have lost my desire for coffee since I've been drinking more herbal tea lately.*

"Thank you, Marian." Rhonda forced a smile as another wave of nausea swept through her. She placed both hands against her stomach, hoping to halt the unpleasant feeling.

"You don't look well, Mrs. Davis." Marian put her hand on Rhonda's shoulder. "Are you sick?"

"I don't think so. For some reason, the strong coffee odor made me feel queasy. I'm sure it'll pass, but would you please take the cup back with you? I haven't had coffee in a while, and I don't think I can drink any right now."

"Oh, I'm sorry." The young employee picked up the mug and started for the door.

"I appreciate the gesture," Rhonda called out to her. "And please let me know if you need anything or any problem arises at the front desk. I'll be in here working on a spreadsheet for a few hours, but feel free to let me know if anything comes up that you can't handle."

Marian turned to Rhonda and smiled. "Thanks, I will."

After the young woman left, Rhonda opened the spreadsheet she'd been working on the day before. The document was related to budget cuts, and it was Rhonda's job to decide what the hotel did or didn't need.

She made a few notations in column B when another wave of nausea hit. With this one, Rhonda knew that if she didn't get to the bathroom quickly, she'd have to use the garbage can to empty her stomach.

Hurrying out of the room and rushing down the hall, Rhonda made it to the women's restroom just in time. Once she'd finished vomiting, she went to the sink to wash her face and rinse out her mouth. Now that she thought about it, Rhonda remembered dealing with a queasy feeling yesterday morning and the day before too. She'd also missed her period but figured it was from stress. Was it possible. . .

No, it can't be, she told herself. *After all these years of hoping for a baby, there's no way I could be pregnant.*

Although the odds were slim, she had been trying to eat healthier in addition to taking several nutritional supplements she'd found at the health food store in Berlin.

Rhonda blotted her face on a paper towel. *If I'm pregnant, it would be no less than a miracle.*

It was probably a waste of time and money, but Rhonda decided she would go to the pharmacy near the hotel during her lunch hour and pick up a pregnancy kit. By this time tomorrow morning, she would hopefully know the truth. *No doubt pregnancy will be ruled out, and I'll have to accept the fact that I have a touch of the flu.*

The following morning, Rhonda woke up early and slipped quietly out of bed, being careful not to wake Jeff. After putting on her robe and slippers, she left their room and went down the hall to the guest bathroom to take the pregnancy test. Not wanting Jeff to see the kit, when Rhonda got home from work yesterday, she'd put her pharmacy purchase in the guest vanity. She wasn't trying to be sneaky, but she didn't want him to know about her suspicions until the test either confirmed or denied them. There was no point in getting Jeff's hopes up only to disappoint him if the test turned out to be negative.

Five minutes later, Rhonda stepped out of the bathroom with a smile on her face. The test had shown a positive result. After all these years, she was going to become a mother. Rhonda couldn't wait for her husband to get out of bed so she could share this super good news with him.

She hurried to the kitchen to start breakfast. Jeff liked bacon and eggs, but the thought of smelling greasy bacon cooking or looking at runny egg whites made Rhonda's stomach lurch. So instead, she would opt for fruit and yogurt parfaits.

As Rhonda reached for the parfait glasses, she heard a crazy rooster crow and realized that Jeff had left his cell phone on the counter. Thinking it might be something important, she picked up the phone to answer, but it went to voice mail. Rhonda typed in Jeff's password to listen to the message.

"Hello, Jeff. This is Reba Sterling, returning your call. I'm available to see you today, so please call me at this number. I look forward to talking to you again."

Rhonda's gaze flitted around the room. *Who is this woman, and why is she calling my husband? I've never heard Jeff mention her name.*

Rhonda saved the message and would tell Jeff about it when he woke up. Surely, he would tell her who Reba Sterling was.

Jeff came into the kitchen a few minutes later, wearing a pair of black slacks and a pale blue dress shirt. "I hope you didn't fix a big breakfast, because I don't have time to eat much this morning. In fact, don't bother to fix anything at all. I'll just grab a cup of coffee for the road."

"Oh? Is there somewhere you need to go?"

His chin dipped slightly, and he looked away. "Yeah, I have an appointment and a few errands to run."

"What appointment is that?"

"It's nothing you need to worry about." Jeff kissed the back of Rhonda's neck. "Is there any coffee made?"

Nearly gagging at the prospect of smelling the strong brew, Rhonda shook her head.

"That's okay. I'll stop somewhere for coffee on the way." He grabbed his cell phone and started for the door. "See you later. I hope you have a good day." Jeff was gone before Rhonda could think of what to say. She'd wanted to ask who the woman was who'd left the message for him. Even more so, Rhonda wanted to tell Jeff about the pregnancy test she'd taken.

Maybe it's best if I don't tell him about the results of the test right now, she thought. *I think it would be better for me to make an appointment with my doctor in Canton and get a blood test. Then I'll know for sure whether I'm really pregnant. In the meantime, I'll keep all this to myself.*

Chapter 37

Canton

Rhonda had reached the supply room at the hotel and was about to open the door when her cell phone rang. Recognizing her doctor's number, she quickly answered. She'd gotten in to see Dr. Gates three days ago and had been anxiously waiting to hear the results of her blood test. Rhonda's heart pounded as she listened to the woman on the other end, and she had to lean against the wall for support when she was given the news that the blood test was positive. Rhonda was indeed pregnant. If everything went according to schedule, the baby would be born during the first week of August.

"Thank you for calling," Rhonda said, barely able to speak around the constriction in her throat. *I can't believe it! This is such a wonderful confirmation, and now I know why I've been feeling so odd lately.* She felt relieved, happy, excited all at once. *Boy, Jeff is going to be surprised when I tell him. Or will he be overwhelmed with losing his business recently and our having a lack of funds on hand?*

"I'll schedule an ultrasound appointment soon, as well any other appointments I'll need during my pregnancy," she said, refocusing.

After Rhonda ended her call, she entered the supply room and took a seat on the wooden stool near the door. She was thrilled about the child growing in her womb but couldn't help feeling some concern. In addition to the fact that she was approaching her mid-thirties and hoping she wouldn't have any complications, she was worried about telling Jeff. He'd been acting so strange lately—like he was keeping something important from her. A week ago, when she'd finally been able to ask him about the woman who'd left a message on his cell phone, he'd been evasive, saying he couldn't tell her right now.

Can't tell me? Rhonda's skin prickled. *If Jeff is involved with another woman and wants to end our marriage, why doesn't he come right out and tell me the truth?*

Either way, Rhonda needed to know, and she planned to question him about it after she got home. In addition, she would need to pray about these matters beforehand. Only then would she feel ready to give Jeff the news that she was pregnant. An overwhelming need to pray swept over her.

She bowed her head. *"Dear Lord, I'm really stressed out right now. Things were going along fairly well until Jeff lost his restaurant, but he hasn't been himself since then. I'm afraid he doesn't love me anymore and may have found someone else."* Rhonda paused a few seconds to wipe away the tears rolling down her cheeks. *"Please give me the courage to talk to Jeff about this, as well as my pregnancy. And I pray that he will be receptive when I tell him that I'm a Christian now."*

~

Walnut Creek

Lois had been baking Christmas cookies all morning and would need to start lunch soon. Their sixteen-year-old neighbor, Gary, and his twin sister, Gayle, had invited Orley to ice skate with them on their parents' pond. Lois had tried to talk him out of it, saying at the age of fifty-five, he wasn't as young as he used to be and could fall and get hurt, but he'd insisted that he would be fine.

"That husband of mine always says he's fine," she murmured. "He could end up with two broken legs, and he'd still proclaim that he was just fine."

The wind-up timer went off, and Lois hurried to open the oven door. The cutout cookies were lightly brown, which meant they were done. She removed the tray and set it on a cooling rack. Once the cookies were cool enough, Lois would frost them with white icing. In addition to the cookies, she'd made some fudge and divinity. They were Orley's favorite candies, so Lois would have to hide them away until Christmas Day, when they would go to Orley's brother Ezra's house for dinner.

Lois had always loved Christmas. In addition to the delicious meal that was served and all the goodies available for snacking and dessert, she liked reading the Bible and focusing on Christ's birth. Although she didn't know for sure the exact date Jesus was born, it was nice to set aside December 25 to celebrate and reflect upon the most wonderful gift God had given when He'd sent His Son to earth.

Lois had often wondered how Jesus' mother, Mary, must have felt when she first held her precious baby. Although Lois had never had an opportunity to hold a child of her own, she'd held many other people's babies, and it was always a joy.

As Lois placed the next batch of cutouts onto the cookie sheet in readiness to be baked, her thoughts went to Rhonda and the conversation they'd had the day Orley and Jeff had enjoyed sledding on their hill. Rhonda's deep yearning for a baby had been obvious, from her pained expression and also the things she'd said. *I hope some of the things I said to her that day helped. I felt bad seeing her so troubled.*

The heavy stomping of boots on the back porch interrupted Lois's thoughts. A few minutes later, Orley stepped into the kitchen, red-cheeked, bright-eyed, and apparently with no injuries.

"How did it go?" she asked.

"It was great. The three of us had a *gut* time, and I never fell once."

"I'm glad to hear that."

He rubbed his hands together briskly and reached for one of the cookies that were done.

Lois shook her finger at him. "Only one, please. The rest I am saving for Christmas."

His bottom lip protruded like a pouty little boy. "But that's almost a week away. How do you expect me to stay away from all these goodies that long?"

She lifted her gaze to the ceiling. "You are incorrigible."

Orley's forehead wrinkled. "What's with the big word? Do I need to get the dictionary to figure out what you mean?"

Lois chuckled. "*Incorrigible* means 'hopeless,' and I read the word you think is big in the newspaper."

"You mean the paper that publishes your Dear Caroline column?"

She nodded.

"How's that going, anyway? You haven't said much about it lately."

Lois paused to put the next tray of cookies into the oven. "It's going okay. I just wish I knew what the people do when they read the answers I give to their questions."

"Hopefully, they listen to your good advice and do what you've suggested."

"I hope so too." Lois grabbed one of the finished cookies and gave another one to Orley. "Let's eat these first, and then I'll fix us some lunch."

He kissed her cheek. "You're a good fraa. I'm sure glad I was smart enough to marry you."

Lois's face warmed at his compliment. "I'm glad I married you too."

Jeff whistled as he set the dining-room table. An organically grown chicken baked in the oven, along with two medium-sized russet potatoes. He'd also bought some fresh broccoli to steam, which he would start cooking as soon as Rhonda got home.

Jeff placed the water glasses on the table as well as napkins and silverware. *I can only imagine what Rhonda's expression will be when I tell her my news. I hope she isn't too upset with me for not telling her before what I've been up to these past few weeks. But it's time, and she deserves to know the truth about everything.*

When Rhonda pulled her car into the yard, she was relieved to see Jeff's SUV parked in the driveway. He'd been gone so much lately, she hadn't expected him to be home. Rhonda was exhausted from working all day and didn't relish the idea of having to cook anything. *Maybe I'll make us some toasted cheese sandwiches and heat a can of tomato soup to go with it.* While it might not be the healthiest meal, it would be quick and easy, and that's all Rhonda had the strength for this evening.

She drove her vehicle into the garage, picked up her purse and briefcase, and made her way into the house. As Rhonda approached the guest room that had once been a nursery, she gave a slow, disbelieving shake of her head. *It doesn't seem possible that by August of next year, this will be a baby's room once again. Her hands tingled as she placed them against her stomach. Oh, thank You, Lord. A thousand times, thank You for the wonderful miracle within me. I only hope that when I tell my husband, he will be as excited as I am.*

Rhonda made her way down the hallway and stopped at her office to put her briefcase and purse in the chair by her desk. When she stepped back into the hall, she couldn't miss the smell of food cooking. Approaching the dining room, Rhonda was surprised to see that the table had been set with their best dishes. Two lit candles had been placed on either side of a vase filled with white roses.

"What's going on?" Rhonda asked when she entered the kitchen where Jeff stood at the stove. "Why is the dining-room table set with our best dishes?"

"Because we have things to talk about, and I wanted to do it in a relaxed atmosphere with good food."

She sniffed the air. "So, you've cooked our meal?"

"Yep. Roasted chicken, baked potatoes, and broccoli."

Her stomach growled at the thought of eating the home-cooked meal, and that was a lot better than the nausea she'd felt earlier today. She moistened her lips with the tip of her tongue. "Thank you for cooking tonight. I'm exhausted and wouldn't have had the energy to fix anything nearly as good as what you've made." She took a few steps closer to him. "I. . .uh. . .have a few things I want to talk to you about too."

"That's good. I'm eager to hear what you have to say." Jeff gestured toward the dining room. "Why don't you take a seat? The broccoli should be done, so I'll bring in the food shortly."

"Okay."

Why is Jeff being so nice to me? Rhonda asked herself as she entered the dining room and took a seat at the table. *Is this his way of preparing me for bad news?* Rhonda glanced around the spacious room. *If Jeff leaves me, I'll have to raise the baby by myself, and I'll never be able to keep this big house.*

She gulped in some air, trying to calm her nerves. There'd been a time when Rhonda thought ending their marriage might be the best thing for both of them, but now, with a baby coming, she couldn't imagine raising their child without his or her father. Besides, she still loved Jeff with all her heart and had hoped by her actions she could win him to the Lord.

"Here we go." Jeff set a plate of succulent-looking chicken on the table. "Be right back."

He returned a few minutes later with two baked potatoes and a bowl of steaming broccoli. "Hang tight. I just have to get the sour cream, butter, and chives."

Rhonda waited for his return. The longer they put off talking, the more apprehensive she became. She wanted desperately to get this conversation over with so she would know where she stood with Jeff.

Jeff returned with the potato toppings and took a seat across from her.

Great. Now I'll have to look right at him while we're talking. Rhonda clasped her hands together in her lap, wanting so badly to pray out loud.

"I hope you don't mind, but I'd like to offer a prayer before we begin eating," Jeff said.

Her heart skipped a beat. "Did I hear that right? You want to pray before our meal?"

"Yeah. Is that okay with you?"

All Rhonda could manage was a quick nod. In the thirteen years of their marriage, she'd never heard her husband offer a prayer for anything.

Jeff bowed his head, and Rhonda did the same. "Heavenly Father, Rhonda and I have some serious things to talk about this evening and some decisions will need to be made. Please bless this time of us being together and help us to make wise decisions. Amen."

Rhonda lifted her head and looked at Jeff. Were those tears she saw in his eyes? Or perhaps the glow from the candlelight had caused his eyes to appear watery.

Jeff cleared his throat. "Would you like to go first, or shall I?"

"I guess I can. Unless you'd rather wait to discuss things until after we've eaten."

"No, we can eat and talk." Jeff forked a piece of chicken onto his plate and pushed the platter closer to her. "Sorry, I should have let you serve yourself first."

Rhonda helped herself to a piece and then moved the platter back to him. After they both had their plates full of food, she drank some water and spoke. "I have two very important things to tell you."

"Okay."

"First of all, you probably won't like this, but a few weeks ago, I accepted Christ as my personal Savior."

His brows shot up. "Seriously?"

"Yes."

"Why didn't you say something sooner?"

"Knowing how you felt about religious things, I was afraid of your reaction."

"I understand."

Rhonda wished she could read Jeff's uncertain expression, as he rubbed the back of his neck.

"I will comment on this," he said, "after you've told me the other thing you wanted to say."

Rhonda's muscles quivered as she drew in several quick breaths and released them slowly. "I'm pregnant."

"What?" His quick exhale through his nose came out sounding like a snort. "After all these years—that's impossible."

"Nothing is impossible with God."

"Are...are you sure about this?"

She nodded. "I took a home pregnancy test, and it was positive. Just to be certain that it was accurate, I followed up by getting a blood test at my doctor's office. I got a call while I was at the hotel today, and the doctor said it was positive." Rhonda touched her stomach and gave it a few pats. "The baby will be born in early August."

A wide grin spread across Jeff's face. "Wow, Rhonda, how exciting! It's a miracle."

"I agree."

"So now are you ready for my news?"

"Yes, please." Rhonda steeled herself for what he might say. She hoped the continued smile on his face meant it wasn't bad news.

"First off—I too am a Christian."

"You are?"

"Yeah. Let me tell you how it happened."

Rhonda ate some of her potato and listened with interest as Jeff told her about the dream he'd had of seeing his mother and how he'd prayed and accepted the Lord afterward.

"Why didn't you tell me about this right away?" she asked.

"For the same reason you didn't say anything to me about becoming a Christian. I was afraid telling you would affect our marriage in a negative way."

Rhonda's thoughts scrambled as she tried to digest all that Jeff had said. It hardly seemed possible that they'd both given their hearts to the Lord and neither of them had caught on.

"Now there's something else I want to say, and I hope you'll be in agreement with what I want to do, because if you are, we'll have to move fast, before it's too late." Jeff looked at Rhonda with a most serious expression.

"What is it?" Her mind raced, searching for answers. "What are you talking about, Jeff?"

"There's an inn for sale here in Walnut Creek, and I've had several meetings with the Realtor, Reba Sterling, in regard to it."

"Did you say Reba Sterling?"

"Yeah, that's right."

Rhonda pushed tightly against the back of her chair and released a sigh of relief. "I listened to a message that a woman named Reba had left on your cell phone one morning while you were still in bed. I didn't know who she was, but I thought. . ." Her voice trailed off.

"What did you think, honey?"

"Oh, nothing. It's not important now." She placed both elbows on the table and leaned closer to Jeff. "So, tell me about this inn and why you met with the Realtor about it."

"We could sell this place and move there. We'd have our own living quarters, and there are several spacious guest rooms. You could take care of the business end of things, and I'd cook the guests a nice breakfast every morning. Since I won't be rebuilding my restaurant, this would be the perfect setup for us."

Jeff had spoken so fast, Rhonda could hardly keep up with him. "Whoa! Wait a minute, please. What about my position at the hotel?"

"How much do you really like that job, Rhonda—not to mention the commute I've heard you complain about?"

"True, but I really like this house, and I thought you did too."

"I do, but I think you might like the living quarters at the inn just as well. And you should see the beautiful grounds that come with the place. It's like one giant park. Will you at least agree to go look at it with me and talk with Reba about the possibilities? I spoke with her again this afternoon, and she said she'd be available to show it to us tomorrow morning."

"I don't have to be at work until noon, so I suppose we could look at the inn around nine, if that's doable." Rhonda couldn't believe she was agreeing to look at the place. The whole idea was a bit overwhelming.

"Great! I'll call Reba and set it up as soon as we finish eating our supper." Jeff reached out a hand, like he was going to take a piece of chicken. Instead, he pushed his chair back and came around to her side of the table. Then, pulling Rhonda gently to her feet, he wrapped his arms around her in a warm embrace. "Even if we don't buy the inn, I want you to know that I love you very much, and I am super excited about becoming a dad. So now, the most important thing we can do is pray and ask God to reveal His will to us so that we'll know with a certainty whether we should make an offer on the inn."

"I agree. Now that we're both believers, we should seek God's will together in all things."

Jeff nodded and placed his hand against Rhonda's belly. "Have you thought of a name for our baby yet?"

She rolled her eyes. "Of course not, silly. We don't even know if it's a boy or a girl."

Rhonda definitely saw moisture in her husband's eyes, just as she felt tears in her own eyes. "Our parents are going to be thrilled when we tell them that we're expecting a baby."

"You're right. Should we wait till Christmas to make the announcement?"

Rhonda nodded. "I think it would be a great Christmas present. I'd also like to stop by the Troyers' and tell them the exciting news."

Jeff nodded. "Let's plan to do that on Christmas Eve. The last time I talked with Orley, he mentioned that he and Lois would be at his brother's house Christmas Day, so I'm sure they'll be home the night before Christmas. I'll give him a call and see if they'll be home Christmas Eve."

"That sounds like a plan." Rhonda gestured to the food on the table. "I'm sure everything is cold by now. Should we heat things up in the microwave?"

He grinned and gave her a kiss. "Yeah, I suppose we should."

As they picked up their plates and headed to the kitchen, Rhonda sent up a silent prayer. *Thank You, Lord, for answered prayer and making my wish for a baby come true.*

Chapter 38

"This is so relaxing." Rhonda breathed in and out as she leaned her head against the back of the sofa and closed her eyes. "Between the warmth of the cozy fire in our gas fireplace and the lull of Christmas music from the CD player, I could almost fall asleep."

She felt the warm touch of her husband's hand. "Better sit up then because I have a gift for you to open."

Rhonda's eyes snapped open, and she giggled. "I thought we'd decided not to open any Christmas gifts until tomorrow morning." She sat forward, looking at his gift and wondering what was inside.

"This one's an exception, because I'd like you to wear it tonight when we go over to the Troyers' for supper." Jeff handed Rhonda a small white box with a red bow stuck on the lid.

"Thank you." She gave the gift a little shake.

"This is the gift I'd planned to give you for our thirteenth anniversary. But I couldn't remember where I'd put it until yesterday, when I was in the garage going through some things to get rid of. I felt really foolish when I found the gift in my toolbox." Jeff chuckled. "I remember thinking it was a safe place to hide it since you probably wouldn't look there, but then I didn't look there either until yesterday."

Rhonda opened the lid and smiled as she removed the pretty daisy pin. "It's lovely, Jeff. Is it a vintage piece of jewelry?"

He nodded. "I bought it at the yard sale we went to this past summer, and don't worry, it wasn't expensive."

"Thank you again. It's beautiful." Rhonda reached over and gave his hand a gentle squeeze.

"Would you like to wear it tonight? Since Orley was with me when I bought the pin and knew that I had lost it, he'll be pleased to see that I finally found it."

"Of course, I want to wear it." She handed the piece of jewelry to Jeff. "Would you pin it on for me?"

"Sure thing." Jeff took hold of the antique pin and secured it close to the neckline on Rhonda's blue solid-colored blouse. "It looks great, honey. I'm glad you like it."

"Definitely." She held her hand against the piece of jewelry and fingered each petal on the daisy. "Would you like to open your gift now?"

"Sure thing. You know me—I'm like a kid at Christmas—always eager to open presents."

Rhonda got up and went over to the tree to retrieve his package from underneath, where their gifts for family members had also been placed. Smiling, she handed him the box. "I hope you like it."

Jeff tore off the paper and then opened the cardboard flaps. His eyes widened when he withdrew the old milk bottle inside. "Wow, thanks! This looks like one that I had put on display at the restaurant before the fire. Did you get it at Memory Keepers?"

She shook her head. "I checked there, but Orley said he didn't have any antique milk bottles at this time. Guess he sold the last of them a week ago. So, I searched the internet and bought the bottle from an antique dealer." Rhonda sat next to Jeff, and he leaned over and gave her a kiss.

"I really appreciate it, but I hope you didn't have to break the bank to get the bottle."

"No, the seller gave me a pretty good deal."

"I'm glad. We need to keep unnecessary spending to a minimum now that we are going to become parents."

Joyful tears sprang to her eyes. "I still can hardly believe the miracle God gave us. It will be exciting to share the news with your dad and my mom tomorrow. I also plan to call my sister, but not until after Mom's been told."

"Same here with my brothers, since they'll be at their in-laws Christmas Day. It'll be a different kind of holiday having it at Dad's and with just us and our parents."

"It'll be quieter than if our nieces and nephews were there, but I'm kind of looking forward to just the four of us enjoying Christmas Day together."

"Same here. Guess it'll be sort of a double date."

"Next year will be different, though. We'll have a son or daughter, so things might be more hectic but oh so fun." Rhonda rubbed both hands against her stomach. "I can hardly wait, and I'm going to do the best I can to be a good mother." She smiled at Jeff. "I'm sure you'll be a good father too."

Jeff slid a little closer to Rhonda. "I have something to confess. Something I should have told you a long time ago."

Fear gripped Rhonda's heart like a vise. She wasn't sure if she wanted to hear his confession.

"Before I say this, I want you to know that I don't feel this way any longer."

"What way? During the worst of our marital problems, did you feel that you no longer loved me?"

He shook his head vigorously. "No, it was never that. I've always loved you, Rhonda, even when I didn't like you too well."

She grimaced. "Thanks for that candid remark."

"You know what I mean, honey. I'm sure there were times when I was being a pain in the neck that you didn't care much for me either."

Rhonda slowly nodded. "Guilty as charged."

Jeff sat quietly for a few seconds before speaking again. "This is what I've never told you before. Early on in our marriage, when you wanted to adopt and I refused, it wasn't for any of the reasons I told you."

"Oh?" She tipped her head. "Why then, Jeff?"

"It was a selfish reason. I wanted you all to myself. I was afraid if we had a baby that you would be consumed with the child and wouldn't have time for me anymore. Quality time is my love language," he added. "And I've always wanted to spend that time with you." Jeff remained silent after admitting how he'd felt and stared at their Christmas tree with its pretty packages underneath.

Meanwhile, the only noise in the room was the soft Christmas music playing in the background.

Rhonda sat, too stunned to say anything. With the way her husband had immersed himself in TV and his hobby of collecting antiques, she never would have guessed that he desired to have more quality time with her. When she could find her voice, she looked at him and said, "Do you still feel that way, Jeff? Do you wish we weren't having this baby?"

"Of course not. I'm excited about becoming a dad. Since becoming a Christian, I've asked God to help me be a loving husband and to not put my selfish needs ahead of yours." Jeff's eyes appeared to be watery as he put his hands against her belly and gave it a few pats. "Please believe me, Rhonda, I want this baby very much."

"I'm so glad you do. I am sure we will make some mistakes while raising our child, just as our parents did, but with God's help, we'll do our best to raise him or her in a Christian home."

"I agree wholeheartedly." Jeff glanced at his watch. "I told Orley that we'd be there by six, so we'd better leave now or we're going to be late."

"You're right. I'll go to the kitchen and get the cucumber dip and veggies from the refrigerator. When the Troyers were here, Lois commented on how much she enjoyed the dip, so I made a big batch this morning. Some I will take to your dad's tomorrow, and the rest I'm taking tonight to enjoy with whatever Lois is planning for supper."

"I'm sure it'll be appreciated."

When Rhonda stood, Jeff did too. Then he pulled her close and gave her a kiss—this one even more meaningful than the last. "I love you, Mrs. Davis."

"I love you too."

~

"I heard a vehicle pull into our yard. Could you please go see if it's Rhonda and Jeff?" Lois asked as she opened the refrigerator door to take out some lunchmeat and cheese for open-faced sandwiches.

"Jah, I'm sure it must be them," Orley responded. "Jeff said they'd be here around this time. I hope you have some cookies or candy to share with them."

"I have both, but not until we've all eaten our sandwiches."

"Of course, I knew that." He gave her a smirk and quickly left the room.

Lois giggled as she shook her head. "That husband of mine is such a kidder, not to mention a tease."

She opened the packages from the refrigerator. The selections of meats and cheeses looked mouthwatering to put on the slices of bread. Once Lois had tossed the discarded packaging away, she began slicing the olives on the cutting board. She heard the front door open and the sounds of her husband and their guests exchanging greetings. She felt joy in her heart knowing that the Lord had moved in their new friends' marriage. *I'm thankful that God hears our prayers. And I'm glad He can use those who want to serve Him.*

Lois got out a loaf of french bread, as well as the condiments to put on the sandwiches. It wasn't long before Orley returned to the kitchen along with Rhonda and Jeff. She stopped working at the counter and wiped the juice from the olives onto her apron. It was good to see them and spend time together on this joyous holiday.

Rhonda had a rosy glow about her, and Lois wondered if it was the chilly evening air or something else. Perhaps the young woman felt the joy that went with it being Christmas Eve.

"Merry Christmas. We're so glad you could join us for supper this evening." Lois gave both Rhonda and Jeff a hug. Normally, she and Orley didn't befriend customers who came into the store unless they already knew them personally, but this couple was different. They'd formed an attachment to them, especially since Jeff had informed Orley the other day that both he and Rhonda had become Christians.

"Thank you for inviting us." Rhonda handed Lois two plastic containers. "I brought some cucumber dip along with cut-up veggies."

"How thoughtful." Lois smiled. "It'll go well with our open-faced sandwiches."

"Are those the kind of sandwiches that have no lids?" Jeff asked.

Orley thumped Jeff's back. "Yes, and Lois makes 'em look and taste so good."

"I'll be eager to try some," Jeff said.

"What can I do to help?" Rhonda asked.

"You can spread mayonnaise on each piece of bread, and then I'll put the slices of lunchmeat and cheese on." Lois gestured to Orley. "The table's all set in the dining room, so why don't you and Jeff relax in the living room until the sandwiches are ready?"

"All right, if you're sure you don't need me for anything."

Lois waved him away. "Rhonda and I can handle things just fine. I'll call you when we're ready to eat."

"Alrighty then." Orley clapped Jeff on the back. "We've had our orders, so to the living room we shall go."

A short time later, they were all seated at the table. Following their silent prayer, Lois passed the tray of sandwiches around as well as the cut-up vegetables, chips, and dip.

"These sandwiches sure look enticing," Jeff commented. "Makes it hard to know which one to pick."

"Don't choose one, take several." Orley reached for a sandwich with ham and cheese. Sliced olives decorated the top, along with a sliver of tomato. On top of that, squiggles of mayonnaise and mustard gave the sandwiches a final, festive touch.

"Lois showed me how to make the fancy sandwiches," Rhonda said. "So, Jeff, anytime you want me to make some, just say the word."

He grinned over at her. "Good to know."

They visited about several topics as they ate their meal, and when they were finished, Jeff looked over at Rhonda and said, "Should we tell them now?"

She nodded. "You can do the honors."

Orley leaned forward with an eager expression. "I'm all ears. What is it you want us to know?"

"We'd like to share two things with you and Lois." Jeff paused and drank some water. "The first and most important announcement we have to make is that Rhonda is expecting a baby. He or she will be born the first part of August."

Lois's fingers touched her parted lips, and Orley's brows shot up. "That's wonderful news," they said simultaneously.

"Yes, we consider it a miracle from God." Jeff looked at Rhonda with an endearing expression. "We are both so happy and can't wait to become parents."

"And well you should be," Orley said. "We are equally happy for you. Right, Lois?"

She smiled while nodding her head. "The good Lord has looked upon you with favor."

Rhonda felt certain that Lois was sincere in her statement, but she couldn't help wondering if the sweet Amish woman might be a bit envious. A couple as kind and loving as Orley and Lois would have certainly made wonderful parents. Rhonda wished the Troyers would have been able to have at least one child.

"Now what's your other piece of news?" Orley questioned. "I'm sure it can't compare to your first announcement."

"On a personal level, it doesn't," Rhonda spoke up, "but it does have to do with the future for us and our baby."

"Rhonda and I made an offer on that inn you told me about,

Orley." Jeff's face broke into a wide smile. "Our offer was accepted, and the same day, I got word from my insurance company that they would be processing the claim I made when my restaurant burned down. So, we'll be using that money to purchase the inn."

Lois clapped her hands, and Orley followed suit. "That is truly wonderful news."

"Will you be selling the home you're living in now?" Lois asked.

"Yes, and we'll miss the place, but our living quarters at the inn, although a bit smaller, are equally nice," Rhonda replied.

"I'm going to do all the cooking for the guests who stay at our inn," Jeff said. "And Rhonda will take care of the business end of things." He reached for her hand and gave her fingers a tender squeeze. "We're excited to not only be a married couple but business partners too."

Orley began to ply Jeff with more questions, and Rhonda and Lois got up to clear the table. When they entered the kitchen and had placed the dishes in the sink, Lois gave Rhonda a hug. "I truly am happy for both of you, and I hope we can continue to keep in touch."

"Of course, we will. Jeff and I want our child to get to know you as we have. Also, we want you to know how much we appreciate all the advice you've given us. I believe your prayers and the things you've shared with us are a big part of the reason we both realized how much we needed the Lord in our lives. So, thank you for that."

"No thanks are needed," Lois said. "Orley and I take no credit for anything. We are just God's instruments and want to share His love and goodness with others."

Holding one hand against her heart, Rhonda said, "I no longer have to wish for things, because now when I have a problem too difficult for me, I'll remember that God is just a simple prayer away."

Epilogue

Eight Months Later

"Oh, Jeff, isn't our sweet Emily the most beautiful baby you've ever seen?"

"Absolutely!" He took a seat on the couch next to Rhonda and leaned over to kiss the top of their daughter's downy head. "She is adorable, and she has her mother's dark hair."

"I enjoy watching her." Rhonda fussed with Emily's soft blanket covered in printed pastel butterflies.

Jeff smiled. "She's melting my heart."

Rhonda had given birth to their precious little girl four days ago with no complications, and they'd come home from the hospital the following day. They had finished setting up the nursery in time for their little one's homecoming. Jeff and his dad had done the majority of the work, painting and setting up the furniture, while her mom helped hang the curtains and took care of anything else that was needed.

Things were falling into place for them better than Rhonda could have ever imagined. They'd sold their house a week after it went on the market and had been living in their private accommodations at the inn ever since. Their new business was doing well, with plenty of satisfied clientele. Rhonda's responsibilities weren't nearly as great as they had been at the hotel, and Jeff seemed to enjoy cooking break-fast for their guests. He also liked visiting with many of the people and talking about some of the antiques he had on display. Running the inn was a big change for them but in a positive way. It brought a lot less stress than their previous jobs had entailed.

"I still can't believe the news my dad and your mom gave us when they stopped by last evening to see the baby."

Jeff's comment pulled Rhonda out of her musings. "I know. Since they've been dating close to a year now, we should have expected that they would end up getting engaged, but their announcement still took me by surprise."

"You're okay with it though, right?"

She bobbed her head. "It strikes me kind of funny, however, to know that my father-in-law will soon become my stepfather."

Jeff laughed. "Yeah, and my mother-in-law will be my stepmom. It's sort of weird but good. I'm happy they found each other." He got up from the couch, left the room for a few minutes, and returned with two plaques in his hands. "I found these when I was going through more boxes we haven't opened yet and figured we should find a place to hang them, either here in our home or in the entryway where our guests come into the inn."

Rhonda smiled as she read the first plaque: GOD BLESS OUR HOME. It had been a housewarming gift from her mother after they'd moved into their previous home. "I think we should hang that one here, where we live," she responded.

Jeff gave a nod. Then he held up the other one that read: BE STILL, AND KNOW THAT I AM GOD. "What about this?"

"Let's hang that plaque so that everyone who enters our inn can see it. As Christians, we should let others know what we believe."

"I agree." Jeff smiled. "And if they ask any questions about the scripture, it'll open the door so we can tell them what that verse truly means to us."

"For sure." Rhonda put the baby over her shoulder and gently patted the infant's back. "I'm glad the Troyers were able to drop by here earlier today to visit with us and greet our daughter. I will think of those two every time I see the Bible verse on that plaque."

"Same here."

Rhonda closed her eyes, listening to her daughter's slow, even breathing. *This sweet child is a wonderful blessing from God, and so are Lois and Orley. I wonder who, in need of mentoring, will walk through the doors of Memory Keepers next.* Rhonda smiled. *Whoever they are, I'm sure that dear Amish couple will be as much of a blessing to them as they have been to us.*

Rhonda's Creamy Cucumber Dip

1 (8-ounce) package cream
cheese, softened

1 cup sour cream

2 tablespoons Miracle Whip
salad dressing

½ teaspoon Worcestershire
sauce

1 medium cucumber, chopped

¼ cup chopped green pepper

1 rounded tablespoon
chopped onion

In mixing bowl, stir together cream cheese, sour cream, Miracle Whip, and Worcestershire sauce. Add cucumber, green pepper, and onion. Refrigerate two hours before serving with your favorite crackers or veggies.

Lois's Bacon Cheese Muffins

2 cups flour

1 cup shredded Cheddar cheese

8 bacon strips, fried
and crumbled

2 tablespoons sugar

½ teaspoon garlic powder

3 teaspoons baking powder

¼ teaspoon salt

1 egg

1 cup milk

¼ cup vegetable oil

Preheat oven to 400 degrees. In large bowl, combine flour, cheese, bacon, sugar, garlic powder, baking powder, and salt. In another bowl, beat egg, milk, and oil. Stir liquid mixture into dry ingredients just until moistened. Fill greased muffin pans two-thirds full. Bake for 15 to 20 minutes or until toothpick inserted in center comes out clean. Cool for 5 minutes before removing from pan. Yield: 1 dozen

Discussion Questions

1. When Rhonda and Jeff first got married, they got along well; but as the years went on, conflict erupted, causing marriage problems. What do you think is the biggest reason some married couples don't get along? Is there anything a husband and wife can do to prevent marital problems?

2. When Rhonda and Jeff's marriage problems first began, she'd wanted him to go with her to see a counselor, but he'd refused. Is it possible for a couple having marriage problems to get help without professional counseling? What other things might they try to get their marriage back on track?

3. Jeff was a collector of antiques, which was a cause of dissension between him and Rhonda because his hobby was expensive. Have you ever known someone who collected high-priced things even when they couldn't afford them? Is there a way this problem can be dealt with?

4. Rhonda desperately wanted a baby, and when it appeared that she and Jeff would not become parents, she threw herself into her work to the point that she was gone more than she was at home. How did this play into the problems she and her husband experienced?

5. In the early part of their marriage, Jeff didn't care about having children because he wanted Rhonda all to himself. He'd never admitted this to her, though, making excuses about why he did not want to adopt. Should he have admitted the real reason, or was he right not to tell his wife the truth until years later?

6. Although Orley and Lois enjoyed selling vintage items and even kept some for themselves, their main focus was on mentoring people who came into the store and seemed to be burdened with a problem. What are some ways we can help others who are troubled and need a touch from God?

7. Lois had been writing a column for the local newspaper for a while before she admitted it to her husband. Why do you think she didn't want him to know? Is there ever a time when a husband or wife should keep a secret from his or her spouse?

8. The relationship Jeff had with his father had been strained since the death of Jeff's mother. Things got worse when Jeff's dad began dating. Even though Jeff was a grown man, he couldn't deal with the possibility of his father getting married again. Have you ever been in a similar situation—either as the adult child of a widowed parent who wanted to begin dating again or as the widowed parent with an adult child who was opposed to the idea? Were you able to work things out so that everyone involved was comfortable with the idea?

9. When Rhonda's mother, June, became a Christian, Rhonda felt uncomfortable around her, because she wanted nothing to do with God. It didn't help that June, eager to have her daughter accept Christ, brought up the topic of religion whenever she talked to Rhonda. How can a Christian witness to a family member who is not a believer without making them feel pressured or uncomfortable about the topic?

10. Rhonda didn't approve of her mother using a dating site to choose a man she might be willing to see socially. She also didn't like the idea of her dating men she'd met at church. Why do you think Rhonda felt this way? Should she have been more understanding of her mother's desire to go out with a Christian man?

11. Jeff felt a bit puffed up when he and Rhonda bought a new house. He wanted to show his brothers that he'd made something of himself. What usually happens when a person takes on more than they can handle financially in order to impress others?

12. In this story, Rhonda experienced what she believed to be a miracle. Has God ever performed a miracle in your life, or have you witnessed a miracle in someone else's life? How did seeing a miracle strengthen your faith?

13. What was Jeff's reason for keeping his conversion to Christianity a secret from Rhonda? Is there a reason or a time when we should not share our Christian beliefs with others? Why?

14. Rhonda was also afraid to tell Jeff that she'd become a Christian. Were her reasons legitimate? Should she have told him right away and given him the chance to accept or reject what she had done?

15. Were there any scriptures in this story that you particularly liked? If so, how do they apply to your own situation?